ISLAM

THE WAY OF REVIVAL

Edited by Riza Mohammed and Dilwar Hussain

Revival

Published by
Revival Publications,
Markfield Conference Centre,
Ratby Lane, Markfield, Leicestershire LE67 9SY, United Kingdom.

Tel: 01530 244944, Fax: 01530 244946
E-mail: revival@islamic-foundation.org.uk

Revival Publications is an imprint of the Islamic Foundation.

British Library Cataloguing in Publication Data
Islam: the way of revival
Vol. 1
1. Islam 2. Religious life – Islam
I. Mohammed, Riza II. Hussain, Dilwar
297

ISBN: 0 9536768 2 x

Typeset in Bembo, 11 point.
Printed and bound in Great Britain by
Antony Rowe Ltd., Chippenham, Wiltshire

Pictures overleaf are of some of the authors from volumes 1 & 2.
Names from top-left: Sayyid Qutb, Yusuf al-Qaradawi, Jamal Badawi, Sayyid Darsh, Sayyid Abul Ala Maududi, Khurram Murad, Anwar Ibrahim, Alija Ali Izetbegovic, Khurshid Ahmad, Rachid Ghannouchi, Tariq Ramadan, Ismail al-Faruqi, Hasan Turabi, Lamya al-Faruqi, Hasan al-Banna.

CONTENTS

TRANSLITERATION TABLE

Arabic Consonants

Initial: unexpressed medial and final:

ء	'	د	d	ض	ḍ	ك	k
ب	b	ذ	dh	ط	ṭ	ل	l
ت	t	ر	r	ظ	ẓ	م	m
ث	th	ز	z	ع	ʿ	ن	n
ج	j	س	s	غ	gh	هـ	h
ح	ḥ	ش	sh	ف	f	و	w
خ	kh	ص	ṣ	ق	q	ي	y

Arabic vowels and diphthongs

Short:	ـَ	a	ـِ	i	ـُ	u
Long:	ـَا	a	ـِي	i	ـُو	u
Diphthongs:			ـَوْ	aw / au		
			ـَيْ	ay / ai		

REFERENCES

- Chapter 1: Muhammad Asad, *Is Religion a thing of the Past?*, Karachi: Islamic Foundation, 1969, pp. 14–36. Originally published in *Arafat*, October 1946.
- Chapter 2: Abul Ala Mawdudi, *Towards Understanding Islam*, Leicester: Islamic Foundation, 1980, pp. 5–13.
- Chapter 3: Jaafar Shaikh Idris, 'These in resume are the basic truths', *Impact International*. London, 25 March – 8 April 1976 & 9–22 April 1976.
- Chapter 4: Hasan al-Banna, *Risalatut Ta'lim* (Arabic: *Message of the Teachings*). London: Ta Ha Publishers, 1981, pp. 6–10. Translated from Arabic by H. Muhammad Najm.
- Chapter 5: Ismail al-Faruqi, 'Why Islam', Islamabad, Pakistan: unpublished audio recording, International Islamic University, Islamabad, Pakistan, date unknown.
- Chapter 6: Fathi Yakan,'Being Muslim', *The Muslim*. London: Federation of Student Islamic Societies, December 1978 – February 1979.
- Chapter 7: Said Ramadan, 'Islam – a liberating Force', *Towards Freedom and Dignity*, London: London Islamic Circle, 1970, pp. 17–22.
- Chapter 8: Alija Ali Izetbegovic, *Islam Between East and West*, Indianapolis: American Trust Publications, 1989, pp. 289–292.
- Chapter 9: Abul Ala Mawdudi, *The Meaning of the Qur'ān Vol. 1*, Leicester, UK: Islamic Foundation, 1998, pp. 8–25. Translated from Urdu by Zafar Ishaq Ansari.
- Chapter 10: Khurram Murad,'Way to the Qur'ān', *The Muslim*. London: Federation of Student Islamic Societies, January – June 1982.
- Chapter 11: Sayyid Qutb, *In the Shade of the Qur'ān Vol. 1*, Leicester, UK: Islamic Foundation, 1999, pp. xvii-xxv. Translated from Arabic by Ashur Shamis and Adil Salahi.
- Chapter 12: Sayyid Qutb, 'The Unique Qur'anic Generation', *Milestones*, Kuwait: International Islamic Federation of Student Organisations, 1980, pp. 21–35.

- Chapter 13: Khurram Murad, *Who is Muhammad?,* Leicester, UK: Islamic Foundation, 1998.
- Chapter 14: Muhammad Qutb, 'The Way of the Messenger', *Islamic Horizons*, Indianapolis, USA: Islamic Society of North America, December 1988.
- Chapter 15: Sayyid Abul Hasan Ali Nadwi, '*Ḥadīth* – Its Relevance to Modern Times', audio recording of a lecture delivered at a seminar on *Ḥadīth* organised by the Muslim Students Association of the US and Canada in Chicago in 1975.
- Chapter 16: Muhammad al-Ghazali, *Remembrance and Prayer: Way of Prophet Muḥammad*, Leicester, UK: Islamic Foundation, 1998, pp. 11–16.
- Chapter 17: Khurshid Ahmad, 'The Technique of the Prophet', *The Muslim*. London: Federation of Student Islamic Societies, July 1969.
- Chapter 18: Mustapha Ahmad al-Zarqa, 'The Islamic concept of Ibadah', *The Muslim*. London: Federation of Student Islamic Societies, March 1968. Translated from Arabic by the Islamic Centre, Geneva.
- Chapter 19: Sayyid Abul Ala Mawdudi, *The Islamic Movement, Dynamics of Values, Power and Change*, Leicester, UK: Islamic Foundation, 1998.
- Chapter 20: Ismail al-Faruqi, *Role of 'Ibadah in the development of the Islamic Personality*, unpublished manuscript.
- Chapter 21: Yusuf al-Qaradawi, 'Halal and Haram in Islam', *The Muslim*. London: Federation of Student Islamic Societies, April – May 1976.
- Chapter 22: Khurram Murad, *Shariah: the Way to God*, Leicester, UK: Islamic Foundation, 1998, pp. 5–11.
- Chapter 23: Khurram Murad, *Shariah: the Way to God*, Leicester, England: Islamic Foundation, 1998, pp. 12–24.
- Chapter 24: Sayyid Sabiq, *Fiqh us-Sunnah Volume 1*, Indianapolis: American Trust Publications, 1986, pp. vii-xiii.
- Chapter 25: Ahmad Zaki Hammad, 'Agreeing to disagree', *Islamic Horizons*. Indianapolis, USA: Islamic Society of North America, January - February 1988.
- Chapter 26: Yusuf al-Qaradawi, *Islamic Awakening between Rejectionism and Extremism*, revised and edited by A. S. Al Shaikh-Ali and Mohamed B. E. Wasfy. Herndon, VA, USA: American Trust Publications and the International Institute of Islamic Thought, 1991, pp. 116–122. First published in Arabic in 1981.

- Chapter 27: Mahmud Rashdan, 'The Islamic Personality', *Al-Ittihad*. Indianapolis, USA: Muslim Student Association of the USA and Canada, January – March 1981.
- Chapter 28: Khurram Murad, 'Revival of the Individual', *The Muslim*. London: Federation of Student Islamic Societies, June – July 1979.
- Chapter 29: Khurshid Ahmad, 'Some Aspects of Character-Building', *The Muslim*. London: Federation of Student Islamic Societies, Nov. 1970.
- Chapter 30: Sayyid Asad Gilani, 'The spiritual training of the Islamic worker', *Al-Ittihad*. Indianapolis, USA: Muslim Student Association of the USA and Canada, July 1976. Translated from Urdu by Kaukab Siddique.
- Chapter 31: Said Ramadan, 'Our Subject is Love', *The Muslim*. London: Federation of Student Islamic Societies, July – August 1976. Translated from Arabic by Abdul Wahid Hamid.
- Chapter 32: Hasan al-Banna, *Risalatut Taʿlim* (Arabic: *Message of the Teachings*). London: Ta Ha Publishers, 1981, pp. 17–21. Translated from Arabic by H. Muhammad Najm.
- Chapter 33: Riza Mohammed, *Islamic Workers' Training Manual Book 1*, Trinidad: Islamic Daʿwah Movement, 1986, pp. 21–24.

ABOUT THE CONTRIBUTORS

Ahmad Zaki Hammad (Egypt–USA)
Founder and President of the *Qur'anic Literary Institute* and the Editor-in-chief of *The Quran Project*. Shaikh Hammad received his Islamic and Arabic training at the world's foremost centre of Islamic learning, Al-Azhar University, Cairo, and was awarded the graduate degree of Alamiyya from the Faculty of Theology. He also holds a PhD in Islamic Studies from the University of Chicago. Author of the well-received *Islamic Law: Understanding Juristic Differences* and the study and translation of al-Ghazālī's quintessential work on Islamic Juriprudence, *al-Mustaṣfā' min ʿIlm al-Uṣūl*. He also wrote the widely acclaimed, *The Opening to the Quran: Commentary and Vocabulary Reference of al-Fatiha.*

Alija Ali Izetbegovic (Bosnia and Herzegovina)
Born in 1925 into a renowned Bosnian Muslim family. Educated in Sarajevo, he got his degrees in law, arts and science. Throughout his life, he has been active in Islamic work, writing and lecturing. He has been a lifelong apponent of Communism and was imprisoned for Islamic activities in 1946–48 and 1983–88 by the totalitarian regime in Yugoslavia. In 1990 he became the President of Bosnia. During the ethnic cleansing of the 90s he stayed with his people and led them through the difficult years. He was the first President of the Republic of Bosnia and Herzegovina and in 2000 he stepped down from the Presidency. Izetbegovic has not only been a statesman but a capable thinker and scholar. His Translated works in English include *Islam Between East and West* and *Inescapable Questions: Autobiographical Notes.*

Fathi Yakan (Lebanon)
Born in 1933, he graduated with a BA in Accounting in 1946. He is a leading figure in the Islamic movement in Lebanon and was elected to the Lebanese Parliament in 1992. He is renowned for his insight into the dynamics of Islamic activism and revival. Translated works in English include: *To be a Muslim* and *The Islamic Movement: Problems and Perspectives.*

Hasan al-Banna (Egypt, 1906–1949)

Born into a family of scholars. In 1928 he formed al-Ikhwān al-Muslimūn (the Muslim Brotherhood). This movement for the revival of Islam soon spread across Egypt and the region. In December 1948, the Muslim Brotherhood organisation was suppressed and thousands of its members arrested. Hasan al-Banna was spared arrest only to be assassinated in February 1949. The Muslim Brotherhood survived and not only did it grow even stronger in Egypt, but it also created branches in most Arab countries.

Ismail al-Faruqi (Palestine–USA, 1921–1986)

Came from a well-known family of Jafa, Palestine. Good education, family name, and his reputation as a capable young man soon brought him into the political limelight. At the age of 24 he became the governor of Galilee. But before he could blossom fully, the creation of the State of Israel forced him to leave his people behind. He moved first to Lebanon where he enrolled in the American University of Beirut and later moved to America for his PhD in philosophy. Until 1960, al-Faruqi was not appreciative of his Islamic legacy. Philosophy awakened in him the desire to know more about Islam. He retreated to the quarters of al-Azhar to study, eventually returning to the US to continue his academic career during which he attained a Professorship in Islamic Studies. He founded the Association of Muslim Social Scientists and the Institute of International Islamic Thought. He also served (1978–1979) as Chairman of the Board of Trustees of the North American Islamic Trust. His works include *Christian Ethics: A Historical and Systematic Analysis of its Dominant Ideas, Islamic Thought and Culture, Historical Atlas of the Religions of the World,* and posthumously, *The Cultural Atlas of Islam.*

Jaafar Shaikh Idris (Sudan–USA)

Born and raised in Sudan, he received his undergraduate degree and PhD from Khartoum University, on 'The Concept of Causality in Islam'. He served as a Professor in Khartoum University and during this time he was very active in the Islamic revival movement in Sudan. He was a founding member of one of the parties attempting to establish an Islamic State in Sudan, now known as The National Front. He also served as a Professor in the department of Islamic Literature, Riyadh University as well as the Department of Research, Imam Mohamed Ibn Saud University. He was also Chairman of the Department of Research in the Institute for Islamic and Arabic Studies in Washington, USA. Currently he is the President of the American Open University. He has authored many articles and Islamic research papers.

Khurram Murad (Pakistan–UK, 1932–1996)
Former Director General of the Islamic Foundation, UK (1978–86). He studied civil engineering at the Universities of Karachi and Minnesota, USA, and worked as a leading consulting engineer at Karachi, Dhaka, Tehran and Riyadh. He was actively involved in the Islamic movement since 1948, he was President, Islāmī Jamiat Ṭalaba, Pakistan (1951–52); a member of the Central Executive, Jamāʿat Islāmī, Pakistan (1963–96) and Amir of its Dhaka (1963–71) and Lahore (1987–89) branches. He became *Nā'ib Amīr* of Jamāʿat Islāmī, Pakistan in 1988 and retained the position till his death in December 1996. In July 1991, he assumed Editorship of the monthly journal, *Tarjumān al-Qur'ān* and until his death strove to make it a platform for reflections on the thought and dynamics of the Islamic movement.

Khurshid Ahmad (Pakistan–UK)
A world-renowned scholar and economist. He is founding Chairman of the Islamic Foundation, UK and Institute of Policy Studies, Pakistan. Besides serving as advisor or member of several international organisations, he has held many key public positions, e.g. Federal Minister for Planning and Development and Deputy Chairman of the Planning Commission, Government of Pakistan (1978–79); Member of the Senate of Pakistan (1985–97; 2003–) and Chairman of the Senate's Standing Committee on Finance and Economic Affairs. A *Nā'ib Amīr* of Jamāʿat Islāmī, Pakistan, he has written or edited over 50 books besides contributing essays and chapters in many others. His books have been translated into Arabic, Persian, Malay and Turkish. He is currently Editor of *Tarjumān al-Qur'ān*. In recognition of his distinguished services in many fields, Khurshid Ahmad has been awarded the First Islamic Development Bank Award for Economics (1988); King Faisal Prize for Services to Islam (1990); the Fifth Annual Prize of the American Finance House, La-Riba (1998), among other awards.

Mahmud Rashdan (Jordan)
Graduated in 1975 from Wisconson University in the field of education. During his stay in North America he was a leading member of the Muslim Students Association of the USA and Canada. Currently he is an Associate Professor in the Faculty of Educational Sciences at Zarqa Private University, Jordan.

Muhammad Qutb (Egypt–Saudi Arabia)
Professor of Islamic Studies at King Abdul Aziz University, Makkah. He is a renowned Islamic scholar and is the author of over a dozen books on

Islam, some of them have been translated into a number of languages, including English, French, German, Urdu and Persian. One of his most famous titles is, *Islam: the Misunderstood Religion*, Kuwait, 1969.

Muhammad al-Ghazali (Egypt, 1917–1996)
One of the most influential Islamic scholars of the twentieth century, both as an author and in the field of *daʿwah*. Born in Buhayra, Egypt, in 1917, he graduated from the University of al-Azhar and in 1943 became an Imam and lecturer in Cairo. During the early 1950s he worked for the Islamic movement in various capacities. Subsequently his work for Islam extended over many parts of Africa, Asia, Europe and America as well as the Arab countries. Between 1971 and 1989, he rose through the ranks of the Egyptian Ministry of Awqaf, to become Under-secretary for Islamic Daʿwah. His academic career included spells of teaching at the universities of Umm al-Qurā' (Makkah) and Qatar and he served as a Chairman of the Academic Council first of al-Amir 'Abd al-Qadir University in Constantine, Algeria, and later of the International Institute of Islamic Thought in Cairo. Shaikh al-Ghazali published over sixty books, several of which have been translated in English. These include, *A Thematic Study of the Qur'an, The Muslims Character* and *Remembrace and Prayer: The Way of Prophet Muḥammad.*

Muhammad Asad (Austria, 1900–1989)
Muhammad Asad was born as Leopold Weiss into a Jewish family of Lemberg (Poland). He established himself as a journalist in Austria and later became a leading Near Eastern correspondent, a job that brought him into contact with the Muslim world. His interest in Islam and Muslims took him through adventurous journies to Egypt, Libya, Palestine, Syria, Iraq, Persia, Pakistan, Afghanistan and Saudi Arabia. Some of which are recorded in his very spiritual autobiography, *The Road to Mecca* which the *Times Literary Supplement* called 'a narrative of great power and beauty'. Muhammad Asad died in Spain in February, 1992. His other works include *The Message of the Qur'an, Islam at the Crossroads, Sahih al-Bukhari: The Early Years of Islam, Islamic Law: Scope and Equity, The Principles of State and Government in Islam* and *This Law of Ours.*

Mustafa Ahmad al-Zarqa (Syria, 1907–1999)
Born in Allepo, Syria into a family well known for its scholars. He received his *Sharīʿah* training in Aleppo from Khusruwiyya school and home tutoring from his father Shaikh Ahmad. He studied law and literature at the Syrian (now Damascus) University, then practised law for some years. He taught

at Damascus University and held the chair of Civil Law and Sharīʿah for nearly 20 years until the mid 1960s. He supervised and designed the initial publication of the Encyclopedia of Sharīʿah at the University of Awqaf in Kuwait. In 1970 he joined the Faculty of Sharīʿah at the University of Jordan where he remained till 1990. Among his numerous publications on *Sharīʿah* and civil law, the most famous is the 3–volume *Introduction to Fiqh* in which he recasts in a modern legal framework the major theories of Islamic jurisprudence, drawing on all the major schools of *fiqh*. For this work especially he received, in 1984, the King Faisal International Award in Islamic Studies.

Riza Mohammed (Trinidad–UK)
Born and brought up in Trinidad, he graduated from the University of the West Indies with a BSc (1988) and an MBBS (1994). A medical doctor by profession, he also graduated with a MRCS from the Royal College of Surgeons Edinburgh (2000). He has been actively involved in developing and organising training programmes for Islamic workers. He is currently in charge of the Tarbiyah Department of the Islamic Society of Britain. His published works include: *Islamic Workers' Training Manual Books* 1 & 2 (1986), *Lots to Do: An educational activity book for Muslim children* (1986). His edited works include: *Journey Through Islam* (1992), and *In the Early Hours: A guide to spiritual and self development* by Khurram Murad (1999).

Said Ramadan (Egypt–Switzerland, 1926–1995)
A pioneer-figure in the renaissance of Islam in Europe, and an outstanding exponent of the ideas of Hasan al-Banna. Egypt. He completed his PhD in Islamic Law at the University of Cologne, Germany. He was a founding Director of the Islamic Centre, Geneva and has published numerous books and articles in Arabic. He was former Editor of the Arabic journal *Al-Muslimūn*. Said Ramadan's translated publications into English include: *Islamic Law: Scope and Equity* (1970).

Sayyid Abul Ala Mawdudi (Pakistan, 1903–1979)
Founder of Jamāʿat Islāmī, which started in 1938 and grew to become a major Islamic movement of the contemporary Muslim world. Mawdudi trained as a journalist and was a prolific writer. Along with his contemporary, Hasan al-Banna, he expounded an ideological framework for Islamic resurgence in the post-*Khilāfah* world. Among his major works are *Tafhīm al-Qur'ān* (Towards Understanding the Qur'ān), *Sunnat ki 'Aini Hathiyat*, (*The Constitutional Role of the Sunnah*), *Khilāfat wa-Mulukīyat* (*Caliphate and*

Monarchy), *Sūd* (Usury), *Maʿāshiyāt-e-Islām* (*The Islamic Economy*), *Islāmi Riyāsat* (The Islamic State) and *Jihād*. A man of tremendous vision, knowledge and enthusiasm, Mawdudi left a lasting impression on the 20th Century and beyond.

Sayyid Abul Hasan Ali Nadwi (India, 1914–1999)
Abul Hasan Ali Nadwi or Ali Mian, as he was lovingly called, was a world famous scholar who had a very wide appeal. He was born and based in India and from 1961 until his death, he was the Rector of Dār ul-ʿUlūm, Nadwatul ʿUlamā' (India), the school his father helped to found. Under his leadership the Nadwah grew into a world renowned Islamic University. He was a powerful, eloquent writer and orator, both in Urdu and Arabic. Though he was a specialist in Islamic history and *Sīrah*, his writing are very diverse, ranging from Islamic faith and literature to the contemporary problems facing Muslims. Many have been translated into English: among them are *Islam and the World, Western Civilisation: Islam and Muslims, Four Pillars of Islam, Saviours of the Islamic Spirit, Glory of Iqbal, Muslims in the West, Faith Versus Materialism, Islamic Concept of Prophethood* and *Muslims in India.*

Sayyid Qutb (Egypt, 1906–66)
Sayyid Qutb was a prominent Muslim thinker of the 20th century. Born in 1906, he came from a deeply religious Egyptian background. He started his career as a literary scholar, and wrote with a profound sense of conviction which eventually led him to give his life for his beliefs. He was executed in August 1966 by the Nasser regime of Egypt for refusing to withdraw his criticisms of corruption in Egyptian society. His translated works in English include *The Islamic Concept and its Characteristics, Milestones, In the Shade of the Qur'an, Islam the Religion of the Future, Social Justice in Islam* and *Islam and Universal Peace.*

Sayyid Asad Gilani (Pakistan, 1922–1992)
A prominent leader of the Jamāʿat Islāmī, he completed his PhD on the Jamāʿat from the University of Punjab, Lahore. He has authored over a hundred books and pamphlets in Urdu and his translated works include *Mawdudi: Thought and Movement, Islam: A Mission and a Movement* and *The Methodology of Prophet Muhammad's Islamic Revolution.*

Sayyid Sabiq (Egypt, 1915–2000)
Born in Egypt he was a prominent member and scholar of the Muslim Brotherhood and a close associate of Hasan al-Banna. His lasting

contribution to the Muslim *Ummah* is his work *Fiqh us-Sunnah* which brings together the opinions of different *madhhabs* in an easy to understand manner and compares their viewpoints.

Yusuf al-Qaradawi (Egypt-Qatar)

Born in 1926, he proved to be a diligent and earnest student of Islam in early life. By his tenth birthday he had memorised the entire Qur'ān. He attended Al-Azhar University and received his PhD in Islamic Jurisprudence with first class honours. He worked with the Muslim Brotherhood organisation in Egypt and was imprisoned for almost 20 years. He is currently Dean of Sharīʿah and Chairman of the Centre of Sunnah and Sīrah Studies, University of Qatar. A prolific author, he has become widely read and acknowledged as one of the foremost Islamic authorities in the contemporary world. His translated works in English include: *The Lawful and the Prohibited in Islam, The Voice of a Woman in Islam, Fiqh az-Zakāh, Islamic Education and Hasan al-Banna, Islamic Awakening between Rejection and Extremism, Priorities of the Islamic Movement in the Coming Phase* and *Time in the Life of a Muslim.*

INTRODUCTION

WHAT IS *ISLAM: THE WAY OF REVIVAL*?

Islam: The Way of Revival is an anthology of writings reflecting various aspects of the Islamic way of life. The chapters and writers have been chosen for their expression of Islam as a holistic way of life and for their perspectives on how Muslims can engage with the modern-day environment. They offer views shared by scholars and activists involved in the Islamic movement, the world over. They represent Islam as Muslims understand it and live it. The word 'revival' is associated with an Islamic tradition that has not only created a spiritual, moral or socio-political vision, but has organised and mobilised people to engage in public life. While Islam is essentially about one's relationship with God, it is by organised action, or by being useful to one's society, that this relationship is given its deepest meaning. The revival of that relationship with God hence implies a revival of society.

THE RATIONALE

It is ironic that this collection should be published at the dawn of the twenty-first century, for in many respects, it looks back at the last hundred years in the *Ummah's* pursuit to regain its lost identity and direction.

We view this publication as appropriate in the light of the grave misunderstanding about Islam which has existed and continues to exist among Muslims and non-Muslims alike. Often what people learn about Islam comes from the electronic and print media and these often provide an interpretation of Islam which lacks objectivity. There are also deliberate distortions. In recent times it has become clear that the misunderstanding of Islam is not just from the outside. There are some Muslims who decide to act in the name of Islam while they have little understanding of the spiritual, moral and peaceful ethos of Islam. We hope that many of these misconceptions will be tackled by the writings in this collection.

THE HISTORY

The present compilation started as articles used in study circles in Trinidad in the 1970s. At that time they were photocopied and circulated as loose sheets. Because of the overwhelming positive feedback we received about their usefulness, it was felt that it would be a good idea to have them in a single text. As a result, the articles were compiled, edited and published in 1992 under the title *Journey Through Islam*.

The collection was circulated to Muslim activists in Trinidad and Tobago, the neighbouring Caribbean Islands, South America, North America and the United Kingdom. All the copies were sold out almost immediately and the reviews were very favourable. The continuing requests for copies meant reprinting it. After some deliberation and consultation, it was decided to publish a new edition that contained additional articles and which addressed various fresh issues and challenges of the Muslim *Ummah* over the last decade.

The current edition is published here in two volumes. *Islam: The Way of Revival, Volume 1* covers the themes: Islamic Worldview; The Qur'ān; The Prophet Muḥammad; Worship, Ethics and Law; and Self-Development. *Volume 2* covers the themes: Islamic Way of Life, Family Life, Islamic Revival, and Society.

THE PROCESS OF COMPILATION

The two main objectives in making the final selections for this anthology were:

- to present all aspects of the Islamic way of life that deal with issues which are relevant to contemporary society.
- to choose a broad spectrum of authors involved in Islamic revival over the last hundred years.

The task of preparing such a compilation presented some difficulties since some of the authors did not communicate in the English language. Additionally, some of the selections in the book were originally speeches. As one may well appreciate, transcribing them and preparing them for publication was indeed an onerous task. Thus, editorial changes had to be made in order to render the text more cohesive, understandable and accessible to English language readers. However the Editors have tried to remain faithful to the spirit of the original text and message of the author. It should also be mentioned that in such a broad collection, not all views expressed will reflect those held by the Editors, or indeed other writers that appear within the two volumes.

As this work will be published in two volumes, a cumulative Index will appear at the end of the second volume. With respect to spellings and references, we have kept 's' and 'z' use (e.g. Islamise/Islamize) as they initially appeared in original texts and as some of these were written in the UK and others in the US, a disparity is visible. We also kept citations of the Qur'ān and *Ḥadīth* in their original quoted form (with corrections where necessary) and did not refer to a standard translation. Diacritical marks have been used to transliterate Arabic words (though not names of authors) in order to help the reader correctly pronounce these words.

THE CONTENT

The theme of this collection is that Islam is an integrated, comprehensive way of life that is dynamic. And so, it is relevant to today's modern world in providing real and lasting solutions to the increasing challenges of modern-day life. In addition, it establishes that Islam is not merely a theoretical religious concept nor any utopian ideal, but must be manifested as a practical reality in the daily lives of Muslims.

In this anthology, we have attempted to concentrate on presenting fundamental Islamic beliefs and values, as well as Islamic perspectives on many topical issues including: education, family life, self development and Islamic culture.

A significant number of selections were taken from *The Muslim*, the magazine of FOSIS (Federation of the Student Islamic Societies of the UK and Eire), *Islamic Horizons*, magazine of the Islamic Society of North America and *Al-Ittihad*, journal of the Muslim Students Association of USA and Canada – three of the leading Muslim English Language publications in their own time, articulating ideas and views of many foremost thinkers and workers of the Islamic movement.

The contributing authors were people who made tremendous sacrifices while working and struggling to share the message of Islam. Indeed, some gave up their lives for the cause of Islam. Also, many of them spent substantial periods of time in the West. This enabled them to understand Western society and, therefore, how to best practise Islam in the West, as well as, how to articulate its message to people in the West. No fewer than 10 chapters have been included from the works of Khurram Murad, who influenced a generation of Muslim youth (in both the East and the West) through his example, training and published works.

WHO SHOULD READ THIS BOOK?

Anyone, Muslim or non-Muslim, wishing to learn more about Islam, especially the revivalist tradition. The chapters are useful to a general audience (including college and university students, teachers, professionals), and any serious student of Islam. In fact, most of the chapters can be easily adapted for *khuṭbahs* or Islamic sermons, short discussions on Islam or as a teacher's guide for Islamic reflections. Furthermore, the chapters are concise enough to be used for self-study and group discussions on Islam.

HOW TO READ THIS BOOK

For the reader who has basic or cursory knowledge of Islam, it is recommended that this book be studied in the same order as the chapters are arranged since there is a sequential development of the ideas. However, those individuals who have a good grounding in Islam and are interested in specific issues, may simply use the table of contents as a guide. In either case, it is recommended that the chapters be studied continuously over time to crystallise the ideas.

One would encounter an inevitable degree of overlap between some chapters. However, we believe that this will serve to benefit the reader since emphasis can make for clearer understanding and appreciation. It is always the case that issues will be addressed from different perspectives by different authors and with such a variety of scholars one would expect different viewpoints.

ACKNOWLEDGEMENTS

Besides the authors of the chapters, the editors and writers of magazines and books which originally published some of the texts contained in this publication and their publishers, there are many individuals who assisted us in ensuring that this publication became a reality. We express our sincerest thanks to all of them and ask Allah's choicest blessings on them. Two individuals deserve special mention, Asim Abdullah and Alyasa Abdullah, who worked on the original version of this collection, *Journey Through Islam*. We would also like to thank the Madina Trust for their kind moral and financial support in the publication of these volumes.

It is our sincere hope that you will benefit from this publication as much as we did. Many of the writings herein have proved invaluable to us and have furnished us with essential tools needed to add value and direction to our individual and collective lives.

May Allah, guide us all in our quest for Truth and our duty to make the world a better place.

The Editors,
March 2003.

ISLAM

THE WAY OF REVIVAL

VOL 1

A. THE ISLAMIC WORLDVIEW

Is Religion Relevant Today?
Muhammad Asad

What is Islam?
Sayyid Abul Ala Mawdudi

The Basic Truths
Jaafar Shaikh Idris

Understanding Faith
Hasan al-Banna

Why Islam?
Ismail al-Faruqi

To be a Muslim
Fathi Yakan

Islam – a Liberating Force
Said Ramadan

Submission to God
Alija Ali Izetbegovic

I

Is Religion Relevant Today?

Muhammad Asad

For many thousands of years – from the earliest, dim beginnings of human consciousness – religion was a mighty power which drove people on and on towards some unknown goal. It was not, however, the only driving power. There was also hunger and human ambition. But throughout history religion was always in the foreground, for good or ill. In its name, kingdoms were built and nations came to life and kingdoms were destroyed and nations made to disappear. Under its spell human beings rose to the most sublime heights of love and self sacrifice while others committed the most cruel deeds of violence for its sake. Whilst it gave a greater joy of living to many, it caused others to despise life as an illusion of vanity. It filled some people with creative fervour and gave them strength to achieve imperishable cultural feats, while in others it gave rise to superstition, obscurantism and stupidity. But to all who followed it sincerely, in this or that form, religion somehow gave happiness.

Therefore, in spite of the great and painfully obvious diversity across different religious faiths and views, something must have been, or must be, common to all of them. It must be a very important 'something': for it gives happiness.

RELIGION: THE SOURCE OF ETHICS AND MORALITY

Obviously, this 'something' is the religious person's conviction, being in agreement with what metaphysics describes as the Ultimate Reality, or the

Absolute. Whatever the tenets of a religion, however sublime or primitive its teaching – whether monotheistic, polytheistic or pantheistic – the innermost core of every religious experience is, firstly, the conviction that all Being and Happening in this world is the outcome of a conscious, creative, all-embracing Power – or, to put it more simply, a Divine Will; and, secondly, the feeling that one is, or desires to be, in spiritual accord with the demands of that Will. On this conviction, on this feeling and desire, was and is based a human being's faculty to judge between Good and Evil. For, unless we presume that an Absolute, planning Will is at the root of all creation, there is no sense in presuming that any of our aims and actions can be intrinsically right or wrong, moral or immoral; in other words, unless we believe in the existence of such a planning Will, we have no definite standard by which to judge our aims and actions. In the absence of a central belief, the concept of morality loses all its precision and resolves itself into a series of vague conventions, which in their turn, become more and more subject to 'expediency' that is, to the question of whether an aim or an action is useful to a particular person (or to the community to which the person belongs), or not. Consequently, Right and Wrong become purely relative terms, arbitrarily interpreted according to one's personal or communal needs and the changing requirements of time as also the economic environment.

These reflections on the role of religious thought in the realm of morality assume paramount importance if we realise that the trend of our own time is definitely antagonistic towards religious thought. Everywhere and every day we are being told by a certain class of intellectuals that religion is nothing but a relic of man's barbaric past, now to be superseded by the 'Age of Science'. Science, they say, is about to take the place of worn-out religious systems; science, so gloriously and irresistibly expanding will teach people to live in accordance with pure reason, and will ultimately help them to evolve new standards of morality without any metaphysical sanction.

Now this naïve optimism with regard to science is in reality not at all 'modern': it is rather extremely old-fashioned, an uncritical copy of the naïve optimism of the Western world during the 18th and 19th centuries. At that time (and particularly during the second half of the 19th century) many Western scientists believed that the solution to the mysteries of the Universe was 'just around the corner', and that, henceforth, nothing would stop people from arranging their life in God-like independence and reasonableness. Thinkers of the 20th century, however, are much more reserved, not to say sceptical. They have found that deterministic science is unable to fulfil the spiritual hopes attached to it in the recent past: for the mysteries of the Universe become more mysterious and more complicated the more our research advances. Every day it becomes more obvious that it will never be possible to answer by purely scientific means the question as to how the Universe came into being and how life originated in it, and, therefore, the question as to the true nature and purpose of human existence. But so long as we are not in a position to answer the latter question we cannot even attempt to define Good and Evil: simply because these terms have no meaning unless they are related to a knowledge, real or imaginary, of the nature and purpose of human existence. And so long as we are not in a position to define Good and Evil there is no sense in talking about standards of morality.

This is just what advanced scientists are now beginning to realise. Faced with the impossibility of deciding metaphysical questions by means of physical research, they have given up the childish hope of the last two centuries that science could ever provide directives in the field of ethics. Not that they discard science as such: on the contrary, they believe that it will lead humankind to ever greater marvels of knowledge and achievement, but at the same time, they realise that science has no direct connection with people's moral life. Science can, and does guide us to a better understanding of the world around us and in us; but, being solely concerned with observations of the facts of Nature, and with the analysis of the laws that appear to govern the inter-relations of those facts, science cannot be called upon to deliver a verdict as to the purpose, if any, of human life, and thus to create moral consciousness in us. No amount of enthusiasm for scientific thinking can hide the fact that the problem of morality is not within the scope of science. It is, on the other hand, entirely within the scope of religion.

It is through religious experience alone that we can arrive, rightly or wrongly, at standards of moral and ethical evaluation independent of the ephemeral changes in our environment; at the recognition of a moral Good worth striving for, and of a moral Evil that must be avoided. I have said, 'rightly or wrongly' for, by all objective canons, there is always the possibility of a religion, any religion, being mistaken in its metaphysical premises. Therefore, our acceptance or rejection of any religion must, in the last resort, be guided by our experience and our reason, which tell us how far that particular religion agrees with people's ultimate needs, physical and spiritual.

But this necessity of exerting our critical faculties with regard to religion does not detract from the fundamental proposition that it is religion alone that can endow our life with a meaning, and can, thus, promote in us the urge to conform our behaviour to a pattern of moral values entirely independent of the momentary constellation of our existence. To phrase it differently, it is religion alone that can provide a broad platform for an agreement, among large groups of people, as to what is Good and therefore desirable, and what is Evil and therefore to be avoided. Could there be any doubt that such an agreement is an absolute, indispensable requirement for any sort of order in human relations?

Considered from this viewpoint, the religious urge (taking the word 'religion' in its widest sense) is not a mere passing phase in the history of human development but rather the ultimate source of ethics and morality; not the outcome of cheap credulity which any age could 'outgrow' but rather the only answer to a real, basic need of people at all times and in all environments. In other words, it is an instinct.

RELIGION TODAY

Nevertheless, there is no getting away from the fact that religion is on a steep decline today. Not because human nature has become 'depraved': it is intrinsically as good or as bad as it always was, capable of reaching the greatest heights of selflessness and idealism or of descending into the deepest abyss of cruelty and greed. Nor is there any sign that the human being has lost his instinctive desire to co-ordinate his individual life with larger, spiritual interests which transcend the material interests of one's private existence: for, what other explanation is there for the semi-religious fervour underlying such modern movements as communism or nationalism? That these movements are but meagre substitutes for religion in its true sense does not in the least disprove our contention that the modern person feels the need for religion exactly as did the thousands of generations before him. But he goes in for substitutes because the real thing is denied to him.

Yes, because it is denied to him. The official 'guardians' of religion, of every religion, have miserably failed in their most cardinal task: to show people how to arrange the practical side of their lives in conformity with religion's moral appeal. Indeed, many conventional religious beliefs have become estranged from the problems and perplexities of present-day life. Furthermore, because, from a social and economic viewpoint, our time is essentially a time of confusion, the failure of religious leaders to guide us in the business of our life is fraught with truly catastrophic consequences.

Owing to the rapid development of science and its practical application to industry, communications, warfare, labour conditions, and so forth, the conventional systems of social co-operation have been thrown out of gear all over the world. The most elementary problems of life: bread and clothing, poverty and security, work and education, have become so complicated that they now constitute problems in the fullest and most baffling sense of the word. Not that there ever was a period when these things were less important than they are now. People always needed bread and clothing, poverty was always a bitter worry, and security always the aim: but in previous epochs, when society did not possess its present complexity, all such problems were comparatively easy of solution and did not, therefore, occupy people's minds as desperately as they do now. By virtue of its stupendous progress in recent times, science has entirely changed the conditions of our existence. It has opened new, unexpected vistas, with all the attending complications, in almost every branch of human activity. It has made possible many things. Some of them creative and full of promise for the future, some of them destructive and full of terror. But none of them dreamt of by previous generations. Furthermore, precisely because these things had not been dreamt of (that is, had not been anticipated in the social concepts evolved in the past) the majority of people had, intellectually and morally, not been properly prepared for them. The net result now is that we possess neither the requisite economic technique nor the ethical maturity to adequately cope with this new situation. The intensity of people's search for new ways and means to resolve this perplexity is mirrored in the emergence of the many social ideologies which are now warring for predominance. Their widely conflicting claims make us realise that the very basis of our conventional thought, the assurance of stability in our social forms and in the relations between one human being and another, has broken down entirely.

This turmoil in socio-economic views did not, and could not, remain confined to the purely material side of our affairs. It has invaded our beliefs as well. Naturally so, for the confusion of our politics and economics gives rise to a very far-reaching criticism of the ethical and religious convictions on which those politics and economics have hitherto rested: the more so as our religious leaders have become accustomed to taking every convention for granted and contributing precious little towards a solution to the perplexities with which modern life is beset. And so the political and socio-economic unrest of our days has its counterpart in deep unrest on the ethical plane.

It is not difficult to see that the question as to what is Good or Evil in a relative, socio-economic sense (in other words, what form of social organisation results in a maximum of common good) is intimately connected with the question of what is Good or Evil in an absolute, spiritual sense. It is for this reason that many people in the East as well as in the West are beginning to feel an uneasiness not exclusively due to the political and economic turmoil of the day. Strong doubts have arisen as to whether the mere re-arrangement of the current economic systems, a mere victory of this or that political ideology, will suffice to resolve the present chaos into something resembling order. Slowly, the conviction is gaining ground that something far deeper than the mere conflicts of political and economic views is ultimately responsible for the confusion evident in the world of today. That 'far deeper' thing is the obvious breakdown of all standards of moral valuation. We now realise that the crisis of our time is, in the last resort, a crisis of moral and ethical ideas.

Almost all the ethical concepts which hitherto were active in the shaping of people's social relations and the idea of 'common good' are now passing through a severe test, and many of them have been found inadequate in meeting the demands of present-day life. Because the majority of the religious leaders all over the world have been wont to regard the prevailing social conventions as identical with religion itself, and have, thus, proved completely ineffectual in their real task of guiding people's practical endeavours, centuries-old religious beliefs have been shaken and are now everywhere in the melting-pot. Many social conventions which were habitually connected with those beliefs and which were, therefore, thought to have been built on eternal foundations are now visibly cracking; not just in this or that community, but in all communities, and in every part of the globe. Generally speaking, religion is everywhere on the retreat, and is being inadequately supplanted by 'substitute' emotions and convictions, like that infantile enthusiasm for the dawning 'Age of Science', or more dangerously by a passionate worship of the gods of nationalism. As already mentioned, the cult of nationalism so characteristic of our time has an emotional, almost mystic colouring which gives it its superficial resemblance to religion. Unlike religion, which starts and ends with the concept of absolute Good and Evil (however different this concept may be in each particular religion), nationalism denies, in its very essence, the existence of absolute Good and Evil. It recognises these terms only in a relative sense; namely, in relation to what is, or seems to be, Good or Evil for the development of a particular nation, and, thus, it destroys the very basis of ethics and morality.

From whatever angle we look at this problem, we must not forget that throughout human history ethics was derived, directly or indirectly, from religious thought. So far, no alternative source of ethics has been discovered. Nor is there the slightest indication that 'non-religious' ethics is at all possible for whatever today goes by this name is in reality a subconscious heritage of past religious thought. Precisely because there is no such indication the space of human life which was once filled, and filled to satisfaction, with religious beliefs and hopes, is now gradually being transformed into a gaping void, an emptiness in which nothing can thrive but despair: unspoken despair as to the future of the human being, as to the purpose and spiritual justification of his life, as to whether there really are such values as Good and Evil.

The bitterness of the struggles, physical and moral, that now shake humanity; the helpless ferocity dictated mainly by fear with which nations, and groups within nations, compete with each other for power; the universal disregard of right and justice, the ruthless exploitation of the weak by the strong, and everybody's distrust of everybody, all these are but symptoms of the ethical frustration from which the majority of people today are suffering. This frustration is ultimately responsible for all the wars and all the civil strife of our time and it causes untold misery in body and mind to untold numbers of people. The feeling not only of social but also of moral insecurity, the feeling that our affairs are rushing wildly, like a river that has burst its banks, into unknown and unpredictable directions, is steadily mounting among the more aware of our generation.

RELIGION AND THE WEST

This holds good for the world of Islam as well. We, like all the others, live in the midst of a whirling flood. For us, as for all the others, the time of moral confusion has come. Our society is in ferment. Many of its time-honoured conventions, some of them irrelevant to Islamic life but many of them indispensable to it, are now dissolving under the pressure of Western cultural influences and of economic necessities arising from our submission to those influences. Despite all the slogans raised in the name of Islam, in spite of the enthusiasm for a re-orientation of Muslim political and economic thought in the direction of Islam, in spite of all this, the fact remains that to the majority of present-day Muslims, the appeal of religion is becoming increasingly theoretical, and that less and less individuals are prepared to apply the principles of Islam (in distinction from Islamic slogans) to their personal behaviour and their social endeavours.

Our Westernised 'progressives' do not even bother to deny this. Most of them maintain, with a self-satisfied smirk, that 'the spirit of the time is against religious thought'.

Now this is perfectly true. The spirit of the time is against religious thought but it is a spirit born and bred in the West, relevant only to the historical experiences of the West, and entirely irrelevant to the problem of Islam. For, if Western thinkers turn against religion they can be understood and excused on the grounds of their experiences with their own religion, namely, (Western) Christianity. No such excuse is, historically speaking, valid for the Muslims. The Islamic concept of, and Muslim experiences with, religion are of a different nature. So different is it that only extreme density can prevent a person from realising that it is not religion as such that has been discredited, but only the peculiar form it attained in the West. It is true that there is a resurgence in Christian thinkers grappling with the notion of faith in the public arena, yet figures such as Augustine and Aquinas were rare in classical Christianity. It is that history that is the focus of my comments, for broadly speaking, Christianity declined because, from the very beginning it divorced itself from the worldly aspect of the human being's existence, from his bodily life, his physical needs and desires, his economics, and his politics. It drew a dividing line between 'that which is God's' (or, ethics and morality) and 'that which is Caesar's' (or, the realm of government, economics and social organisation). This was the logical outcome of Christianity's central teaching which postulates a gulf between the alleged Evil of the 'natural' life in this world and the Good of 'supernatural' spirituality.

In Christian theology, spirit and matter were entities, essentially opposed to one another. Matter was essentially a domain of Evil, and a person's attachment to it synonymous with his attachment to Evil. Consequently 'redemption' was conditional upon a person's spirit freeing itself from the entanglements of matter and returning to its ideal state from which it has lapsed by an act of perversity called Original Sin. According to St. Paul, the real founder of Christian metaphysics, the source of all sin is the 'flesh'.

Thus, Christian ethics rested on a condemnation of the physical, sensual aspect of a human being's life. Whatever modern Christian theology may have made or is trying to make of its original attitude in this respect there can be no doubt that contempt of sensual life was at the root of its early teachings. In the Middle Ages, when the Church was the only fount of the Europeans' ethical concepts, the correctness of this attitude was never questioned, and the life of the body, with all its sensations and desires, was regarded not only as inferior but as opposed to spiritual life. And even in our days, when Christianity has lost a good deal of its influence on the Western mind, and the rights of the body tend to be more and more exalted, even exaggerated, the derogatory meaning still attached in all European languages to the word 'sensuality' bears ample evidence to its ethical background. An example thereof can be seen in the naïve assumption, so popular in the West, that the Prophet Muḥammad could not have been a person of 'high spirituality' because he enjoyed, and advised his followers to enjoy, the most intense of all sensual experiences: sexual-life. Modern interpretations cannot hide the anti-sensual and anti-physical attitude of Christianity, and none of the concessions which Christian theologians now make to the changing mentality of the West can alter that historical fact.

But, as was only to be expected, the Church could not achieve the impossible. It could not in reality eliminate the 'urges of the flesh' from people's life. Similarly, in spite of its insistence on the 'devilish' aspect of the world of Matter, the Church could not suppress a person's natural interest in worldly affairs and his desire for material progress. And so, quite early in the Middle Ages, a compromise was reached between a person's ineradicable tendencies on the one hand, and the teachings of the Church, on the other. The Church made it silently understood that all those vital aspects of the human nature are some sort of 'necessary' Evil; and, further, that they need not always run counter to the demands of religion, but have simply nothing to do with religion. By thus relegating all practical concerns of life outside the realm of religion, the Church gave birth to that typically Western idea that religion and worldly affairs belong to different compartments of life.

It is, therefore, not due to any moral defect on the part of Europeans or Americans that in practice they never conformed to the ideals of Christianity. They never could conform to these principles. Nor did the Church, in point of fact, ever seriously insist on a practical application of all its teachings. It was, always, fully satisfied with merely postulating them as a theoretical, unattainable idea.

To a Muslim, nurtured on quite a different concept of religion, it may sound strange that people could ever have been satisfied with ethics as something apart from the practical problems of life. Nevertheless this is how ethics was usually, with some exceptions, conceived of in Christian society.

Despite all the assertions to the contrary, few of the Western economists or politicians would ever allow his moral convictions to overrule 'expediency': for history taught them that ethics and morality deal with beautiful ideals, fit to be discussed in edifying sermons in the church, but 'business is business'.

Since Christianity was the only religious experience of the Western world for so many centuries, the West grew accustomed to identifying it with 'religion' in general. Furthermore the West's modern, obvious disappointment with Christianity has assumed the colour of disappointment with the religious principle as such. In reality, however, Westerners have become disappointed with the only form of religion they have ever known.

And at the same time they remember that the Church only too often lent a helping hand to oppression and exploitation, to secular power holders anxious to keep intact social conditions that were manifestly unjust to the many but very profitable to the power-holders themselves. What wonder then that to many people in the West the very name of religion has become suspect? This simply because of their fear that religious interest might once again be used as a cloak for the forces of darkness and oppression.

WHAT ABOUT ISLAM?

My purpose is not to make a comparison of Christianity and Islam as religions, but to look at one specific issue, namely: why the notion of religion became irrelevent to so many people?

Firstly, Islam knows nothing of a division of human life into 'physical' and 'spiritual' compartments, and has never reduced religion to a mere spiritual cult. The system which the Prophet Muḥammad enunciated in the twenty-three years of his ministry refers not only to matters spiritual, and aims not only at individual righteousness, but provides a framework for all our individual and social activities as well. It embraces life in all its aspects, moral and physical, individual and communal, the problems of the flesh and of the mind, of sex and economics, of morality and aesthetics. Side by side with problems of worship and theology, these aspects of our daily lives find legitimate place in the Prophet's teachings. We have been offered by him the vision of an equitable society, and of the type of person, which such a society presupposes. We have been given the outline of a political scheme (the outline only, because the details of peoples' political and economic needs are time-bound and, therefore, variable) as well as a scheme of individual rights and social duties in which all possibilities of historical evolution are duly anticipated. And as there is no division of reality into 'physical' and 'spiritual' compartments, there is no possibility of dividing it into 'natural' and 'supernatural' planes. To a Muslim, everything that is or happens is within the natural sphere; for Nature is the sum total of all Creation, visible and invisible, concrete and abstract; and the so-called laws of Nature are but the way in which the Will of God becomes manifest. In such a scheme of things there can be no conflict between the moral and physical aspects of people's existence; they are inseparable, and therefore equally 'justified'.

Secondly, the great exponents of Islamic theology and jurisprudence were the most jealous guardians of human rights. It is they who always stood up – frequently at the cost of great personal sacrifice and sometimes even martyrdom – against tyranny and oppression, and, thus, imposed the most severe checks on the power-holders' will to exploit. It is entirely to the credit of such *ʿulamāʾ* or religious scholars of the past and of the religion which inspired them, that the Muslim nations were spared the miseries which were the common people's lot in Europe for many centuries.

Thirdly, while there was always a conflict between Christianity and science – manifested, on the one hand, in fantastic, irrational dogmas and, on the other, in the most atrocious persecution of scientific thought and of scientists down to modern times – we are unable to discover the slightest trace of a conflict between Islam and science, be it in the teachings themselves or in the attitude of Muslim *ʿulamāʾ* towards scientists.

This latter point has an important bearing on our discussion: for it is undeniable that the main Western objection to religion is Christianity's other-worldliness in general, and its historic opposition to the march of science, in particular. If we add to this the severe strain which most of the Christian dogmas imposed on the intellect, we can easily understand the slogan, 'Religion is opposed to Science'. But we rarely stop to inquire whether the historical outlook and the attitude of the Christian Church are symptomatic of religion as such – that is of every religion. Is it not possible that other religions may have been built on the idea that there is no conflict between science and religion? In point of fact, Islamic history shows, with regard to science, a picture quite different from the one offered by Christendom. Not only was Islam never opposed to science: it even conferred on science, and on intellectual endeavours generally, something of the sanctity of worship. In contrast with the burning and torturing of scholars, the destruction of so many works of science, the suppression of independent thought in different spheres of life, history does not furnish a single instance of a scientist (of whatever description) having been persecuted under Muslim rule because of his scientific findings. Persecution of theologians and scholars there have been – occasional attempts at suppression of individuals who deviated from the 'orthodox' theology of the day, but of scientists never. Simply because Islam inculcated in its followers the greatest respect for learning and made 'the search after knowledge the sacred duty (*farḍ*) of every Muslim' (*Bukhārī*). No accident, therefore, that many of the Muslim pioneers of science whose names are now household words the world over, were, at the same time, outstanding theologians and *fuqahā'*. They had only to turn their eyes to the Qur'ān and the *Sunnah* of the Prophet in order to find that by acquiring scientific knowledge they would truly worship their Lord. When they read of the Prophet's teachings that, 'God sends down no disease without sending down a cure for it as well' (*Bukhārī*), they understood that by searching for unknown cures they would contribute to a fulfilment of God's Will; and so medical research became invested with the Holiness of a religious duty. They read the verse of the Qur'ān, *We have created everything out of water* (21: 30), and in their endeavour to penetrate the depths of these words they began to study living organisms and so developed the science of biology. The Qur'ān pointed to the harmony of the stars and their movements as witnesses of their Creator's Glory, and, thereupon, the sciences of astronomy and mathematics were taken up by the Muslims with the fervour which in other religions is reserved only for Prayer. In the same way they took to physiology, chemistry, zoology, and to all the other sciences in which the Muslim genius was to find its most lasting monument.

In those far-away times, every Muslim was accustomed to the view that 'the scientist walks in the Path of God', as the Prophet had so beautifully expressed it. Instances of the highest honours awarded by Muslim rulers and

Muslim society to seekers after scientific Truth, and of the greatest practical encouragement given to scientific research, are beyond counting. Throughout the whole creative period of Muslim history, that is to say, during the first five centuries after the *Hijrah*, science had no greater champion than Muslim civilisation, and no home more secure than the lands in which Islam was supreme. In a word, it was Islam that gave incentive to the cultural achievements which constitute one of the proudest pages in the history of humankind and it gave that incentive by saying 'Yes' to life and 'No' to asceticism. 'Yes' to the intellect and 'No' to obscurantism. 'Yes' to action and 'No' to quietism.

2

What is Islam?

Abul Ala Mawdudi

Every religion of the world has been named either after its founder or after the community or nation in which it was born. For instance, Christianity takes its name from its Prophet Jesus Christ; Buddhism from its founder, Gautama Buddha; Zoroastrianism from its founder Zoroaster; and Judaism, the religion of the Jews, from the name of the tribe of Judah (of the land of Judea) where it originated. The same is true of all other religions except Islam, which enjoys the unique distinction of having no such association with any particular person or people or country. Nor is it the product of any human mind. It is a universal religion and its objective is to create and cultivate in human beings the quality and attitude of Islam.

Islam in fact, is an attributive title. Anyone who possesses this attribute, whatever race, community, country or group he belongs to, is a Muslim. According to the Qur'ān, among every people and in all ages there have been good and righteous people who possessed this attribute and all of them were and are Muslims.

ISLAM – WHAT DOES IT MEAN?

Islam is an Arabic word and connotes submission, surrender and obedience. As a religion, Islam stands for complete submission and obedience to God.

Everyone can see that we live in an orderly universe, where everything is assigned a place in a grand scheme. The moon, the stars and all the heavenly bodies are knit together in a magnificent system. They follow unalterable laws and make not even the slightest deviation from their ordained courses. Similarly, everything in the world, from the minute whirling electron to the mighty nebulae, invariably follows its own laws. Matter, energy and life – all obey their laws and grow and change and live and die in accordance with those laws. Even in the human world the laws of nature are paramount. Each person's birth, growth and life are all regulated by a set of biological laws. He derives sustenance from nature in accordance with an unalterable law. All the organs of his body, from the smallest tissues to the heart and brain, are governed by the laws prescribed for them. In short, ours is a law-governed universe and everything in it follows its assigned course.

The powerful, all-pervasive law, which governs all that comprises the universe, from the tiniest specks of dust to the magnificent galaxies, is the law of God, the Creator and Ruler of the universe. As the whole of creation obeys the law of God, the whole universe, therefore, literally follows the religion of Islam – for Islam signifies nothing but obedience and submission to God, the Lord of the Universe. The sun, the moon, the earth and all other heavenly bodies are thus Muslim. So are the air, water, heat, stones, trees and animals. Everything in the universe is 'Muslim' for it obeys God by submission to His laws. Even a person who refuses to believe in God, or offers his worship to someone other than God, has necessarily to be a 'Muslim' as far as his existence is concerned.

For his entire life, from the embryonic stage to the body's dissolution into dust after death, every tissue of a person's muscles and every limb of his body follows the course prescribed by God's law. His very tongue, which, on account of his ignorance advocates the denial of God or professes multiple deities, is in its very nature 'Muslim'. His head which he wantonly bows to others besides God is born 'Muslim'. His heart, which, through his lack of true knowledge, cherishes love and reverence for others, is 'Muslim' by intuition. These are all obedient to the Divine law, and their functions and movements are governed by the injunctions of that law alone.

Let us now examine the situation from a different angle. The human being is so constituted that there are two distinct spheres of his activity. One is the sphere in which he finds himself totally regulated by the Divine law. Like other creatures, he is completely caught in the grip of the physical laws of nature and is bound to follow them. But there is another sphere of his activity. He has been endowed with reason and intellect. He has the power to think and form judgements, to choose and reject, to approve and spurn. He is free to adopt whatever course of life he chooses. He can embrace any faith, and live by any ideology he likes. He may prepare his own code of conduct or accept one formulated by others. Unlike other creatures, he has been given freedom of thought, choice and action. In short, the human being has been bestowed with free will. Both these aspects co-exist side by side in a person's life.

In the first instance, the human being like all other creatures, is a born Muslim, invariably obeying the natural laws of God, and is bound to remain one. As far as the second aspect is concerned, he is free to become or not to become a Muslim. It is the way a person exercises this freedom which divides people into believers and non-believers. An individual, who chooses to acknowledge his Creator, accepts Him as his real Master, honestly and scrupulously submits to His laws and injunctions. He has achieved completeness in his Islam by consciously deciding to obey God in the domain in which he was endowed with freedom of choice. He is a perfect Muslim: his submission of his entire self to the will of God is Islam and nothing but Islam.

The human being has now consciously submitted to Him Whom he had already been unconsciously obeying. He has now willingly offered obedience to the Master Whom he already owed obedience to involuntarily. His knowledge is now real for he has acknowledged the Being Who endowed him with the power to learn and to know. Now his reason and judgement is balanced, for he has rightly decided to obey the Being Who bestowed upon him the faculty of thinking and judging. His tongue is also truthful for it expresses its belief in the Lord Who gave it the faculty of speech. Now the whole of his existence is an embodiment of Truth for in all spheres of life, he voluntarily as well as involuntarily obeys the laws of the One God – the Lord of the universe. Now he is at peace with the whole universe for he worships Him whom the whole universe worships. Such a person is God's vicegerent on earth. The whole world is for him and he is for God.

THE NATURE OF DISBELIEF

In contrast to the individual described above, there is the person who, although a born Muslim and unconsciously remaining one throughout his life, does not exercise his faculties of reason, intellect and intuition to recognise his Lord and Creator and misuses his freedom of choice by choosing to deny Him. Such a person becomes a disbeliever – in the language of Islam, a *kāfir*.

Kufr literally means 'to cover' or 'to conceal'. The person who denies God is called a *kāfir* or concealer because he conceals by his disbelief what is inherent in his nature and embalmed in his own soul – for his nature is instinctively imbued with 'Islam'. His whole body functions in obedience to that instinct. Each and every particle of existence – living or lifeless – functions in accordance with 'Islam' and fulfils the duty that has been assigned to it. But the vision of this person has been blurred, his intellect has been befogged, and he is unable to see the obvious. His own nature has become concealed from his eyes and he thinks and acts in utter disregard of it. Reality becomes estranged from him and he gropes in the dark. Such is the nature of *kufr*.

Kufr is a form of ignorance, or, rather, it is ignorance. What ignorance can be greater than to be ignorant of God, the Creator, the Lord of the universe? A person observes the vast panorama of nature, the superb mechanism that is ceaselessly working, the grand design that is manifest in every aspect of creation – he observes this vast machine, but he does not know anything of its maker and director. He knows what a wonderful organism his body is but is unable to comprehend the force that brought it into existence, the engineer who designed and produced it, the Creator Who made the unique living being out of lifeless stuff: carbon, calcium, sodium and the like. He witnesses a superb plan in the universe – but fails to see the planner behind it. He sees great beauty and harmony in its working – but not the Creator. He observes a wonderful design in nature – but not the Designer! How can such a person, who has so blinded himself to reality, approach true knowledge? How can one who has made the wrong beginning reach the right destination? He will fail to find the key to Reality. The Right Path will remain concealed from him and whatever his endeavours in science and arts, he will never be able to attain the Truth. He will be groping in the darkness of ignorance.

Not only that; *kufr* is a tyranny, the worst of all tyrannies. And what is 'tyranny'? It is an unjust use of force or power. It is when you compel a thing to act unjustly or against its true nature, its real will and its inherent attitude.

We have seen that all that is in the universe is obedient to God, the Creator. To obey, to live in accordance with His will and His law or (to put it more precisely) to be a Muslim is ingrained in the nature of things. God has given people power over these things, but it is incumbent that they should be used for the fulfilment of His will and not otherwise. Anyone who disobeys God and resorts to *kufr* perpetrates the greatest injustice, for he uses his powers of body and mind to rebel against the course of nature and becomes an instrument in the drama of disobedience. He bows his head before deities other than God and cherishes in his heart the love, reverence and fear of other powers in utter disregard of the instinctive urge of these organs. He uses his own powers and all those things over which he has authority against the explicit Will of God and thus establishes a reign of tyranny.

Can there be any greater injustice, tyranny and cruelty than that exhibited by this individual who exploits and misuses everything under the sun and unscrupulously forces them to a course which affronts nature and justice?

Kufr is not mere tyranny; it is rebellion, ingratitude and infidelity. After all, what is the reality of the human being? Where do his power and authority come from? Is he himself the creator of his mind, his heart, his soul and other organs of his body, or has God created them? Has he himself created the universe and all that is in it, or has God created it? Who has harnessed all the powers and energies for the service of mankind, people or God? If everything has been created by God and God alone, then to whom do they belong? Who is their rightful sovereign? It is God and none else. And if God is the Creator, the Master and the Sovereign, then who would be a greater rebel than the person who uses God's creation against His injunctions, makes his mind think against God, harbours in his heart thoughts against Him, and uses his various faculties against the Sovereign's Will.

All that a person has and all that he uses for the benefit of others is a gift of God. The greatest obligation that a person owes on this earth is to his parents. But who has implanted the love of children in the parents' heart? Who endowed the mother with the will and power to nurture, nourish and feed her children? Who inspired the parent with the passion to spend everything in their possession for the well-being of their children? A little reflection would reveal that God is the greatest benefactor of mankind. He is his Creator, Lord, Nourisher, Sustainer, as well as Sovereign. So what can be greater betrayal, ingratitude, rebellion and treason than *kufr* – through which a person denies and disobeys his real Lord and Sovereign?

Do you think that by committing *kufr* a person does or can do the least harm to Almighty God? An insignificant speck on the face of a tiny ball in this limitless universe is what the human being is. What harm can he do to the Lord of the Universe whose dominions are so infinitely vast that we have not yet been able to explore their boundaries even with the help of the most powerful probes? His power is so great that the myriad of heavenly bodies, like the earth, the moon, the stars and the sun are at His bidding, whirling like tiny balls. His wealth is so boundless that He is the sole Master of the whole universe, and He provides for all. A human being's revolt against God can do Him no harm. On the other hand, by his disobedience, the human being treads the path of ruin and disgrace.

The inevitable consequence of this revolt and denial of reality is a failure to recognise and live up to the ultimate ideals of life. Such a rebel will never find the thread of real knowledge and vision, for knowledge that fails to reveal its own Creator can reveal no Truth. Such a human being's intellect and reason always go astray, for reason which errs about its own Creator cannot illumine the paths of life.

Such a person will meet with failures in all the affairs of his life. His morality, his civic and social life, his struggle for livelihood and his family life, in short, his entire existence, will be unsatisfactory. He will spread confusion and disorder. He will, without the least compunction, shed blood, violate other people's rights and generally act destructively. His perverted thoughts and ambitions, his blurred vision and distorted scale of values, and his evil activities will make life bitter for him and for all around him.

Such a person destroys the calm and balance of life on earth. In the life hereafter he will be accountable for the crimes he committed against his nature. Every organ of his body will testify against the injustice and cruelty he had subjected them to. Every tissue of his being will denounce him before God who, as the fountain of justice, will punish him, as he deserves. This is the inglorious consequence of *kufr.* It leads to the blind alleys of utter failure, both in this world and the hereafter. These are the evils and disadvantages of *kufr.*

THE BLESSINGS OF ISLAM

Let us now look at some of the blessings of Islam. You find in the world around you and in the small kingdom of your own self innumerable manifestations of God's power. This grand universe, which ceaselessly works with matchless order and in accordance with unalterable laws, is in itself a witness to the fact that its designer, creator and governor is a being with infinite power, knowledge and wisdom, whom nothing in the universe dares disobey. It is in the very nature of the human being, as it is with every other thing in this universe, to obey Him.

Besides endowing the human being with the capacity to acquire knowledge, the faculty to think and reflect, and the ability to distinguish right from wrong, God has granted him a certain amount of freedom of will and action. In this freedom lies a person's real trial. His knowledge, his wisdom, his power of discrimination and his freedom of will and action are all being tried and tested. A person has not been obliged to adopt any particular course, for by compulsion the very object of the trial would have been defeated. If in an examination you are compelled to write a certain answer to a question, the examination will be of no use. Your merit can be properly judged only if you are allowed to answer questions freely, according to your own knowledge and understanding. If your answer is correct you will succeed; if it is wrong you will fail, and your failure will bar the way to further progress.

The situation which a person faces is similar. God has given him freedom of will and action so that he may choose whatever attitude in life he likes and considers proper for himself – Islam or *kufr.*

By the correct use of his knowledge and intellect a person recognises his Creator, reposes belief in Him, and, in spite of being under no compulsion to do so, chooses the path of obedience to Him. He understands both his own nature and the laws and realities of nature itself. Despite the power and freedom to adopt any course, he adopts the way of obedience and loyalty to God, the Creator. He is successful in his trial because he has used his intellect and all other faculties properly. He uses his eyes to see the reality, his ears to listen to the Truth and his mind to form correct opinions. He puts all his heart and soul into following the right way he has so chosen. He chooses Truth, sees the reality, and willingly and joyfully submits to his Lord and Master. He is intelligent, truthful and dutiful, for he has chosen light over darkness. Thus he has proved by his conduct that he is not only a seeker after Truth but is the knower and worshipper as well. Such a person is on the right path, and is destined to succeed in this world and in the world to come.

Such a person will always choose the right path in every field of knowledge and action. The one who knows God with all His attributes knows the beginning as well as the ultimate end of reality. He can never be led astray, for his first step is on the right path, and he is sure of the direction and destination of his journey in life. He will reflect on the secrets of the universe, and will try to fathom the mysteries of nature, but he will not lose his way in mazes of doubt and scepticism. His path is illumined with Divine grandeur, and so his every step will be in the right direction. In science he will endeavour to learn the laws of nature and uncover the hidden treasures of the earth for the betterment of humanity. He will try his level best to explore all avenues of knowledge and power and to harness all that exists on earth and in the heavens in the interests of mankind.

At every stage of his enquiry, his God-consciousness will save him from making evil and destructive uses of science and the scientific method. He will never think of himself as the master of all these objects, boasting to be the conqueror of nature, arrogating to himself godly and sovereign powers and nourishing the ambition of subverting the world, subduing the human race and establishing his supremacy over all and sundry by fair means or foul. Such an attitude of revolt and defiance can never be entertained by a Muslim scientist – only a scientist who rejects God can fall prey to such illusions and by submitting to them expose, the entire human race to the danger of total destruction and annihilation.

A Muslim scientist, on the other hand, will behave in an altogether different way. The deeper his insight into the world of science, the stronger will be his faith in God. His head will bow down before Him in gratitude. He will feel that, since his Master has blessed him with power and knowledge, he must exert himself for his own good and for the good of humanity. Instead of arrogance there will be humility. Instead of drunkenness on power there will be a strong realisation of the need to serve humanity. His freedom will not be unbridled. He will be guided by the tenets of morality and Divine revelation. Thus science in his hands will become an agency for human welfare and moral regeneration instead of becoming an instrument of destruction. This is the way in which he will express his gratitude to his Master for the gifts and blessings He has bestowed on him.

Similarly, in history, economics, politics, law and other branches of arts and science, a Muslim will nowhere lag behind one who rejects God in the fields of enquiry and struggle, but their perspectives and consequently their *modus operandi* will be vastly different. A Muslim will study every branch of knowledge in its true perspective. He will strive to arrive at the right conclusions.

In history he will draw correct lessons from the past experiences of people, and will uncover the true causes of the rise and fall of civilisations. He will try to benefit from all that was good and right in the past and will scrupulously avoid all that led to the decline and fall of nations. In politics his sole objective will be to strive for the establishment of policies where peace, justice and goodness reign, where each person is a brother or sister, where there is respect for everyone's humanity, where no exploitation or slavery is allowed, where the rights of the individual are upheld, and where the powers of the state are considered as a sacred trust from God and are used for the common welfare of all. In the field of law, the endeavour of a Muslim will be to make it the true embodiment of justice and the real protector of the rights of all particularly of the weak. He will see that everybody gets his due share and no injustice or oppression is inflicted on anyone. He will respect the law, encourage to make others respect it, and will see that it is administered equitably.

The life of a Muslim will always be filled with godliness, piety, righteousness and truthfulness. He will live in the belief that God alone is the Master of all, that whatever he and other men possess has been given by God, that the powers he wields are only a trust from God, that the freedom he has been endowed with is not to be used indiscriminately, and that it is in his own interest to use it in accordance with God's Will. He will constantly keep in view that one day he will have to return to the Lord and submit an account of his entire life. The sense of accountability will always remain implanted in his mind and he will never behave irresponsibly.

Think of the moral excellence of the person who lives with this mental attitude – his will be a life of purity and piety and love and altruism. He will be a blessing unto mankind. His thinking will not be polluted with evil thoughts and perverted ambitions. He will abstain from seeing evil, hearing evil, and doing evil. He will guard his tongue and will never utter a false word. He will earn his living through just and fair means and will prefer hunger to a food acquired unfairly through exploitation or injustice. He will never be a party to any form of oppression or violation of human life and honour. He will never yield to evil, whatever the cost of defiance. He will be an embodiment of goodness and nobility and will defend righteousness and truth even at the cost of his life. Such a person will be a power to be reckoned with. He is bound to succeed.

He will be highly honoured and respected. How can humiliation ever visit a person who is not prepared to bow his head before anyone except God the Almighty, the Sovereign of the universe? No one can be more powerful than he, for he fears none but God and seeks blessings from none but Him. What power can make him deviate from the right path? What wealth can buy his faith? What force can shape his conscience? What power can compel him to behave, as he does not want to?

He will be the wealthiest. No one in the world can be richer or more independent than he, for he will live a life of austerity and contentment. He will be neither a sensualist, nor indulgent, nor greedy. He will be content with whatever he earns fairly and honestly and however much ill-gotten wealth is heaped before him he will not even look at it. He will have peace and contentment of heart and what can be a greater wealth than this?

He will be the most beloved and respected person, for he lives a life of charity and benevolence. He will be just to everyone, discharge his duties honestly, and work for the good of others. People's hearts will be naturally drawn towards him.

No one can be more trustworthy than he, for he will not betray his trust, nor will he stray from righteousness. He will be true to his word, and straightforward and honest in his dealings. He will be fair and just in all his affairs, for he is sure that God is ever-present, ever vigilant. The credit and good-will which such a person commands will be immense. Can there be anyone who will not trust him? Such is the life and character of a Muslim.

If you understand the true character of a Muslim, you will be convinced that he cannot live in humiliation, abasement or subjugation. He is bound to prevail and no power on earth can overwhelm him. For Islam inculcates in him the qualities which cannot be driven out.

And after living a respectable and honourable life on this earth, he will return to his Creator who will shower on him the choicest of His blessings – for he will have discharged his duty ably, fulfilled his mission successfully and emerged from his trial triumphantly. He is successful in the life in this world and in the hereafter will live in eternal peace, joy and bliss.

This is Islam, the natural religion of all human beings, the religion which is not associated with any person, people, period or place. It is the way of nature. In every age, in every country and among every people, all God-knowing and truth-loving individuals have believed and lived this very religion. They were all Muslims, irrespective of whether they called that way Islam. Whatever its name was, it signified Islam and nothing but Islam.

3

The Basic Truths

Jaafar Shaikh Idris

One of the myths of our century, a myth that is believed by almost all atheists as well as many theists, is that rationality and science are on the side of disbelief. As a corollary of this myth, disbelief is taken to be the normal position, that demands no mental effort because it needs no justification. It is the believer who is taken to task, who is required to justify his position and who is, therefore, on the defensive.

But why is disbelief taken to be normal? Purely and simply because it is wrongly thought that while a positive claim, the disbeliever, as the name indicates, is only denying that the believer has any evidence to support his claim. The two positions are, therefore, mistakenly likened to those, say, of accuser and accused. The latter does not have to prove that he is innocent, since he is assumed to be so until the contrary is proven. This picture is misleading because in it, only one of the parties, the accuser, has a problem that he wants to resolve. The accused has no problem, and is, therefore making no claim or even if he had one, it is different from that of the accuser.

A better comparison to the position of the believer and the disbeliever would be that of two politicians or economists, 'A' and 'B', arguing about inflation, a problem that affects them both. 'A' suggests that the cause of inflation is the sudden and tremendous increase in oil prices and, therefore, that it can only be stopped by such measures. The other, 'B', denies that this is the cause. He sees no causal link between the two phenomena, and has not been helped by 'A' to see one. We may sympathise with 'B', but we would certainly not think that he had done his job merely by rejecting the analysis of 'A'. Why? This is because inflation is a serious problem that affects us all and we consider that those who conduct our affairs have a responsibility to look for its cause and to seek a solution to it.

Thus, the position of the believer is not like that of the accuser and the accused. The solution to the problem of whether a creator exits, does not concern him alone. Like inflation, it affects both the one who advances a solution to it and the one who rejects that solution.

THE PROBLEM

What is this problem? Essentially it is expressed in the question, 'Where did we come from?' There are other related issues but let us first examine this central question.

The disbeliever reacts to this question in one of three ways, all of which are irrational and unscientific. Hence, his claim that science and rationality are on his side is unfounded.

1. He may say: 'I neither know nor do I care. All that I know is that I am here and that I am free to decide for myself what role to play. And this I am going to do.' 'I neither know': to admit one's ignorance is surely a mark of rationality and is in the spirit of science. But what about 'nor do I care'? The disbeliever is not in this instance, dismissing the possibility of there being a creator who assigned for him a role to play in this world, and who would, therefore, hold him accountable for his deeds in a hereafter. Does he really mean that it does not matter or that it would make no difference to him whether this was true or not? This is clearly not rational, because it surely does make a difference whether a person goes to heaven or to hell. Turning away from a fact does not make it disappear. Years of indulgence in the pleasures of this life would hardly make up for punishment in the hereafter.

2. A second response the disbeliever might make would be to say: 'We could have come from nothing.' To this one could ask: 'Are you saying that this is the only possibility as your statements indicate or are you affirming that we did come from nothing?' If it is said that this is the only possibility, then one cannot rule out the possibility of our having been created. Given this possibility, and considering the gravity of the problem, one should try to make up one's mind as to which of the two possible alternatives seems to be the more likely and reasonable. If, however, it is claimed that the world really

did come from nothing, then one could suggest the following points: firstly, how do you know this? And secondly, do you have any evidence?

Without evidence, is it either rational or scientific to opt for the view that anything like ourselves that is not eternal can be caused by or produced from nothing? Is it not a scientific principle, I am not saying a scientific fact, as well as a principle of ordinary life, that every event has a cause and, hence, that nothing comes out of nothing? If so, then why is the position of the disbeliever considered to be the more rational and the more scientific?

3. Having realised the irrationality of these two responses, the disbeliever might now choose the only alternative that is left to him if he insists on continuing in his disbelief. He will now admit that it is more reasonable to believe that there is a cause. But since he rejects the idea of a transcendent Creator he will maintain that this cause must be inside the world.

THE SEARCH FOR THE CAUSE

What can that cause be? It is sometimes taken to be an object on this earth, an idol, an animal or a human being. Since the foolishness of such a belief is now clear, we should not allow it to detain us. It has only been mentioned to draw attention to the fact that idol worship and belief in magic belong to the history of disbelief, and not to that of true religion, which advocates belief in a transcendent Creator.

Seeing that a perishable object or person could not be a Creator, some disbelievers thought that the heavenly bodies, which for them seemed to be eternal, were more worthy of such a role, and, thus, worshipped them. But science has proved that none of these celestial bodies are eternal. The believers' claim that they cannot be gods is, thus, vindicated.

Having despaired of finding their Creator in the larger physical bodies, and having been told that these are, in fact, built up of smaller units, the disbelievers now turned to another direction and began to look for the ultimate and eternal building unit of which everything we know is made. This, they felt, would explain everything and, thus, render the idea of a transcendent God obsolete. But these eternal building blocks have turned out to be will-o'-the-wisps. It is not the mixtures and compounds, but the elements of which they are made. It is not even these, because they in their turn are made of molecules which are made of atoms. Atoms are made up of subatomic particles. Could these be what we are looking for? But these are not solid material things. They are strange creatures that change their mass whenever they move. Moreover these tiny 'things' cannot be directly observed. Their existence is deduced only from their behaviour.

THE ETERNAL CREATOR

One of the basic arguments raised by earlier disbelievers against there being a transcendent God was that He could not be seen. It was no use telling them that as rational beings they did not have to see to believe; that they could also believe in something whose existence could be deduced from what they observed. Science has again vindicated the believers' argument since this method of deduction turns out to be the only way we know about subatomic particles, the phenomena that disbelievers wish to see as the ultimate cause or Creator. But this they cannot do. The Creator, or if you like the ultimate cause we are looking for must be eternal, that is, it must have no beginning. If a thing is eternal in the sense of having no beginning then it must be self-sufficient, that is, it cannot logically depend for its existence or continuance on anything outside itself. But if this is so then it will not perish. Nothing that perishes or is perishable can be eternal. All forms of matter, even subatomic particles, are perishable. Since matter in every form is necessarily affected by other forms of matter, then matter in any form cannot be eternal. The disbeliever cannot, therefore, console himself by putting his faith in the progress of science to discover a solution to the problem of creation. Science cannot do for them what is logically impossible.

THE NATURAL SOLUTION

Some disbelievers say: 'Why look for the eternal? If what we want is an explanation of the finite things of which our world is made up, then this can be obtained without recourse to a belief in an eternal Creator. If I want to explain how 'A' came to be, I look for its natural and finite cause, 'B'; and if asked about 'B', I look for 'C' and so on. The series of cause and effect need not terminate in an ultimate cause but can be infinite.'

To demonstrate how untenable this position is, let us take the example of a dictator who hears that a derogatory rumour about him is being spread. He orders his secret police to discover its origin and they, devoted to their master, start to interrogate suspects. 'A' tells them that he heard it from 'B', who in turn tells them that he heard it from 'C', who heard it from 'D' and so on. If we assume this series of hearer-relator to be infinite, it would not explain the ultimate and real source of the rumour, which can only be someone who invented it, someone who did not hear it from someone else. The rumour, therefore, clearly had a creator: the chain is not infinite. The fact of coming into being cannot be explained by something which has itself come to be. It can only be explained by something which causes others to be but is not itself caused to be.

THE ULTIMATE CAUSE

So much for the alleged rationality and scientific attitude of the disbeliever towards the question: where do we come from? The position of the believer, on the other hand, is based on reason and is not contradicted by science. He says that since perishable things cannot come from nothing, they must be caused by something that is eternal and, therefore, self-sufficient. Since it is eternal and therefore infinite, all its attributes must be infinite.

How does this eternal cause bring about its effect – that is, the things of this world? Things are produced by others in two ways. Either they follow naturally from them, or, they are intentionally made by them. All natural causes produce their effects in the former way, while rational beings have the ability to do the latter. Thus fire does not intentionally boil water; the boiling is a natural result of the water container being exposed to heat. But a human being makes tea intentionally. There is nothing in his nature as a result of which tea is naturally produced, so he can choose whether or not to do so.

A natural effect does not depend solely on what we normally call its cause. Its happening is conditional upon many other factors. For example, for water to boil it is not enough that there should be heat. The water must be put in a container which must be brought near the heat, there must be oxygen etc. Our eternal cause, on the other hand, is by definition self-sufficient and, thus, does not depend on any factors external to itself. If this is so, then it does not act in the way natural causes act; thus, it must act with intention. Since a being that acts with intention must also act knowingly and must, therefore, be a living being and not an inanimate thing, the true Creator of whatever exists in the world must possess these attributes, as well as others that can be deduced in the same manner.

This is what unbiased reason tells us. What it tells us is confirmed and elaborated and brought to completion by what the Creator Himself tells us in what He reveals to His Prophets.

A person's answers to the questions, 'Why are we here?' and 'Where do we go from here?' are bound to depend on his answer to the basic question: 'Where do we come from?' Because the disbeliever fails to give a satisfactory answer to the basic question his answers to the others are doomed to be unsatisfactory, both rationally and psychologically.

THE ISLAMIC BELIEF SYSTEM

The foundation of the Islamic Faith is the belief that the Creator is one in Being and attributes. The other pillars of the Faith (belief in life after death, in God's angels, His books, His messengers and His *qadar* or will) and the external expressions of this faith (*ṣalāh* or prayer, *zakāh* or purification tax, *ṣawm* or fasting and *ḥajj* or pilgrimage) are built on this belief in the one true God.

Muḥammad (570–632) was sent to invite people to God and to teach them how to perform the task for which they were created, namely, to worship Him. Many of the people whom he addressed had a hazy idea about God, Some of them believed in God, but they also associated lesser gods with Him. Some others were atheists or pagans. The Qur'ān, declares: *Their creed was 'we live and we die, and nothing causes our death except time'* (45: 24).

The Qur'ān therefore asks such people: *Were they created out of nothing? Or were they the creation* [of themselves]*? Or did they create the heavens and the earth?* (52: 35–6). In other words, the Qur'ān states that for everything that has a beginning in time, such as a human being, there are only three ways of explaining how it came to be:

- Either it is created, or made, or caused by nothing at all i.e. it came out of nothing
- It is the creator of itself
- It has a Creator, cause, or maker outside itself.

Obviously it is inconceivable for something to come out of, or be made by nothing at all, and since it is even more inconceivable that it should bring itself into being, then the only conclusion is that it must have a creator outside itself.

THE TRUTH ABOUT GOD

The Creator must be of a different nature to the things created because if He is the same nature as they are, He will have to be temporal and, therefore, need a maker. It follows that nothing is like Him. If the maker is not temporal, then He must be eternal. But if He is eternal, he cannot be caused, and if nothing caused Him to come into existence, nothing outside of Him causes Him to continue to exist, which means that He must be self-sufficient. And if He does not depend on anything for the continuance of His existence, then that existence can have no end. The Creator, is therefore Eternal and Everlasting: 'He is the first and the last'.

He is *al-Qayyūm* or self-Sufficient and self-Subsistent (2: 255). The Creator does not create only in the sense of bringing things into being; He also preserves them and takes them out of existence and is the Ultimate Cause of whatever happens to them.

God is the Creator of everything. He is Guardian over everything. Unto Him belongs the keys of the heavens and the earth, but its provision rests on God. He knows its resting place and its repository (11: 6).

If the Creator is Eternal and Everlasting, then His attributes must also be eternal and everlasting. He should not lose an attribute that He had nor acquire a new one. His attributes must be absolute. Can there be more than one Creator with such absolute attributes? Can there be, for example, two absolutely powerful creators? A moment's thought shows that it cannot be so.

If a maker is absolutely powerful then it follows that He is absolutely free to do whatever he likes. But if another maker with similar powers exists and they differ over the making of something, then either one of them overcomes the other, in which case the latter will not be absolutely powerful; or, they neutralise each other, in which case they will both be limited in power. And if we assume that they agree on everything, still they cannot both be absolutely powerful because, for one of them at least, the execution of his intention shall not depend solely on his power, but on the condition, though a passive one, that the other does not interfere.

The Qur'ān summarises this argument in the following verse: *God has not taken to Himself any son, nor is there any god with Him: For then each god would have taken off with that which he created and some of them would have risen up over others* (23: 91), and: *were there gods in the earth and heaven other than God, they* [heaven and earth] *would surely go to ruin* (21: 22). The fact that the Creator is One in being and in attributes is the foundation of the Islamic edifice.

THE POWER OF GOD

There are two ways in which causes produce their effects. Either they produce them naturally or intentionally. The Maker which has the attributes enumerated above cannot be a natural cause, because if things of this world flow from it naturally and spontaneously, they cannot be but of the same nature as it is. And if, like all natural causes, it causes only under certain conditions, then its power is limited. It follows that it must be a wilful agent. But intention implies knowledge and both imply life. So, that maker must be a living, knowing agent with a will that is absolutely free.

Thus, God according to the Qur'ān, does everything with intention and for a purpose: *Surely We have created everything in due measure* (54:49). *Did you think that We created you only for sport?* (23:115). He is absolutely free to do whatever He wills: *Surely your Lord accomplishes what He desires* (11:107). He is aware of every detail of His creation. *He knows what is in the land and sea; not a leaf falls but He knows it. Not a grain in the earth's shadow, not a thing fresh or withered, but it is in a book manifest. It is He who recalls you by night, and He knows what you work by day* (6:59 60).

God is a living being with all that this implies: *There is no god but He, the Living, the Everlasting. Slumber seizes Him not, neither sleep; to Him belongs all that is in the heavens and the earth. Who is there that shall intercede with Him save by His leave? He knows what lies before them and what is after them, and they comprehend not anything of His knowledge save such as He Wills. His Throne comprises the heavens and the earth; the preserving of them oppresses Him not; He is the all-High, the all-Glorious* (2:255).

God is not only willing and powerful; He is also just, in that He does not punish a sinner for more than his crime. He is Merciful and His mercy, in the words of the Prophet 'overcomes His punishment'. So He does not punish us for whatever we do, but forgives and erases our sins, and magnifies and multiplies our good deeds.

These, and many others which can be arrived at in a similar way, are the attributes which the true creator must possess. Any other being or object which is alleged to be a god or an ultimate cause and which lacks at least some of them cannot in actual fact be what it is believed to be.

THE ONENESS OF GOD

Having shown clearly what the true God should be like, the Qur'ān goes on to show why there cannot be any other god but He, and recalls the falsity of all alleged gods.

To the worshippers of man-made objects it asks: *Do you worship what you have carved yourself or have you taken unto you others beside Him to be your protectors, even such as have no power to protect themselves?* (7:197).

To the worshippers of heavenly bodies it relates the story of Abraham: *When night overspread him he saw a star and said, 'This is my Lord.' But when it set he said, 'I love not the setters.' When he saw the moon rising he said, 'This is my Lord.' But when it set he said, 'If my Lord does not guide me I shall surely be of the people gone astray.' When he saw the sun rising he said, 'This is my Lord, this is greater.' But when it set he said, 'O my people I am quit of that which you associate. I have turned my face to Him who originated the heavens and the earth; a person of pure faith, I am not of the idolaters'* (6:76–9).

The Qur'ān also refutes the belief in the Divine nature of human beings: *The Jews say, 'Ezra is the son of God.' The Christians say, 'The Messiah is the son of God.' That is the utterance of their mouths, conforming to the disbelievers before them. God assail them! How they are perverted* (9:30). The Qur'ān states that if God creates everything, then it must be His subordinate and cannot, therefore, be His son. *And they say, 'The All Merciful has taken unto Himself a son!' You have indeed advanced something hideous! The heavens behove not the all-Merciful to take a son* (19:88–90). It then goes on to explain to Christians the real nature of Jesus. *Truly, the likeness of Jesus in God's sight is as Adam's likeness; He created him of dust, then He said unto him 'Be', and he was* (3:59).

THE BELIEVER'S ATTITUDE

To be a Muslim, to surrender oneself to God, is to necessarily believe in the Oneness of God, in the sense of His being the only Creator, Preserver and

Nourisher. But this belief, later on called *tawḥīd ar-rubūbiyyah*, is not enough. In fact, many of the idolaters did know and believe that it is the Supreme God alone who can do all this. But that was not enough to make them Muslims. To *tawḥīd ar-rubūbiyyah* one must add *tawḥīd al-ulūhiyyah* or the acknowledgement that God alone is the One who deserves to be worshipped, and, therefore, the abstinence from directing any act of worship to someone or something else.

Having known the true God, a person should acknowledge what he knows and believes and have faith in Him, and not allow any ulterior motive to induce him to deny a fact which he realises to be true.

When faith enters a person's heart, it causes therein, certain mental states, which result in certain actions, both of which are the proof of true faith. The Prophet said, 'Faith is that which resides firmly in the heart and which is proved by deeds.' Foremost among those mental states is the feeling of gratitude towards God, which could be said to be the essence of *ʿibādah* or true worship of God.

This feeling of gratitude is so important that a disbeliever is called *kāfir* meaning 'one who denies a Truth' and also 'one who is ungrateful'. The Qur'ān says that the main motive underlying one's denial of the existence of God is vanity. Such a person does not think that it befits him to be created and governed by a being whom he must thus acknowledge to be greater than himself and to whom he must be grateful.

A believer loves and is grateful to God for the bounties He bestows upon him. But he is aware that his good deeds, whether mental or physical, are far from commensurate with any Divine favours; he is always anxious lest God should punish him, whether here or in the hereafter. He, therefore, fears Him, surrenders himself to Him and serves Him with great humility. One cannot be in such a mental state, without being almost all the time mindful of God. Remembering God is, thus, the life force of faith, without which it fades and might even wither away.

The Qur'ān, therefore, prescribes and describes in great detail, the ways and means to help a person remember God and keep his faith alive. All Qur'ānic and Prophetic injunctions and prohibitions which extend to all aspects of human life – acts of worship and personal conduct as well as behavioural, social relations and political order – are designed to put a person in a state which is conducive to the remembrance of God. The details of this Islamic way of life were expounded in Madinah, but the main principles of this new order were already laid down during the Makkan period.

The other pillars of the Faith is the belief in life after death, in God's angels, His books, His messengers and His *qadar*. The argument for all these is based almost entirely on the assumption that the addressee believes in God.

RESURRECTION

The Qur'ānic reasoning about the fact of another life after death is intended to show that it is possible and also desirable that there should be such a life, and that without believing in it, our belief in the true God cannot be complete.

Many of the people whom the Prophet addressed in Makkah did believe in the Supreme God, but many of them thought that it was impossible for their dead and decayed bodies to be resurrected. They, therefore, mocked and laughed at the Prophet when he told them so. The Qur'ānic reply was that there was no reason for such astonishment and mockery because resurrection is not only logical but a physical possibility for the following reason: if it is God who created the human being in the first place, why should it be impossible for Him to re-create him when he dies? Resurrection should be easier than original creation!

Why is resurrection desirable? Simply because without it, God would not be the just and wise and merciful God that He is. God created people and made them responsible for their actions, some behaved well and others committed wrongs. If there is no future life in which the virtuous are rewarded and the vicious reprimanded, there would be no justice and the creation of people in that way and the sending of the Prophets to them would have been for no purpose at all. But this kind of behaviour is not expected of a human being known to be rational and just, let alone the perfect Creator. The Qur'ān says, *What, does the human being reckon he shall be left to roam at will?* (75: 36). And again, *What, did you think that We created you only for sport and that you would not be returned to Us?* (23: 115).

Is the real and only motive for denying life after death the one expressed by those who deny and to which the Qur'ān replied? By no means, says the Qur'ān. The real motive is often a psychological one. Those who do evil do not wish to be punished and it is this wishful thinking that leads them to deny the reality of a time when such punishment will take place. *What, does a human being reckon We shall not gather his bones? Yes, We are able to put together in perfect order the tips of his fingers. Nay, but a human being desires to continue on as a libertine, asking, 'When shall be the Day of Resurrection?'* (75: 3–6).

A question that naturally arises in connection with reward and punishment in the hereafter is: 'Do we do what is good because it is good or for fear of punishment and expectation of reward?'

The answer to this depends on whether God enjoins us to do an act because of this Divine injunction. It seems to me to be very clear that the goodness of an act is logically prior to its being an object of Divine order otherwise it would be a tautology to say 'God enjoins what is good' because it would only mean God enjoins what He enjoins.

The answer to our original question then is that we do what is good because it is good. But since to give good for good is itself good, there is no contradiction in saying that one does good because God, whom he loves and in whom he puts his trus, tells him to do it, and because he expects to be rewarded by God for doing it.

According to the Qur'ān, God created the human being in a natural state called *fiṭrah*. We possess what may be described as a moral sense, which enables him to recognise without any external aid certain acts, like telling the truth and being grateful, as good qualities, and by reason of which he is inclined to do good once he comes to know it. True religion is built on the basis of this original human nature. It strengthens it and brings to fruition the seeds of virtue that reside in it. That is why Islam is said in the Qur'ān to be *fiṭratullāh* and why the Prophet said that he was sent only to perfect good conduct. The Qur'ān praises those in whom this moral sense is sharp and condemns those in whom it has become so blunt that the ugliness of vice becomes, in their eyes, the model of beauty.

So a Muslim does good because it is endeared to him, and eschews vice because it is detestable to him. But since a Muslim surrenders himself to God and loves and fears Him, and since God loves virtue and enjoins it and hates vice and forbids it, he does the former and avoids the latter in obedience to his Lord. Those who do good shall, in the hereafter, live a life of bliss, the highest type of which would be a state of being near to God and of enjoying His sight, while those who lead an evil life shall suffer all kinds of chastisement the most terrible of which would be a state of being deprived from that sight. A Muslim would be wise to always have that future and eternal life in mind and endeavour to do here all kinds of work that help to elevate his position there.

ANGELS

Angels are beings of a different kind from human beings. While human beings are created from soil, angels are created from light. Thus human beings, except Prophets, cannot see them in their original form, but may see them if they take a material form. Our knowledge of them is, therefore, almost entirely based on what God and His Prophets tell us about them. But why should we bother to know about them? Because they play a large role in our affairs. To know about them could perhaps be said to be as useful to us as knowledge of the working of natural causes and other people's behaviour.

We are told that these almost innumerable beings who are endowed with great power are created in such a way that they always obey and never go against Divine Commands (66: 6), and that they never tire of serving their Lord (21: 20).

But in spite of this they are, as a species, of a lower degree than humans, and this is symbolised by the fact that when Adam was created they were ordered to prostrate themselves before him as a sign of greeting and respect.

One of the activities of angels is the task of conveying God's messages to His chosen Prophets. This great honour is assigned mainly to their leader Gabriel, *a noble Messenger* (81: 19). *They attend to and watch over us* (6: 61). They keep a record of our good and bad deeds, and never a word we mention, passes without being registered by them either for or against us (50: 18). They play a role in the causation and happening of seemingly purely natural phenomena, like wind and rain, and death (32: 11). And to them is assigned the role of helping the believers to the extent of fighting on their side in times of war and of praying for them (42: 5).

REVEALED BOOKS

A Muslim believes that the Qur'ān is the word of God. But it is not the only revelation. God sent many Prophets before Muḥammad and He spoke to them as He spoke to him. So a Muslim also believes in the Torah and the Injīl. In fact, he would not be a Muslim if he did not believe in these earlier books, since *the true believers are those who believe in what has been sent down to you* [Muḥammad] *and what has been sent down before you* (2: 4).

God created humans so that they may serve Him. Being a servant of God, thus constitutes the essence of one's 'humanity'. But you cannot attain true humanity and acquire peace of mind unless you realise the purpose of your creation. But, how can you do this?

God, being merciful and just, has helped in many ways. He granted us, as we said before, an originally good nature that is inclined to know and serve Him. He granted us a mind that possesses a moral sense and has the ability to reason. He made the whole universe a natural book full of signs that leads a thinking person to God. To make things more specific, to give him a more detailed knowledge of God, and to show him in a more comprehensive manner how to serve Him, He has, sent down verbal messages through chosen Prophets since the creation of mankind. Hence the description of the scriptures in the Qur'ān as guidance, Light, Signs, Reminders, etc.

All these Books basically advocate the same message, *And We sent never a Messenger before you except that We revealed to him, saying, 'There is no God but I; so serve Me.' And the religion which they all expounded is Islam* [i.e. surrender to God]. *The true religion with God is Islam* (10: 70). Thus Noah, Abraham, Jacob and his sons and the other Prophets were all Muslims.

If the religion of all Prophets is the same in its essence and basic foundation, so are the ways of life based upon it. One last important point about God's

Books is that, with the exception of the Qur'ān, they have not been preserved intact, but have either been completely lost or have been subjected to distortion. As for the Qur'ān, God has decreed that it shall never be subjected to such distortion, but shall be preserved by God Himself.

PROPHETS

Messengers are people chosen by God to have the honour of conveying His message to other people. Being such a Messenger is not a position that one attains by any consciously designed effort. It is a grace from God, but God grants this grace to those who are deserving of it. Messengers are not, then, like the rank and file of us. True, they are human beings but they are people of an extremely high moral, spiritual and intellectual standard that qualifies them, in the eyes of God, to be the bearers of His Light to the world. When God chooses any of them, He supports him with a clear 'sign'; that proves the truth of his claim, and distinguishes him from false Prophets, sorcerers and soothsayers.

None of them betrays the message or falls short of being exemplary in practising what he preaches. Asked about the conduct of the Prophet Muḥammad, one of his wives said 'it was the Qur'ān', meaning that he embodied all the ideals which the Qur'ān called for.

Two related points about messengers which the Qur'ān stresses, and which, therefore, deserve some elaboration are the humanity of Prophets and the nature of their task. Despite the vast spiritual, moral and intellectual difference between them and ordinary people, and despite the special relation with God that they enjoy, Prophets are nonetheless humans with all that this term implies. They beget and are begotten; they eat and drink and go about in market places; they sleep and they die, they forget and they err. Their knowledge is limited and they can only tell that part of the future that God reveals to them. They cannot intercede with God on behalf of any person except with His permission, and it is not left to them to cause people to go on the right path. In short, they have no part to play in the running of the affairs of the universe.

A Prophet whose humanity is specially emphasised is that of Jesus. He was created in the same manner as Adam was created, from soil; he was the son of Mary not of God; he and his mother ate food; he was indeed the word of God but since he was a human being in the full sense of the word, this should not be interpreted to mean that there was or is a Divine element in him. He is 'the word of God' only in the sense that God said 'Be' and he was. But in that sense everything is the 'word of God' and Jesus was especially so called because he came more directly as a result of this Word. Jesus is, thus, a loyal servant of God who never claimed that he was in any sense Divine.

Messengers are entrusted, as we said, with the task of conveying God's word to other people. But this is not as simple as it looks. It implies many things which are not at first sight clear, and which the Qur'ān, therefore, expounds and elaborates upon.

The most important point which all messengers are reminded of, and which is very easy to forget or be heedless of, is that since their duty is only to convey the message, they are not responsible for people's response to it once they have made it clear to them. God has given people the power to understand the difference between truth and falsehood, especially in religious matters, once this has been explained to them. He has also given them the ability, by reason of their free will, either to accept or reject it. And since it is only God who knows what goes on in peoples' minds, it is only He who can judge who is worthy of being guided and who deserves to be left groping in the darkness. A Prophet has no such power, and cannot, therefore, guide whom he likes. *You are only a reminder, you are not charged to oversee them* (88: 21–22).

FREE WILL

The original meaning of the word *Qadar* is specified measure or amount whether of quantity or quality. It has many other usages which branch out from this core. Thus *yuqaddir* means, among other things, to measure or decide the quantity, quality or position of something before you actually make it. And it is this latter sense which interests us here.

God is the Creator of everything, but whatever He creates, He creates with *Qadar*, i.e. He knows before creating it, that He is going to create it and that it shall be of such and such magnitude, quality or nature. Further, He specifies the time of its coming into being and passing away, and the place of its occurrence (54: 49). Hence, he who believes in the true God believes that there are no accidents in nature. If something disagreeable happens to him, he says 'God *qaddara* (ordained it), and He did what He willed,' and he does not waste time wishing that it had been otherwise. If on the other hand something agreeable happens to him, he should not boast of it, but instead thank God for it.

No affliction befalls in the earth or in yourselves, but it is in a Book, before We create it; that is easy for God; that you may not grieve for what escapes you, nor rejoice (vainglory) in what has been given to you, God loves not any a person proud and boastful (57: 22–23).

If God *yuqaddir* (pre-destines and pre-determines) everything, that includes our so-called free actions, then in what way can they be said to be free, and how are we responsible for them? This question occasioned the appearance, in the very early history of Islam, two extreme theological schools. One of them, called the *Qadariyyah*, asserts a human being's free will and responsibility at the expense of God's foreknowledge, by denying the latter, and claim that God knows our 'free' actions only after we have performed them. The other, called the *Jabariyyah*, does just the opposite and claims that there is no difference between the motions of inanimate things and our movements in performing so called free action, and that when we use intentional language we speak only metaphorically.

But there is no need to go to such extremes, since it is not difficult to reconcile Divine *Qadar* and human responsibility. God decreed to create a human being as a free agent, but He knows (and how can He not know?) before creating him how he is going to use his free will. What, for instance, his reaction will be when a Prophet clarifies God's message to him. This foreknowledge and the recording of it in a 'Book' is called *Qadar*. 'But if we are free to use our will', a *Qadarī* might say, 'We may use it in ways that contradict God's Will, and in that case we would still be right in claiming that not everything is willed or decreed by God.' The Qur'ān answers this question by reminding us that it was God who Willed that we shall be wilful, and it is He who allows us to use our will.

Surely, this is a Reminder; so he who wills, takes unto his Lord a Way. But you will not unless God Wills. 'If so', says a *Jabarī*, 'He could have prevented us from doing evil'. Yes, indeed, He could. But He Willed that people shall be free especially in regard to matters of belief and disbelief. And people would not be so free if whenever any of them wills to do evil God prevents him from doing it and compels him to do good.

'If our actions are willed by God' someone might say, 'then they are in fact His Actions.' This objection, however, is based on confusion. God Wills what we will in the sense of granting us the will to choose and enabling us to execute that will i.e. He creates all that makes it possible for us to do it. Otherwise, it would be in order to say, when we drink or eat or sleep, for instance, that God performed these actions. God creates them; He does not do or perform them.

Another objection, based on another confusion, is that if God allows us to do evil, then He approves of it and likes it. But, to will something in the sense of giving a person the permission and power to do it is one thing; to approve of his action and commend it, is quite another. Not everything that God Wills He likes. He has, as we have just read in the Qur'ān, granted people the choice between belief and disbelief, but He does not, of course, like them to disbelieve.

CONCLUSION

These, then, are the basic truths to which the Prophet Muḥammad invited mankind. The best proof, besides the foregoing arguments of their being truths, is the good effect which they produce in our internal state, and thus our outward behaviour.

Since our attitude to others is very much connected with our attitude towards God, belief in God with its outcome of feelings towards the Divine is bound to produce in one's heart feelings towards others that are appropriate to it. And since our outward behaviour regarding God and other humans is generated, when it is honest, by our beliefs about and feelings towards them, it is only to be expected of true religion to call for a code of behaviour that is both a natural outcome of its beliefs. The internal state to which Muḥammad invited people is called *īmān* or faith. The external behaviour based on it is called Islam, meaning Self-surrender.

4

Understanding Faith

Hasan al-Banna

The essential beliefs of Islam can be summarised into the following twenty concise principles. These help us understand Islam more clearly. If you understand your religion according to these principles, then you will also grasp the meaning of the motto: 'The Qur'ān is our constitution, and the Prophet is our example'.

1. Islam is a comprehensive system which deals with all spheres of life: it is a state and a homeland or a government and an *ummah*; it is morality and power or mercy and justice; it is a culture and law or knowledge and jurisprudence; it is material, wealth or gain and prosperity; it is *jihād* and *daʿwah* or an army and a cause; and it is true belief and worship.

2. The glorious Qur'ān and the *Sunnah* or purified tradition of the Prophet Muḥammad are the references of every Muslim for the realisation of the rules of Islam. The Qur'ān can be understood according to the principles of the Arabic language without affectation or controversy, and the *Sunnah* can be acquired by reference to the trustworthy transmitters of *aḥādīth* or collected sayings of the Prophet.

3. True belief, proper worship, and *jihād* in the way of Allah have a light and warmth that Allah casts in the hearts of whomever He chooses from among His servants. Though they may be blessed, visions, notions, inspirations, and dreams are not authentic references for Islamic law, and therefore should

not be given any consideration except when they do not conflict with the authentic references and established principles of Islam.

4. Talismans, incantations, the placing of shells around the neck, fortune-telling whether by drawing lines in the sand or astrology, sorcery and claiming to have knowledge of the Unseen, and similar practices are all evils that must be fought, except what is mentioned in the Qur'ān or transmitted to us as an authentic narration of the Prophet.

5. The opinion of an Islamic scholar is acceptable in matters which are of proven benefit to the public, provided that his opinion does not conflict with any established principle of Islam. It may change in light of circumstances, customs, and habits. The basis of worship is purely devotional without asking why. However, in other areas there is scope to prod into the 'whys' and 'wherefores' of matters.

6. Everyone's opinion, except the infallible words of the Prophet, is liable to change and modification. We accept all that has reached us of the opinions and rulings of the pious predecessors as long as it is in agreement with the Qur'ān and the *Sunnah*. If this is not the case, the Book of Allah and the practice of His Prophet are more deserving of our adherence. However, we do not scorn and attack those individuals who differed, since we do not know what their intentions were nor the circumstances that necessitated their decision.

7. Any Muslim who has not reached a complete understanding of the different branches of Islamic jurisprudence should follow one of the scholars. Thus, he should try his best to get to grips with the evidences put forward, while being open to the opinions, supported by evidence, of trustworthy people. This will provide him with enough knowledge to find Islamic solutions to the contemporary problems of society. At the same time, those Muslims who are deficient in knowledge, and who wish to seek knowledge, are advised to exert the necessary efforts to acquire such understanding.

8. Differences in opinion regarding secondary matters should not be allowed to cause division, contention, or hatred within the ranks of the Muslims. To every seeker of knowledge is a reward. In cases of disagreement, however, there is no harm in objective scientific investigation in an atmosphere of love (for the sake of Allah) and co-operation with the aim of realising the Truth. Fanaticism, obstinacy and controversy have no place among true Muslims.

9. Wasting time and effort in investigating trivial matters that will not lead to action is prohibited in Islam. This category includes debating minute aspects of rulings in cases which have never occurred, investigating the meaning of the Qur'ānic verses which are still beyond the scope of human knowledge

(the *mutashābihāt* verses), and differentiating between the Companions (*Saḥābah*) of the Prophet or investigating the instances of disagreement that took place among them. Every *Saḥābī*, may Allah be pleased with them all, has the honour and distinction of being a Companion of the Messenger of Allah, and to each is the recompense of his motives.

10. Recognising Allah's existence, believing in His Oneness, and glorifying Him are the most sublime beliefs of Islam. We believe in the Qur'ānic verses and authentic traditions of the Prophet which describe the exalted attributes of Allah and glorify His Name. We also believe in the *mutashābihāt* or allegorical Qur'ānic verses, which serve this same purpose, without rejecting any part of them or attempting to interpret them on our own. We stand aloof from the disagreement which exists among the scholars concerning these verses; it is enough for us to adopt the attitude of the Prophet and his Companions: *And those who are established in knowledge say: 'We believe in the Book; the whole of it is from our Lord'* (3: 7).

11. Every innovation introduced by the people into the religion of Allah on the grounds of whim or without authentic foundation, whether by adding to the principles of Islam or taking from them, is a serious deviation from the path of Truth and must, therefore, be fought and abolished by the best means as long as it does not lead to a greater evil.

12. There is a difference of opinion regarding innovations which do not contradict established Islamic principles, such as praising *Imāms* and religious figures with pronouncements of their credibility and binding people to acts of worship left open to one's choice. We should adopt what can be confirmed by sound evidence.

13. Love of pious people, respecting them, and honouring their righteous achievements bring one closer to Allah. The favourites of Allah are described in the Qur'ānic verse: *those who believed and were fearful of Allah* (10: 65). Honour and prestige are due to them with the conditions prescribed in Islamic law, but we must firmly believe that they, may Allah be pleased with them, had no power over their own fates and, thereby, cannot avail or harm anyone after their death.

14. Visiting gravesides and tombs is an authentic *Sunnah* if done in the manner prescribed by the Prophet. But seeking the help of the dead, whoever they may be, appealing to them, asking them to fulfil certain requests, building high tombs, covering graves with curtains, illuminating them, wiping (ones hands) on them, vowing to the dead, swearing with their names instead of the name of Allah, and all such gross innovations must be fought. We do not need to find excuses for these matters.

15. There is a difference of opinion regarding use of the names of Allah's favourites in supplication. However, this is a matter of secondary importance and does not pertain to matters of *ʿaqīdah*.

16. Erroneous practices should be restrained irrespective of the names or titles under which they may be disguised. If something contradicts an Islamic principle in its essence, it should be opposed without regard to what people call it. In Islam, consideration is given to the significance and meaning of appellations and not to the appellations themselves.

17. Belief is the basis of action. Sincere intentions are more important than good actions with bad or no intentions. However, the Muslim is urged to improve through purification of the heart and the performance of righteous deeds.

18. Islam liberates the mind, promotes contemplation of the universe, honours science and scientists, and welcomes all that is good and beneficial to mankind: 'Wisdom is the lost property of the believer. Wherever he finds it, he is more deserving of it' (*Ibn Mājah*).

19. Islamic principles may be evident or uncertain, as are pure scientific principles. The evident principles of both will never conflict; that is, it is impossible for an established scientific fact to contradict an authentic Islamic principle. However, this may happen if one or both of them are uncertain. If one of them is uncertain, then it should be reinterpreted so as to remove the contradiction. If both are uncertain, then the uncertain Islamic principle should be given precedence over the uncertain scientific notion until the latter is proven.

20. Never label as a *kāfir* or disbeliever any Muslim who has confessed the two *Shahādah* or Declarations of Faith, who acts accordingly and performs the *farḍ* or obligatory duties of Islam unless he clearly professes the word of disbelief, refuses to acknowledge a fundamental principle of Islam, belies the verses of the Qur'ān, or commits an evident act of disbelief.

5

Why Islam?

Ismail al-Faruqi

Within Islam it is both legitimate and right to ask the question: 'why Islam?' Every tenet in Islam is subject to analysis and contention. No other religion is willing to subject its basic fundamentals of faith to such questioning. For example, Saint Thomas Aquinas, the most rational of Christian theologians, stopped the use of reason when it came to the basic fundamentals of Christian Faith. He then tried to justify faith. So to ask 'why Christianity?' was seen as an illegitimate question. However, Allah invites the question as to 'why Islam?'.

RATIONAL SYSTEM

Islam is also a rational system which not only allows questions but raises knowledge to a new level of dignity and respect. No other religion has exalted knowledge and its pursuit, as has Islam. In fact, for the first time in human history, a religious book invited people to question the creation of the universe and stated that in it (the universe) were signs for people of knowledge. Everything in Islam is subject to rational pursuit.

Islam has only forbidden the questioning of one thing and this is something which reason cannot handle. However, this does not imply an anti-intellectual attitude. The only thing which Islam has said is not within the capacity of the human mind to question is the essence (*dhāt*) of God. This will always escape a person, as He, Allah, is transcendent. However, His will, His purpose, His works, His intentions and His effects can be known.

Even the rites of Islam can be examined rationally. For example, logical and rational explanations can be made for the time of Prayer, the number of *rakāʿāt* or units in Prayer and even why we must bend our toes when we do. Of course the Muslim will always be aware that the answer he has obtained by rational enquiry is not exhaustive. It cannot be definitely accepted as explaining all the facts. It could be erroneous or incomplete. However, Islam encourages its followers to ask 'why Islam?'. Islam is an intellectual and historical religion. There are no secrets and no mysteries which cannot be understood by an ordinary person.

EASILY UNDERSTANDABLE

Islam does not present stumbling blocks to the mind. It does not make claims which overwhelm the mind. Islam does not present to a person that which the human intellect cannot grasp. Anyone can understand Islam as it is a universal religion. However, for example, Hinduism legitimises idolatry for the less educated, as it says, not all people can understand the higher religion of the Brahmans.

UNIVERSAL MESSAGE

Islam does not force a person to choose between various religions as it has included the essential teachings of all religions in its universal message. The Islamic concept is that, to every people, Allah sends a Messenger and that in their present religion or ideology they must have retained some kernel of Truth from the original teachings of that religion which was, of course, the teachings of the primordial religion (*dīn al-fiṭrah*) or, in other words, Islam.

Islam views inter-religious dialogue as an internal discussion, not as a discussion with outsiders because, from its perspective, all mankind are members of a universal religious brotherhood. So the differences Islam has with other religions are regarded as internal differences. Of course, Islam criticises some Jews and Christians who have wrongly interpreted their faith, however, this criticism is based on the fact that they have strayed from the original teachings of their religion.

Islam, therefore, was the first religion in the world to call for the critical examination of religious texts. The Muslim says, in effect, to other religions: 'Let us together examine the Holy Books of our religions and compare the contents with the original teachings of our respective religions and examine how far we have adhered to, or gone astray from these original teachings.' Muslims, therefore, never attack other religions.

Islam accepts the personal morality and values of Jesus, the concept of liberating a human being from materialism found in Hinduism, as well as the practical ethics for harmony in human society as found in Confucianism.

RELIGIOUS TOLERANCE

Islam is tolerant of other religions and regards them as religiously legitimate or *de jure*. In accepting other religions as legitimate, Islam, therefore, accepts their adherents. No other religion has given equal treatment to other religions as has Islam for over 1400 years. As we well know, Judaism and Roman Catholicism were illegal in the time of Queen Elizabeth I. In Spain under Ferdinand and Isabella, it was illegal to have any religion other than Catholicism, and Muslims and Jews had to choose baptism, exile or death. In the Middle East, some Christian sects, which were brutally eliminated by their fellow Christians in Europe, have survived after fourteen centuries of Muslim rule. Secular regimes do not respect religion. They look down upon religion; either they believe any religion will do or they believe no religion is acceptable. The tolerance of other religions in Islam comes from respect because Islam says in every person there is an embryonic *fiṭrah* or purity planted in all human beings at birth and in every religion there is a basic kind of the original *dīn al-fiṭrah*.

THE HUMAN BEING'S INNOCENCE

Islam declares a person to be born with a clean slate. The human being was not born evil but rather he was created good and equipped by nature to fulfil his duties. From the Islamic point of view, the drama of a person's life is something that takes place after birth and not before. Islam does not record a human being as a degradation of the Divine as it regards a human being as having instincts which are pure and good.

THE HUMAN BEING: AN INTEGRAL WHOLE

Islam does not divide the soul and life of a person into two compartments, i.e. religious or ethical and verbal or material. Islam regards the human being as an integral whole. All of his actions and instincts are part and parcel of his being together with his hopes, fears, certitude, faith and conviction. Islam wants all these to cohere and, therefore, we could say that Islam is mental health *par excellence*. Islam considers a person's work or even sex in this world as an act of worship.

LIFE FILLED WITH PURPOSE AND MEANING

Islam takes the world of life and existence seriously, declaring it to be full of meaning and purpose. Life is not a sport, nor is it purposeless. From the Islamic perspective, everything has meaning because the concept of God's purpose in creation gives meaning to human life. The Muslim is never bored with life; there is no existential anxiety in Islam. The Muslim can see the working of the good purposes of the Divine Creator in everything. The Muslim lives in a world where life is full of meaning and purpose and this means the Muslim never looses his mental balance. In fact, mental illness is very rare in the Muslim community.

WORLD-AFFIRMATIVE

Islam is world-affirmative. For the Muslim the world is good. It is a blessing, it has been created good, to be enjoyed. Islam does not view the world as a demon, it is not valued as being satanic or evil. It is not a degraded kingdom. The world is the only kingdom; the hereafter is not a kingdom but merely a place of Judgement for a human person's actions during his life. For Muslims, the world is a beautiful place; pearls, clothes and horses are to be enjoyed. What is wrong, is its misuse under moral law. The world is good and Muslims are obliged to cultivate it and make it into a garden. The process of organising people as a community is a religious duty.

No 'ism', ideology or religion matches Islam in its world-affirmative stance. All Muslims should be wealthy and affluent. It is Satan who promises poverty, not God. In fact, the Qur'ān criticises those who were lazy and who failed to migrate, who could not pull themselves up by their bootstraps. To be a Muslim is to live in and to be loyal to this world but not above and beyond our loyalty to Allah.

A SOCIAL FAITH

In building this world and conforming it to God's desire, Muslims are told that they must work with each other and not alone. Islam establishes a social order not a mystical order. Islam's social order has teeth, regulated by law, the *Sharīʿah*. Islam wants to establish a social order to enjoin the good and prevent the evil. However, every Muslim must correct evil. It is his duty, just as much as it is his duty to pray five times a day.

In Islam, it is of the highest degree of faith to plunge into space and time and bring about the transformation of the world in accordance with God's desire. Islam is affirmative action in a social setting; it is neither abstract nor isolationist. Islam establishes justice and an ordered society, regulated by law. Islam guarantees justice for all; Madinah was that class of model society. In those days justice had no price. For several centuries under Islamic rule any citizen who voiced a complaint could be sure that justice would be done. No theory of society can give as much as the Islamic theory of society has given. Society, based on race, language or history are prototypes of the animal world where dog eats dog. The social order of Islam ends this and brings justice to all. A Muslim's mission is to bring order and this international society established by Islam must be carried to the world and, therefore, the Islamic social order seeks universality.

UNIVERSAL SYSTEM

Islam provides a social order which cannot only tend to be universal but must become universal. The Islamic system is a system for world order and it must spread around the world. Unless it is spread around the world, it will degenerate into a form of nationalism which is *ḥarām* or unlawful in Islam. Islam is built on the basis of values which are not only for the group which adheres to them, but for the whole of mankind. Allah is the deity of all people.

Does Islam deny the value of national, ethnic or linguistic identity and culture? No! Islam recognises the worth of these national and ethnic groups. Islam does not only tolerate but encourages the development of different ethnic groups. The group has a special perspective on the values affecting people's lives. Insofar as it exists, national culture is encouraged by Islam, but it is subject to the universal law of Allah. The interests of the nation or group must be subject to the moral law, the *Sharīʿah*, which encompasses the whole of mankind. Islam created a world society and it was Islam, over 1400 years ago, that first established a working system of international law.

It was only in the 20th century that the West started to develop international law. Grotius contributed only wishful thinking. In the West, international law existed only in the imagination until after World War I when the League of Nations was established. The present system of international law is far inferior to the Islamic system of international law because, under the Islamic system, the law of nations is backed by a court and not just a single court in the Hague. Any *Sharīʿah* court in any part of the world can hear any international dispute to which the parties are not only nations but also individuals. If we want to solve international problems we must make justice under international law possible for everyone.

PROMOTING HARMONY WITH THE ENVIRONMENT

Islam is a religion that enables us to live our lives in harmony with nature, ourselves and God. Islam does not compartmentalise but rather unites the life of a person. This is the *summum bonum,* supreme good, of Islam because Islam assures us of happiness in this world and the next. Presently, people are so madly in pursuit of this world that it has resulted in upsetting the ecology of nature; this because of the decay in the inner nature of human beings. In this age of unprecedented advancements in science and technology, the pursuit of worldly gain has turned sour and self-destructive because it is devoid of all ethical values. Therefore the pursuit of *dunyā* (worldly affairs) without *dīn* can only lead to, and has led to, disaster. On the other hand, pursuit of *dīn* without *dunyā* is merely daydreaming. Islam asks people to cultivate the world without robbing, usury, stealing and raping the environment and insists that people must carry out their tasks subject to moral law. For the Muslim, involvement and success in the world will ensure success in the hereafter. Islam guarantees happiness in this world and the next. Having granted this great gift of God to humanity what else could we do but say 'we hear and we obey and all praise is due to Allah, Lord of the Worlds.'

6

To be a Muslim

Fathi Yakan

The first condition for you to become a true Muslim is to have the correct *ʿaqīdah* or belief. Your belief must be in accordance with the Qur'ān and the *Sunnah* (practices) of the Prophet Muḥammad, may the peace and blessings of Allah be upon him. To be a true Muslim in your belief means:

1. You must believe that the Creator of this universe is the Great, Wise, Capable, all-Knowing and self-Subsisting God. The proof of that, is this perfect and delicately balanced universe itself. If part of this universe is altered it would not be suitable for any life. Allah says, *Had there been in heaven or on earth any deities other than Allah, both would surely have fallen into ruin!* (21: 22).

2. You must believe that Allah did not create this universe for play or in vain, because it is impossible for the Perfect to be seeking amusement. Allah says, *Did you then think that We had created you aimless and that you shall not be returned to Us?* (23: 115).

3. You must believe that Allah sent Prophets to all people and with some Prophets he sent written Scriptures or Messages. The mission of His Prophets was to tell their people about Allah and to teach them what He, Allah, expects of them: *And indeed within every community We have raised up an Apostle* [entrusted with this message]: *'Worship God, and shun the powers of evil'* (16: 36). The last of these messengers was Muḥammad, whom Allah supported with the Eternal Miracle, the Qur'ān.

4. You must believe that the reason for your existence is to know Allah and to obey and worship Him, as He states: *I have not created jinn and mankind except that they should worship Me* (51: 56).

5. You must believe that the reward for the believer is Paradise, and the punishment for the disbeliever is Hell: *And warn* [them] *of the Day of Gathering, of which there is no doubt:* [when] *some shall find themselves in the Paradise, and some in the blazing Flame* (42: 7).

6. You must believe that a person does good and bad deeds by his own choice: *Consider the human self, and how it is formed in accordance with what it is meant to be, and how it is imbued with moral failings as well as with the consciousness of God! To a happy state shall indeed attain he who causes this* [self] *to grow in purity, and truly lost is he who buries it* [in darkness] (91: 7–10). And again, *Every soul shall be pledged for what it has earned* (74: 38).

7. You must believe that legislation is for Allah Alone. A Muslim is limited to *ijtihād* or intellectual effort in deriving laws from the *Sharīʿah*, the Islamic legal code. You must reflect continuously on the verse: *Whatever it be you differ, the decision thereof is with Allah: 'Such is Allah my Lord, in Him I trust, and to Him I turn'* (42: 10).

8. You must ponder upon the creation of Allah and not upon the Creator Himself. In this respect, the Prophet said, 'Ponder the creation of Allah and not about the person of Allah, because you will not be able to comprehend it' (cited in *At-Targhīb wa-Tarhīb*).

9. You must learn about Allah from His beautiful Names and from His creation. The Prophet said: 'There are ninety-nine Names of Allah, everyone of you who remembers them will enter Paradise, and Allah is One' (*Bukhārī*). In the Qur'ān, many of these attributes are mentioned. For example, He is the Eternal, the Everlasting, the Absolute, the Unique, He begetteth not nor is He begotten, the self-Subsisting, the all-Knowing, the Living.

10. You must worship Allah and Allah alone. This is the message which Allah sent with every Prophet: *For We assuredly sent amongst every people a Messenger* [with the command]: *'Serve Allah and eschew Evil'* (16: 36).

11. You must fear Allah, and only Allah. This fear should prevent you from doing anything unacceptable to Him. *Whoso obeys God and His Messenger, and fears God and has awe of Him, those – they are the triumphant* (24: 52).

12. You must remember Allah at all times. This is the best treatment for affliction and distress. *Those who believe and whose hearts find satisfaction in the remembrance of Allah. For without doubt, in the remembrance of Allah hearts do find*

satisfaction (13: 28). Thus, the true believer is less likely to suffer from mental illnesses, for close adherence to the Islamic Way of Life is an added bonus in alleviating fears, tension and disturbances in life.

13. You must love Allah with a love that makes your heart connected to Him. This love should motivate you to do more and more good, and enable you to sacrifice everything for His sake. Nothing should stop you from *jihād* (struggle), be they the vanities of the world, or close relationships, as Allah, Himself declares: *Say: if it be that your fathers, your sons, your brothers, your mates, or your kindred, the wealth that you have gained, the commerce in which you fear a decline, or the dwellings in which you delight, are dearer to you than Allah and His Messenger, or the striving in His cause, then wait until Allah comes with His judgement: and Allah guides not the rebellious* (9: 24).

The Prophet further emphasised: 'There are three types of people who will experience the sweetness of faith: he to whom Allah and His Messenger are dearer than all else; he who loves a person for Allah's sake alone; and he who has as great an abhorrence of returning to disbelief after Allah has rescued him from it, as he has of being cast into Hell' (*Bukhārī*).

14. You must put your trust in Allah in everything you do. This will encourage you in everything you do no matter how difficult it is. *And if anyone puts his trust in Allah, Sufficient is* [Allah] *for him* (65: 3).

Ibn Abbas narrated that the Prophet once told him: 'Young man, shall I teach you some words [of advice]: Be mindful of God's [Commands] and God will protect you. Remember God and you will find Him in front of you. [Know God in prosperity and He will know you in adversity.] If you have to ask, ask of God; if you have to seek help, seek help from God. Remember that if all the people were to join hands to bring you some benefit, they cannot bring you any benefit except that which God had already decreed for you. And if they were to join hands to harm you, they would harm you only with that which God had already decreed for you. The pens have been lifted and the pages have been dried' (*Tirmidhī*).

15. You must thank Allah for His innumerable graces, His favour and His mercy: *And God Has brought you forth from your mothers' wombs knowing nothing – but He Has endowed you with hearing, and sight, and minds, so that you might have cause to be grateful* (16: 78); *And a Sign for them is the dead earth: We give life to it and bring forth from it grain from which they eat. And We have made on it* [the earth] *gardens of date-palms and grapes, and We have caused springs to gush forth in it. That they may eat of its fruit, though their hands did not make it. Will they not then be grateful?* (36: 33–35). And again: *Allah has promised those who give thanks ever*

increasing grace and those who do not, ever increasing loss; And [remember the time] *when your Sustainer made* [this promise] *known: 'If you are grateful* [to Me], *I shall most certainly give you more and more; but if you are ungrateful, verily, My chastisement will be severe indeed!'* (14: 7).

16. You must seek Allah's forgiveness all the time. This will help absolve your sins, renew your repentance and bring you peace and tranquillity: *Whosoever does evil, or wrongs himself, and then prays for God's forgiveness, he shall find God is all-Forgiving, all-Compassionate* (4: 110).

17. All your actions must be done with full awareness of Allah's presence, for He says: *Never can there be a secret consultation between three persons without His being the fourth of them, nor between five without His being the sixth of them; and neither between less than that, or more, without His being with them wherever they may be. But in the end, on Resurrection Day, He will make them truly understand what they did: for, verily God has full knowledge of everything* (58: 7).

7

Islam – a Liberating Force

Said Ramadan

The birth of Islam was in reality a strong declaration of the birth of higher humanity. For Islam is, in essence, a great liberation movement encompassing the manifold aspects of human life, emanating from the conscience of the individual and oriented towards the life of society. It was a revolution which destroyed in its march all the spiritual, intellectual and social chains which had encumbered people, and declared over fourteen centuries ago the full gamut of human rights.

A REVOLUTION IN BELIEF

1. Emancipation from Superstition

The advent of Islam heralded a revolution in the realm of belief. It emancipated the human conscience from superstition and fancy; it established the absolute transcendence of the Divine essence beyond polytheistic and anthropomorphic aberrations and it formed a direct relationship between God and His subjects without any intermediary.

The absolute transcendence of God and the direct link between God and subject, are the crossroads between order and chaos in the realm of belief, as well as between freedom and slavery. This is a considerable achievement if we recall the sufferings of mankind as a result of the power of clerical intermediaries, the persecution of scientists and free thinkers in the Middle

Ages, and if we recall the revolutions which broke out in Europe to destroy the hegemony of those claiming to be the vicegerents of God on earth.

As a corollary to this basic approach, freedom of thought had been an indigenous attribute of the Islamic creed because Islam does not recognise the existence of a clerical hierarchy or group in the sense commonly understood today.

2. Revolution Against Religious Intolerance

The birth of Islam constituted a revolution in another facet of belief: it was a revolution against religious intolerance by virtue of its declaration of the freedom of belief and of worship in their fullest manifestations. The Qur'ān says, *There is no compulsion in religion* (2:256). *And if your Lord willed, all who are in the earth would have believed together. Would you then compel people until they are believers?* (10:99).

Religious fanaticism and intolerance gave way to liberality and tolerance. Indeed, the freedom of belief and of worship became a duty imposed upon the Muslim towards believers in other revealed religions in the Muslim world. When the duty of *jihād* was ordained for the first time in Islam, the Qur'ān expressed it in the following manner: *Sanction is given unto those who fight because they have been wronged, and God is indeed able to give them victory. Those who have been driven from their homes unjustly only because they said, Our Lord is God: for had it not been for God's repelling some people by means of others, cloisters and churches and oratories and masjids, wherein the name of God is oft mentioned would assuredly have been pulled down* (22: 39–40).

Indeed, the tolerance went so far as to accord protection even to the infidel who does not believe in any Divine religion at all, provided he refrains from molesting the Muslims in their faith and from enticing them away from their religion. The Qur'ān declares: *And if anyone of the idolaters seeks your protection, then protect him so that he may hear the word of God, and afterward convey him to his place of safety. That is because they are a folk who know not* (9:5).

Islam emphasised the ethnological unity and equality of all races, thus destroying the heinous monstrosity of racial discrimination. It ordained one immutable standard of virtue and excellence, having nothing to do with the colour of the skin, birthplace or family genealogy. That criterion of judgement was made relational to fear of God and to good deeds in this world. These pertain to the conduct of the individual and are completely divested of colour or race. God says: *O human beings! We have created you all from a male and a female, and have made you nations and tribes that you may know one another. Indeed the most honourable of you in the sight of God is the one among you most deeply conscious of Him. Indeed God is all-Knowing, all-Aware* (49:13).

3. Revolution Against Class Distinctions

The birth of Islam represented a revolution against class distinctions, as well as against tyrannical rulers: for it divested the ruling classes of all privileges and personal powers. Divine law became the source of all legislation, while the selection of those in charge of implementing that law was vested entirely in the people. It is necessary to dwell further on the profound implications of this unique system in guaranteeing rights and equality for all.

Firstly, by depriving human beings of the right to lay down basic legislation and in recognising God the Almighty as the sole legislator, no person, or a group or a class is, thereby, afforded an opportunity to rule arbitrarily over others. Sovereignty is recognised in the Supreme Being, the God of all. Human beings are merely assigned the implementation and execution of Divine law. Consequently, legislation is freed of discrimination: no one feels that in submitting to the law he is submitting to the will of any other human. All are equal before God.

Secondly, the administrator of this legislation derives his authority from the people who chose him: obedience is not to his person but to the Divine law, the implementation of which he is entrusted with. His right to obedience is forfeited if he oversteps his jurisdiction. Thus, the Islamic system stands unique in realising equality and justice, and in destroying all forms of individual, class or state tyranny.

A SYSTEM OF SOLIDARITY

Social life in Islam is based upon social co-operation and cohesion amongst its constituent elements. Such co-operation has been embodied in systematic legislation outlining its nature and methods. But above all, stress is laid upon the cultivation of individual conscience and upon the preponderance of moral imperatives in society.

In discussing social co-operation and the role of religious belief therein, many are inclined to cite such words as charity, philanthropy and most of all the institution of *zakāh*. But these words and their connotations do not represent the true role of the Islamic creed in the field of social cohesion. Social cohesion in Islam is a fully-fledged social system. It does not refer merely to financial aid in its various forms, as is implied in such concepts as 'social security' and 'social insurance'. Financial assistance is only one aspect of aid, ordained by the principle of co-operation and cohesion in Islam.

The term 'social cohesion' in Islam is intended as a system for training the spirit and the conscience of the individual, and the cultivation of his personal endowments and capabilities for useful and productive endeavour. It encompasses the family as well as social relations. And finally, it covers financial and economic relationships within society.

Thus, the connotations of charity, philanthropy and even *zakāh* are dwarfed in comparison with this all-embracing concept of social cohesion as laid down by Islam and observed as a living reality as history so testifies. Islam begins by making this co-operation and cohesion a relationship between the individual and his own self. The individual is made responsible for his self before God. He is duty bound to cleanse it from evil, to afford it the good things in life, to give it a fair share of work and rest so that it does not fall into disuse from idleness, nor succumbs to exhaustion from overwork. This equilibrium within the individual and his inner self is designed to awaken the individual's conscience and sensitivities, and to assert his personality and will. Freedom and obligation are the prerequisites of an independent personality. But this apparently individual cohesion is in reality a social one in the wider sense of the concept in Islam. For the training of the individual in this manner is a preparation for the part which he is called upon to play within the social matrix.

Islam then moves from the realm of the individual to that of the family. Again, the family structure is based upon solid cohesion in which advantages and liabilities, rights and obligations are equalised. The family is the cornerstone in the establishment of society; if its edifice is based upon this principle of cohesion and balance, the social obligations of the state are to that extent lightened and reduced, because a substantial portion of such obligations can be shouldered within the orbit of the family.

Such cohesion in the family does not pertain merely to economic affairs; it is all-embracing in scope and includes protection of motherhood, the duty of caring for children and their adequate preparation physically, mentally and spiritually, the duty imposed upon offspring towards their parents in their old age and senility, in addition to the normal financial obligations incurred by every family.

With a view to safeguarding motherhood and in order to maintain a healthy 'home' environment in which the young may be adequately brought up, Islam has imposed the financial duties of maintenance upon men, exempting women from the same. This is designed to afford the mother the necessary time and energy for rearing her young.

Islam does not forbid women the opportunity to work. Instead it does not make such work obligatory upon her as it does upon a man. This is to equalise the burden for males and females. Islam recognises a woman's right to gain full employment if she so desires; it also safeguards her inheritance rights, her right for unrestricted financial dealings, her right to choose her life partner, and her right to revoke the marriage contract when life becomes intolerable.

Moving from the family to the social structure we find social cohesion an imperative in all social relationships and not merely in the spheres of finance and economics. There is a reciprocal relationship of interdependence between the individual and the group, as regards both rights and obligations. Islam goes so far in this regard that the two interests are inseparably integrated.

Every individual is duty bound to perform his own job satisfactorily, because the fruits of his toil register their impact upon society as a whole. He is also obliged to refrain from evil deeds and to prevail upon others to do likewise. It is his duty to respect the rights of the community and to struggle towards its preservation and survival.

On the other hand, the individual is entitled to certain rights from the community or the state which represents it – for example the provision of training both theoretical and practical for gainful and productive employment. The right to a job is also mandatory upon the state towards all able-bodied citizens.

Every worker is entitled to adequate housing facilities, to protection from heat, cold and rain and to privacy; he is also entitled to adequate clothing, food and transportation commensurate with the needs of the time. If he wishes to marry and does not possess the means to do so, the state is duty-bound to help him satisfy this instinctive calling so as to safeguard him from indulging in illicit and immoral practices.

The individual is held responsible for any delinquency in meeting his obligations, and the state is responsible likewise for any failure to meet its obligations towards the individual.

It is thus clear that social cohesion in Islam is not a system of philanthropy and charity; it is a system designed to prepare the citizen for productive endeavour. Only those who are partially or totally incapacitated, whether temporarily or permanently, qualify for help through *zakāh* and charity.

Zakāh is only one aspect of the manifold ramifications of the principle of social cohesion. It is not a mere personal charity left to the private conscience of the individual. It is a right exacted and spent by the state in ways very similar to those which in the modern era come under the umbrella of 'social security' and 'social insurance'; it is administered, however, on the basis of decentralisation. The *zakāh* funds of each region should be allocated principally towards meeting the needs of that particular locality. Any surplus should be returned to the *bayt-ul-māl* (treasury) for distribution in all parts of the Muslim world without discrimination of creed or colour.

A PERFECT WAY OF LIFE

Islam legislates for mankind a complete and equitable system, for while it holds the human spirit in an exalted position and prescribes ideal ethical principles, it does not deny the importance of the material in life. Islam's legislation is a balanced admixture of the spiritual and the material.

Thus, Islam is not a mere religion in the sense denoted by the equivalent term in English. It is rather a comprehensive way of life spiritually and materially, in the conscience of the individual as well as in the matrix of the group, including the principles of obligation to the state, and dealings of all sorts whether they be economic, political or international.

Such expressions as religion and state, faith and politics, as they are understood in the West, have no equivalent in the Islamic lexicography. The term 'Islamic religion' embraces all these concepts in their totality, both integrally and indissolubly. The Muslim performs his Prayers in the *masjid*, sells his commodities in the market, decides between litigants in a court of law, manages the affairs of state, concludes treaties and covenants with other states, fights for justice and right on the battlefield. He does all these things motivated by one spirit, and in accordance with one *Sharīʿah*, and in the inspiration of one creed and system – the system of Islam.

Islam builds this imposing edifice on the basis of a belief in God and places the God-fearing conscience as a guardian over legislation and implementation. It makes the link between this conscience and God, the pillar of this system, for it is always possible to evade and cheat the law, but the externally vigilant eye of God is always on the watch for those who dare violate upright conduct.

8

Submission to God

Alija Ali Izetbegovic

THE DESTINY OF THE HUMAN BEING

Nature has determinism, the human being has destiny. Acceptance of this destiny is the supreme and final idea of Islam. Does destiny exist and if so what form does it take? Let us look at our own lives and see what remains of our most precious plans and dreams from our youth. Do we not come helplessly into the world faced with our own personality, with higher or lower intelligence, with attractive or repulsive looks, with an athletic or dwarfish stature, in a king's palace or in a beggar's hut, in a tumultuous or peaceful time, under the reign of a tyrant or a noble prince, and generally in geographical and historical circumstances about which we have not been consulted? How limited is what we call our will, how tremendous and unlimited is our destiny! A human being has been cast down upon this world and made dependent on many factors over which he has no power. His life is influenced by both very remote and very near factors.

During the Allied invasion of Europe in 1944, there was, for a moment, a general disturbance in radio communications which could have been fatal for the operations under way. Many years later, the disturbance was explained as a huge explosion in the Andromeda constellation, several million light years away from our planet. One type of catastrophic earthquake on the earth is due to changes on the sun's surface. As our knowledge of the world grows, so does our realisation that we will never be complete masters of our fate. Even supposing the greatest possible progress of science, the number of factors under our control will always be insignificant compared to those beyond it. A human being is not proportional to the world. He and his lifetime are not the measuring units of the pace of things. This is the cause of a human being's eternal insecurity, which is psychologically reflected in pessimism, revolt, despair, apathy, or in submission to God's will. Islam arranges the world by means of upbringing, education, and laws – that is its narrower scope; submission to God is the broader one. Individual justice can never be fully satisfied within the conditions of existence. We can follow all Islamic rules which, in their ultimate result, should provide us with the 'happiness in both worlds'; moreover, we can follow all other norms, medical, social and moral but, because of the terrific entanglement of destinies, desires and accidents, we can still suffer in body and soul. What can console a mother who has lost her only son? Is there any solace for a human being who has been disabled in an accident?

We ought to become conscious of our human condition. We are immersed in certain situations. I can work to change my situation, but there are situations which are essentially unchangeable, even when their appearance takes a new turn, and when their victorious power is veiled: I must die; I must suffer; I must fight; I am a victim of chance; I inevitably become entangled in guilt. These basic conditions of our existence are referred to as 'the border situations' (Karl Jaspers, *An Introduction to Philosophy*, Vol. 2). Sure, 'man is bound to improve everything that can be improved in this world. After that, children will still go on dying unjustly even in the most perfect of societies. A human being, at best, can only give himself the task of reducing arithmetically the sufferings of this world. Still, injustice and pain will continue and, however limited, they will never cease to be blasphemy' (Albert Camus, *L'Hommé révolté*).

SUBMISSION TO GOD OR REVOLT

Submission to God or revolt: these are two different answers to the same dilemma. In submission to God, there is an element of every (human) wisdom except one: shallow optimism. Submission is the story of human destiny, and that is why it is inevitably permeated with pessimism.

Recognition of destiny is a moving reply to the great human theme of inevitable suffering. It is the recognition of life as it is and a conscious decision to bear and to endure. In this point, Islam differs radically from the superficial idealism and optimism of European philosophy and its naïve story about 'the best of all possible worlds.' Submission to God is a mellow light coming from beyond pessimism.

As a result of one's recognition of one's own impotence and insecurity, submission to God itself becomes a new potency and a new security. Belief in God and His providence offers a feeling of security which cannot be made up for with anything else. Submission to God does not imply passivity as many people wrongly believe. Obedience to God excludes obedience to a human being. It is a new relation between a human being and God and, therefore, between one person and another.

Submission to God is also a freedom which is attained by following through with one's own destiny. Our involvement and our struggle are human and reasonable and have the token of moderation and serenity only through the belief that the ultimate result is not in our hands. It is up to us to work, the rest is in God's Hands.

Therefore, to properly understand our position in the world means to submit to God, to find peace, not to start making a more positive effort to encompass and overcome everything, but rather a negative effort to accept the place and the time of our birth, the place and the time that are our destiny and God's will. Submission to God is the only human and dignified way out of the unsolvable senselessness of life, a way out without revolt, despair, nihilism, or suicide. It is a heroic feeling not of a hero, but of an ordinary human being who has done his duty and accepted his destiny.

Islam does not get its name from its laws, orders, or prohibitions, nor from the efforts of the body and soul it claims, but from something that encompasses and surmounts all that: from a moment of cognition, from the strength of the soul to face the times, from the readiness to endure everything that an existence can offer, from the Truth of submission to God. Submission to God, thy name is Islam!

B. THE QUR'ĀN

9

Introducing the Qur'ān

Sayyid Abul Ala Mawdudi

What kind of book is the Qur'ān? In what manner was it revealed? What underlies its arrangement? What is its subject? What is its true purpose? What is the central theme to which its multifarious topics are intrinsically related? What kind of reasoning and style does it adopt in elucidating its central theme? If we could obtain clear, lucid answers to these and other related questions we might avoid some dangerous pitfalls, thus making it easier to reflect upon and to grasp the meaning and purpose of the Qur'ānic verses. If we begin studying the Qur'ān with the expectation of reading a book on religion we shall find it hard, since our notions of religion and of a book are naturally circumscribed by our range of experience.

We need, therefore, to be told in advance that the Qur'ān is unique in the manner of its composition, in its theme and in its contents and arrangement. We should be forewarned that the concept of a book which we have formed from our previous readings is likely to be a hindrance, rather than a help, towards a deep understanding of the Qur'ān. We should realise that as a first step towards understanding it we must disabuse our minds of all preconceived notions.

FUNDAMENTAL CLAIMS OF THE QUR'ĀN

The student of the Qur'ān should grasp, from the outset, the fundamental claims that the Qur'ān makes for itself. Whether one ultimately decides to believe in the Qur'ān or not, one must recognise the fundamental statements made by the Qur'ān and by the man to whom it was revealed, the Prophet Muḥammad, to be the starting point of one's study. These claims are:

1. The Lord of creation, the Creator and Sovereign of the entire Universe, created people on earth – which is merely a part of His boundless realm. He also endowed them with the capacity for cognition, reflection and understanding, with the ability to distinguish between good and evil, with the freedom of choice and volition, and with the power to exercise their latent potentialities. In short, God bestowed upon people a kind of autonomy and appointed them His vicegerent on earth.

2. Although man enjoys this status, God made it abundantly plain to him that He alone is His Lord and Sovereign, just as He is the Lord and Sovereign of the whole universe. Man was told that he was not entitled to consider himself independent and that only God was entitled to claim absolute obedience, service and worship. It was also made clear to him that life in this world, in which he had been placed and bestowed with a certain honour and authority, was in fact a temporary term, and was meant to test him. After the end of this earthly life he must return to God, Who will judge him on the basis of his performance, declaring who has succeeded and who has failed.

The right way for a human being is to regard God as his only Sovereign and the only object of his worship and adoration, to follow the guidance revealed by God, to act in this world in the consciousness that earthly life is merely a period of trial, and to keep his eyes fixed on the ultimate objective – success in God's Final Judgement. Every other way is wrong.

It was also explained to man that if he chose to adopt the right way of life – and in this choice he was free – he would enjoy peace and contentment in this world and be assigned, on his return to God, the abode of eternal bliss and happiness known as Paradise. Should he follow any other way – although he was free to do so – he would experience the evil effects of corruption and disorder in the life of this world and be consigned to eternal grief and torment when he crossed the borders of the present world and arrived in the hereafter.

3. Having explained all this, the Lord of the Universe placed people on earth and communicated to Adam and Eve, the first human beings to live on earth, the guidance which they and their offspring were required to follow. These first people were not born in a state of ignorance and darkness. On the contrary, they began their life in the broad daylight of Divine guidance. They had intimate knowledge of reality and the law which they

were to follow was communicated to them. Their way of life consisted of obedience to God, that is Islam, and they taught their children to live in obedience to Him, that is to live as Muslims.

In the course of time, however, people gradually deviated from this true way of life and began to follow their various and erroneous ways. They allowed true guidance to be lost through heedlessness and negligence and sometimes, even deliberately, distorted it out of evil perversity. They associated with God a number of beings, human and non-human, real as well as imaginary, and adored them as deities. They adulterated the God-given knowledge of reality (*al-ʿilm*) with all kinds of fanciful ideas, superstitions and philosophical concepts, thereby giving birth to innumerable religions. They disregarded or distorted the sound and equitable principles of individual morality and of collective conduct (*Sharīʿah*) and made their own laws in accordance with their base desires and prejudices. As a result, the world became filled with wrong and injustice.

4. It was inconsistent with the limited autonomy conferred upon people by God that He should exercise His overwhelming power and compel them to righteousness. It was also inconsistent with the fact that God had granted a term to the human species in which to show their worth that He should afflict people with catastrophic destruction as soon as they showed signs of rebellion. Moreover, God had undertaken from the beginning of creation that true guidance would be made available to people throughout the term granted to them and that this guidance would be available in a manner consistent with a person's autonomy. To fulfil this self-assumed responsibility, God chose to appoint those human beings whose faith in Him was outstanding and who followed the way pleasing to Him. God chose these people to be his envoys. He had His Messages communicated to them, honoured them with an intimate knowledge of reality, provided them with the true laws of life and entrusted them with the task of recalling people to the Original Path from which they had strayed.

5. These Prophets were sent to different people in different lands and over a period of time covering thousands and thousands of years. They all had the same religion; the one originally revealed to man as the right way for him. All of them followed the same guidance; those principles of morality and collective life prescribed for people at the very outset of their existence. All these Prophets had the same mission, to call people to this true religion and subsequently to organise all who accepted this message into a community (*Ummah*) which would be bound by the law of God, which would strive to establish its observance and would seek to prevent its violation. Each of the Prophets discharged their missions creditably in their

own time. However, there were always many who refused to accept their guidance and consequently those who did accept it and became a 'Muslim' community gradually degenerated, causing the Divine guidance either to be lost, distorted or adulterated.

6. In the sixth century (CE) the Lord of the Universe sent Muḥammad to Arabia and entrusted him with the same mission that He had entrusted to the earlier Prophets. This last Messenger of God addressed the followers of the earlier Prophets (who had by this time deviated from their original teachings) as well as the rest of humanity. The mission of each Prophet was to call people to the right way of life, to communicate God's true guidance afresh and to organise into one community all who responded to his mission and accepted the guidance vouchsafed to him. Such a community was to be dedicated to the two-fold task of moulding its own life in accordance with God's guidance and striving for the reform of the world. The Qur'ān is the Book which embodies this mission and guidance, as revealed by God to Muḥammad.

SUBJECT, THEME AND OBJECTIVE OF THE QUR'ĀN

If we remember these basic facts about the Qur'ān it becomes easy to grasp its true subject, its central theme and the objective it seeks to achieve. Insofar as it seeks to explain the ultimate causes of a person's success or failure the subject of the Book is the human being.

Its central theme is that concepts relating to God, the universe and people which have emanated from a person's own limited knowledge run counter to reality. The same applies to concepts which have been either woven by a person's intellectual fancies or which have evolved through a human being's obsession with animal desires. The ways of life which rest on these false foundations are both contrary to reality and ruinous for a human being. The essence of true knowledge is that which God revealed to the human being when He appointed him his vicegerent. Hence, the way of life which is in accordance with reality and conducive to human good is the right way. The real object of the Book is to call people to this right way and to illuminate God's true guidance, which has often been lost either through a people's negligence and heedlessness or distorted by their wicked perversity.

All the various themes occurring in the Qur'ān are related to this central theme; just as beads of different sizes and colour may be strung together to form a necklace. The Qur'ān speaks of the structure of the heavens and the earth and of the human being, refers to the signs of reality in the various phenomena of the universe, relates anecdotes of bygone nations, criticises the beliefs, morals and deeds of different peoples, elucidates supernatural truths and deals with many other themes. All this the Qur'ān does, not in order to provide instruction in physics, history, philosophy or any other particular branch of knowledge, but rather to remove the misconceptions people have about reality and to make that reality clear. It emphasises that the various ways people follow, which do not conform to reality, are essentially false, and full of harmful consequences for mankind. It calls on people to shun all such ways and to follow instead, the way which both conforms to reality and yields the best practical results. The entire content consistently revolve around this call.

The Qur'ān is not a book in the conventional sense of the term. God did not compose and entrust it in one piece to Muḥammad so that he could spread its message and call people to adopt an attitude to life consonant with its teachings.

THE MAKKAN REVELATIONS

The nature of the Qur'ān is that God chose a human being in Makkah to serve as His Messenger and asked him to preach His message, starting in his own city, Makkah, and with his own tribe, the Quraysh. At this initial stage, instructions were confined to what was necessary at this particular juncture of the mission. Three themes in particular stand out:

- Directives were given to the Prophet on how he should prepare himself for his great mission and how he should begin working for the fulfilment of his task.
- A fundamental knowledge of reality was furnished and misconceptions commonly held by people in that regard – misconceptions which gave rise to wrong orientations in life – were removed.
- People were exhorted to adopt the right attitude toward life. Moreover, the Qur'ān also elucidated those fundamental principles which, if followed, lead to a person's success and happiness.

In keeping with the character of the mission at this stage the early revelations generally consisted of short verses, in language of uncommon grace and power, and in a literary style suited to the taste and temperament of the people to whom they were originally addressed, and whose hearts they were meant to penetrate. The rhythm, melody and vitality of these verses drew rapt attention, and such was their stylistic grace and charm that people began to recite them involuntarily.

The local colour of these early Messages were conspicuous, for while the truth they contained were universal, the arguments and illustrations used to elucidate them were drawn from the immediate environment familiar to the first listeners. Allusions were made to their history and traditions and to the visible traces of the past which had crept into the beliefs, and into the moral and social life of Arabia. All this was calculated to enhance the appeal the message held for its immediate audience. This early stage lasted for four or five years, during which period the following reactions to the Prophet's message manifested themselves:

- A few people responded to the call and agreed to join the *Ummah*, community, which committed itself to submit to the Will of God.
- Many people reacted with hostility, either from ignorance or egotism, or because of their chauvinistic attachment to the way of life of their forefathers.
- It began to meet with favourable responses beyond Makkah and among other tribes.

The next stage of the mission was marked by a hard, vigorous struggle between the Islamic movement and the age-old ignorance (*jāhiliyyah*) of Arabia. The pagan Makkans were not only bent upon preserving their inherited way of life, but resolved to suppress the new movement by force. They stopped at nothing in the pursuit of this objective. They resorted to false propaganda. They spread doubt and suspicion and used subtle, malicious insinuations to sow distrust in people's minds. They tried to prevent people from listening to the Prophet's message. They perpetrated savage cruelties on those who embraced Islam. They subjected them to economic and social boycott, and persecuted them to such an extent that on two occasions a number of them were forced to leave home and emigrate to Abyssinia, and finally they had to emigrate *en masse* to Madinah.

In spite of this strong and growing resistance and opposition, the Islamic movement continued to spread. There was hardly a family left in Makkah in which at least one of its members had not embraced Islam. Indeed, the violence and bitterness of the enemies of Islam was due to the fact that their own kith and kin – brothers and sisters, sons and daughters, fathers and mothers – had not only embraced Islam, but were even ready to sacrifice their lives for its sake. Their resistance, therefore, brought them into conflict with their own nearest and dearest. Moreover, those who had forsaken the age-old ignorance of Arabia included many who were outstanding members of their society. After accepting Islam, they distinguished their moral uprightness, their truthfulness and their purity of character that the world could hardly fail to notice the superiority of the message which was attracting people of such qualities.

During the Prophet's long and arduous struggle, God continued to inspire him with revelations possessing at once the smooth, natural flow of a river, the violent force of a flood and the overpowering effect of a fierce fire. These Messages instructed the believers in their basic duties and inculcated in them a sense of community and belonging. They exhorted them to piety, moral excellence and purity of character. These messages taught them how to preach the true Faith, sustained their spirit by promises of success and Paradise in the hereafter, aroused them to struggle in the cause of God with patience, fortitude, high spirits, and filled their hearts with such zeal and enthusiasm that they were prepared to endure every sacrifice, brave every hardship and face every adversity.

At the same time, those who were bent on opposition, or who had deviated from the right way, or who had immersed themselves in frivolity and wickedness, were warned by reminding them of the tragic ends of nations with whose fates they were familiar. They were asked to draw lessons from the ruins of those localities through which they passed every day in the course of their wanderings. Evidence for the Oneness of God and the existence of the After-life was pointed to in signs visible to their own eyes and within the range of their ordinary experience. The weaknesses inherent in polytheism, the vanity of a human being's ambition to become independent even of God, the folly of denying the After-life, the perversity of blind adherence to the ways of one's ancestors regardless of right or wrong, were all fully elucidated with the help of arguments cogent enough to penetrate the minds and hearts of the audience.

Moreover, every misgiving was removed, a reasonable answer was provided to every objection, all confusion and perplexity was cleared up, and ignorance was besieged from all sides till its irrationality was totally exposed. Along with all this went the warning of the wrath of God. People were reminded of the horrors of Doomsday and the tormenting punishment of Hell. They were also censured for their moral corruption, for their erroneous ways of life, for their clinging to the ways of ignorance, for their opposition to Truth and their persecution of the believers. Furthermore, these messages enunciated those fundamental principles of morality and collective life on which all sound and healthy civilisations enjoying God's approval had always rested.

This stage was unfolded in several phases. In each phase, the preaching of the message assumed ever-wider proportions, as the struggle for the cause of Islam and opposition to it became increasingly intense and severe, and as the believers encountered people of varying outlooks and beliefs.

All these factors had the effect of increasing the variety of the topics treated in the Messages revealed during this period.

BACKGROUND TO THE MADINAN REVELATIONS

For thirteen years the Islamic movement strove in Makkah. It then obtained, in Madinah, a haven of refuge in which to concentrate its followers and its strength. The Prophet's movement now entered its third stage. During this stage, circumstances changed drastically. The Muslim community succeeded in establishing a fully-fledged state; its creation was followed by prolonged armed conflict with the representatives of the ancient ignorance of Arabia. The community also encountered followers of the former Prophets, i.e. the Jews and Christians. An additional problem was that the hypocrites, themselves, even began to join the fold of the Muslim community; their machinations inevitably then needed to be resisted. After a severe struggle, lasting ten years, the Islamic movement reached a high point of achievement when the entire Arabian peninsula came under its sway and the door was open to worldwide preaching and reform. This stage, like the preceding one, passed through various phases each of which had its peculiar problems and demands.

It was in the context of these problems that God continued to reveal Messages to the Prophet. At times, these Messages were couched in the form of fiery speeches; at other times, they were characterised by the grandeur and stateliness of majestic proclamations and ordinances. At times, they had the air of instructions from a teacher; at others, the style of preaching of a reformer. These Messages explained how a healthy society, state and civilisation could be established and the principles on which the various aspects of human life should be based.

They also dealt with matters directly related to the specific problems facing the Muslims. For example, how should they deal with the hypocrites who were harming the Muslim community from within and with the non-Muslims who were living under the care of the Muslim society? How should they relate to the People of the Book? What treatment should be meted out to those with whom the Muslims were at war, and how should they deal with those with whom they were bound by treaties and agreements? How should the believers, as a community, prepare to discharge their obligations as vicegerents of the Lord of the Universe? Through the Qur'ān the Muslims were guided on questions like these, were instructed and trained, made aware of their weaknesses, urged to risk their lives and property for the cause of God, and taught the code of morality they should observe in all circumstances – in times of victory and defeat, ease and distress, prosperity and adversity, peace and security, peril and danger.

In short, they were being trained to serve as the successors of the mission of the Prophet, with the task of carrying on the message of Islam and bringing about reform in human life. The Qur'ān also addressed itself to those outside the fold of Islam, to the People of the Book, the hypocrites, the disbelievers, the polytheists. Each group was addressed according to its own particular circumstances and attitudes. Sometimes the Qur'ān invited them to the True Faith with tenderness and delicacy; on other occasions, it rebuked and severely admonished them. It also warned them against, and threatened them with, punishment from God. It attempted to make them take heed by drawing their attention to instructive historical events. In short, people were left with no valid reason for refusing the call of the Prophet.

Such, briefly, is the background to the Madinan *Sūrahs* of the Qur'ān.

THE QUR'ĀN: RESPONDING TO PEOPLE'S NEEDS

It is now clear to us that the revelation of the Qur'ān began and went hand in hand with the preaching of the message. This message passed through many stages and met with diverse situations from the very beginning and throughout a period of twenty-three years. The different parts of the Qur'ān were revealed step by step according to the multifarious, changing needs and requirements of the Islamic movement during these stages. It, therefore, could not possibly possess the kind of coherence and systematic sequence of a doctoral dissertation. Moreover, these various fragments that made up the Islamic movement were not published in the form of written treatises, but were rather spread orally. Their style, therefore, bore an oratorical flavour rather than the characteristics of literary composition.

Furthermore, these orations were delivered by one whose task meant he had to appeal simultaneously to the mind, to the heart and to the emotions, and to people of different mental levels and dispositions. He had to revolutionise people's thinking, to arouse in them a storm of noble emotions in support of his Cause, to persuade his Companions and inspire them with devotion and zeal, and with the desire to improve and reform their lives. He had to raise their morale and steel their determination, turn enemies into friends and opponents into admirers, disarm those out to oppose his message and show their position to be morally untenable. In short, he had to do everything necessary to carry his movement through to a successful conclusion. Orations revealed in conformity with the requirements of a message and movement will inevitably have a style different from that of a professorial lecture.

This explains the repetitions we encounter in the Qur'ān. The interests of a message and a movement demand that during a particular stage emphasis should be placed only on those subjects which are appropriate at that stage, to the exclusion of matters pertaining to later stages. As a result, certain subjects may require continual emphasis for months or even years. On the other hand, constant repetition in the same manner becomes exhausting. Whenever a subject is repeated, it should therefore be expressed in different phraseology, in new forms and with variations so stylistic as to ensure that the ideas and beliefs being put over find their way into peoples' hearts.

At the same time, it was essential that the fundamental beliefs and principles on which the movement was based should always be kept fresh in people's minds; a necessity which dictated that they should be repeated continually through all stages of the movement. For this reason, certain basic Islamic concepts about the Unity of God and His attributes, about the hereafter, about a person's accountability and about reward and punishment, about Prophethood and belief in the revealed Scriptures, about basic moral attributes such as piety, patience, trust in God and so on, recur throughout the Qur'ān. If these ideas had lost their hold on the hearts and minds of people, the Islamic movement could not have moved forward in its true spirit.

THE QUR'ĀN'S ARRANGEMENT

When we reflect on recurrent themes in the Qur'ān, it becomes evident why the Prophet did not arrange the Qur'ān in the sequence in which it was revealed. As we have noted, the context in which the Qur'ān was revealed over the course of twenty-three years was the mission and movement of the Prophet; the revelations correspond with the various stages of this mission and movement. Now, it is evident that when the Prophet's mission was completed, the chronological sequence of the various parts of the Qur'ān – revealed in accordance with the growth of the Prophet's mission – could in no way be suitable to the changed situation. What was now required was a different sequence in tune with the changed context resulting from the completion of the mission.

Initially, the Prophet's message was addressed to people totally ignorant of Islam. Their instruction had to start with the most elementary things. After the mission had been successfully completed, the Qur'ān acquired a compelling relevance for those who had decided to believe in the Prophet.

By virtue of that belief they had become a new religious community – the Muslim *Ummah*. Not only that, they had been made responsible for carrying on the Prophet's mission, which he had bequeathed to them, in a perfected form on both conceptual and practical levels. It was no longer necessary for the Qur'ānic verses to be arranged in chronological sequence. In the changed context, it had become necessary for the bearers of the mission of the Prophet to be informed of their duties and of the true principles and laws governing their lives. They also had to be warned against the deviation and corruption which had appeared among the followers of earlier Prophets. All this was necessary in order to equip the Muslims to go out and offer the Light of Divine guidance to a world steeped in darkness.

It would be foreign to the very nature of the Qur'ān to group together in one place all verses relating to a specific subject; the nature of the Qur'ān requires that the reader should find teachings revealed during the Madinan period interspersed with those of the Makkan period, and vice versa. It requires the juxtaposition of early discourses with instructions from the later period of the life of the Prophet. This blending of teachings from different periods helps to provide an overall view and an integrated perspective of Islam, and acts as a safeguard against lopsidedness. Furthermore, a chronological arrangement of the Qur'ān would have been meaningful to later generations only if it had been supplemented with explanatory notes and these would have had to be treated as inseparable appendices to the Qur'ān. This would have been quite contrary to God's purpose in revealing the Qur'ān; the main purpose of its revelation was that all people – children and young people, old men and women, town and country dwellers, laymen and scholars – should be able to refer to the Divine guidance available to them in composite form and providentially secured against adulteration. This was necessary to enable people of every level of intelligence and understanding to know what God required of them. This purpose would have been defeated had the reader been obliged solemnly to recite detailed historical notes and explanatory comments along with the Book of God.

Those who object to the present arrangement of the Qur'ān appear to be suffering from a misapprehension as to its true purpose. They sometimes almost seem under the illusion that it was revealed merely for the benefit of students of history and sociology!

HISTORICAL PRESERVATION OF THE QUR'ĀN

The present arrangement of the Qur'ān is not the work of later generations, but was made by the Prophet under God's Direction. Whenever a *Sūrah* was revealed, the Prophet summoned his scribes, to whom he carefully dictated its contents, and instructed them where to place it in relation to the other *Sūrahs.* The Prophet followed the same order of *Sūrahs* and verses when reciting during ritual Prayer as on other occasions, and his Companions followed the same practice in memorising the Qur'ān. It is, therefore, a historical fact that the collection of the Qur'ān came to an end on the very day that its revelation ceased. The One who was responsible for its revelation was also the One who fixed its arrangement. The one whose heart was the receptacle of the Qur'ān was also responsible for arranging its sequence. This was far too important and too delicate a matter for anyone else to dare to become involved in. Since Prayers were obligatory for the Muslims from the very outset of the Prophet's mission, and the recitation of the Qur'ān was an obligatory part of those Prayers, Muslims were committing the Qur'ān to memory while its revelation continued. Thus, as soon as a fragment of the Qur'ān was revealed, it was memorised by some of the Companions. Hence the preservation of the Qur'ān was not solely dependent on its verses being inscribed on palm leaves, pieces of bone, leather and scraps of parchment – the materials used by the Prophet's scribes for writing down Qur'ānic verses. Instead those verses came to be inscribed upon scores, then hundreds, then thousands, then hundreds of thousands of human hearts, soon after they had been revealed, so that no scope was left for any devil to alter so much as one word of them.

When, after the death of the Prophet, the storm of apostasy convulsed Arabia and the Companions had to plunge into battles to suppress it, many Companions who had memorised the Qur'ān suffered martyrdom. This led ʿUmar to plead that the Qur'ān ought to be preserved in writing, as well as orally. He therefore impressed the urgency of this upon Abū Bakr. After some slight hesitation, the latter agreed and entrusted that task to Zayd ibn Thābit, who had worked as one of the Prophet's scribes. The procedure decided upon was to try and collect all written pieces of the Qur'ān left behind by the Prophet, as well as those in the possession of his Companions. When all this had been done, assistance was sought from those who had memorised the Qur'ān. No verse was incorporated into the Qur'ānic codex unless all three sources were found to be in complete agreement and every criterion of verification had been satisfied. Thus, an authentic version of the Qur'ān was prepared. It was kept in the custody of Ḥafṣa, one of the Prophet's wives and people were permitted to make copies of it and also to use it as the standard of comparison when rectifying the mistakes they might have made in writing down the Qur'ān.

In different parts of Arabia and among its numerous tribes there existed a diversity of dialects. The Qur'ān was revealed in the language spoken by the Quraysh of Makkah. Nevertheless, in the beginning, people of other areas and other tribes were permitted to recite it according to their own dialects and idiom, since this facilitated its recitation without affecting its substantive meaning. In the course of time, in the wake of the conquest of a sizeable part of the world outside of the Arabian peninsula, a large number of non-Arabs entered the fold of Islam. These developments affected the Arabic idiom and it was feared that the continuing use of various dialects in the recitation of the Qur'ān might give rise to grave problems. It was possible, for instance, that someone hearing the Qur'ān recited in an unfamiliar dialect might pick a fight with the reciter, thinking that the latter was deliberately distorting the Word of God. It was also possible that such differences might gradually lead to tampering with the Qur'ān itself. It was also not inconceivable that the hybridisation of the Arabic language, due to the intermixture between Arabs and non-Arabs, might lead people to introduce modifications into the Qur'ānic text, thus impairing the Grace of the Speech of God. As a result of such considerations, and after consultation with the Prophet's Companions, ʿUthmān decided that copies of the standard edition of the Qur'ān, prepared earlier on the order of Abū Bakr, should be published, and that publication of the Qur'ānic text in any other dialect or idiom should be proscribed.

The Qur'ān that we possess today corresponds exactly to the edition which was prepared on the orders of Abū Bakr and copies of which were officially sent, on the orders of ʿUthmān, to various cities and provinces. Several copies of this original edition of the Qur'ān still exist today. Anyone who entertains any doubt as to the authenticity of the Qur'ān can satisfy himself by obtaining a copy of the Qur'ān from any bookseller, say in West Africa, and then have a *ḥāfiẓ* (memorizer of the Qur'ān) recite it from memory, compare the two, and then compare these with the copies of the Qur'ān published through the centuries since the time of ʿUthmān. If he detects any discrepancy, even in a single letter or syllable, he should inform the whole world of his great discovery!

Not even the most sceptical person has any reason to doubt that the Qur'ān as we know it today is identical with the Qur'ān which Muḥammad set before the world; this is an unquestionable, objective, historical fact, and there is nothing in human history on which the evidence is so overwhelmingly strong and conclusive. To doubt the authenticity of the Qur'ān is like doubting the existence of the Roman Empire, the Mughals of India, or Napoleon! To doubt historical facts like these is a sign of stark ignorance, not a mark of erudition and scholarship.

HOW TO BENEFIT FROM THE QUR'ĀN

Anyone who really wishes to understand the Qur'ān, irrespective of whether or not he believes in it, must divest his mind, as far as possible, of every preconceived notion, bias and prejudice, in order to embark upon his study with an open mind. Anyone who begins to study the Qur'ān with a set of preconceived ideas is likely to read those very ideas into the Book. No book can be profitably studied with this kind of attitude, let alone the Qur'ān which refuses to open its treasure house to such readers.

For those who want only a superficial acquaintance with the doctrines of the Qur'ān one reading is perhaps sufficient. For those who want to fathom its depths several readings are not even enough. These people need to study the Qur'ān over and over again, taking notes of everything that strikes them as significant. Those who are willing to study the Qur'ān in this manner should do so at least twice to begin with, so as to obtain a broad grasp of the system of beliefs and practical prescriptions that it offers. In this preliminary survey, they should try to gain an overall perspective of the Qur'ān and to grasp the basic ideas which it expounds, and the system of life that it seeks to build on the basis of those ideas. If, during the course of this study, anything agitates the mind of the reader, he should note down the point concerned and patiently persevere with his study. He is likely to find that, as he proceeds, the difficulties are resolved. (When a problem has been solved, it is advisable to note down the solution alongside the problem.) Experience suggests that any problems still unsolved after a first reading of the Qur'ān are likely to be resolved by a careful second reading.

Only after acquiring a total perspective of the Qur'ān should a more detailed study be attempted. Again the reader is well advised to keep noting down the various aspects of the Qur'ānic teachings. For instance, he should note the human model that the Qur'ān extols as praiseworthy, and the model it denounces. It might be helpful to make two columns, one headed 'praiseworthy qualities', the other headed 'blameworthy qualities', and then to enter into the respective columns all that is found relevant in the Qur'ān. To take another instance, the reader might proceed to investigate the Qur'ānic point of view on what is conducive to human success and felicity, as against what leads to a person's ultimate failure and perdition. An efficient way to carry out this investigation would be to note under separate headings, such as 'conducive to success' and 'conducive to failure', any relevant material encountered. In the same way, the reader should take down notes about Qur'ānic teachings on questions of belief and morals, a person's rights and obligations, family life and collective behaviour, economic and political life, law and social organisation, war and peace, and so on. Then he should use these various teachings to try to develop an image of the Qur'ānic teachings *vis-à-vis* each particular aspect of human life. This should be followed by an attempt at integrating these images so that he comes to grasp the total scheme of life envisaged by the Qur'ān.

Moreover, anyone wishing to study, in depth, the Qur'ānic viewpoint on any particular problem of life should, first of all, study all the significant strands of human thought concerning that problem. Ancient and modern works on the subject should be studied. Unresolved problems where human thinking seems to have got stuck should be noted. The Qur'ān should then be studied with these unresolved problems in mind, with a view to finding out what solutions the Qur'ān has to offer. Personal experience again suggests that anyone who studies the Qur'ān in this manner will find his problem solved with the help of verses which he may have read scores of times without it ever crossing his mind that they could have any relevance to the problems at hand.

It should be remembered, nevertheless, that full appreciation of the spirit of the Qur'ān demands practical involvement with the struggle to fulfil its mission. The Qur'ān is neither a book of abstract theories and cold doctrines which the reader can grasp while seated in a cosy armchair, nor is it merely a religious book like other religious books, the secrets of which can be grasped in seminaries and oratories. On the contrary, it is the Blueprint and Guidebook of a message, of a mission, of a movement. As soon as this Book was revealed, it drove a quiet, kind-hearted man from his isolation and seclusion, and placed him upon the battlefield of life to challenge a world that had gone astray. It inspired him to raise his voice against falsehood, and pitted him in a grim struggle against the standard-bearers of disbelief, of disobedience to God, of waywardness and error. One after the other, it sought out everyone who had a pure and noble soul, mustering them together under the standard of the Messenger. It also infuriated all those who by their nature were bent on mischief and drove them to wage war against the bearers of the Truth.

This is the Book which inspired and directed that great movement which began with the preaching of a message by an individual, and continued for no fewer than twenty-three years, until the Kingdom of God was truly established on earth. In this long and heart-rending struggle between truth and falsehood, this Book unfailingly guided its followers to the eradication of the latter and the consolidation and enthronement of the former. How then could one expect to get to the heart of the Qur'ānic Truths merely by reciting its verses, without so much as stepping upon the field of battle between faith and disbelief, between Islam and ignorance? To appreciate the Qur'ān fully one must take it up and launch into the task of calling people to God, making it one's guide at every stage.

Then, and only then, does one meet the various experiences encountered at the time of its revelation. One experiences the initial rejection of the message of Islam by the city of Makkah, the persistent hostility leading to the quest for a haven of refuge in Abyssinia, and the attempt to win a favourable response from Taif which led, instead, to cruel persecution of the bearer of the Qur'ānic message. One experiences also the campaigns of Badr, of Uḥud, of Ḥunayn and of Tabūk. One comes face to face with Abū Jahl and Abū Lahab, with hypocrites, with people of other faiths, with those who instantly responded to this call as well as those who, lacking clarity of perception and moral strength, were drawn into Islam only at a later stage.

This will be an experience different from any so-called 'mystic experience'. I designate it the 'Qur'ānic mystic experience'. One of the characteristics of this 'experience' is that at each stage one almost automatically finds certain Qur'ānic verses to guide one, since they were revealed at a similar stage and, therefore, contain the guidance appropriate to it. A person engaged in this struggle may not grasp all the linguistic and grammatical subtleties, he may also miss certain finer points in the rhetoric and semantics of the Qur'ān, yet it is impossible for the Qur'ān to fail to reveal its true spirit to him.

Again, in keeping with the same principle, a person can neither understand the laws, the moral teachings, and the economic and political principles which the Qur'ān embodies, nor appreciate the full import of the Qur'ānic laws and regulations, unless he tries to implement them in his own life. Hence the individual who fails to translate the Qur'ānic precepts into personal practice will fail to understand the Book. The same must be said of any nation that allows the institutions of its collective life to run contrary to the teachings of the Qur'ān.

10

Way to the Qur'ān

Khurram Murad

A MOMENTOUS JOURNEY

You are about to undertake a momentous journey – a journey that will take you through the endless joys and riches of the words that your Creator and Lord has sent to you and all mankind. As you come to the Qur'ān, you will come to a new world – a world of untold treasures of knowledge and wisdom to guide you on the pathways of life, of thought and action; of deep insights to capture your imagination; of radiant light to illumine the deeper reaches of your soul; of profound emotions and glowing warmth to melt your heart and bring tears running down your cheeks. It is the Qur'ān, and only the Qur'ān which can lead you on and on to success and glory in this world and the hereafter.

It is beyond the power of a human being to comprehend or even to describe the greatness and importance of what the Qur'ān holds for him. Yet you must have some idea of what it means to you, to inspire you, to immerse the whole of your self in the Qur'ān, in total commitment and complete dedication, as it demands. The Qur'ān is Allah's greatest blessing for you. It is the fulfilment of His promise to Adam and his descendants: *There shall come to you guidance from Me, and whosoever follows My guidance no fear shall be on them, neither shall they sorrow* (2: 38).

It is the only weapon to help your frail existence as you struggle against the forces of evil and temptation in this world. It is the only light, as you grope in the darkness, with which to find your way to success and salvation. It is your only sanctuary as you are tossed around in the stormy sea of life. It has been brought down by one who is powerful and trustworthy in the Heavens – the angel Gabriel. Its first abode was that pure and sublime heart, the like of which people had never seen – the heart of the Prophet Muḥammad. More than anything, it is the only 'way' to come nearer and closer to your Creator. It tells you of Him; of His attributes; of how He rules over the cosmos and history; of how He relates Himself to you and how you should relate to Him, to yourself, to others and to every other being.

What you read in the Qur'ān is the word of Allah, the Lord of the Worlds, which He has conveyed to you in a human language, only because of His infinite mercy, care and providence for you. This act of Divine mercy is enough to awe and overwhelm you and inspire you to ever-greater heights of gratitude, yearnings and endeavours to enter the world of the Qur'ān. The majesty of the Qur'ān is so overpowering that, *If We had sent down this Qur'ān upon a mountain, you would have seen it humbled, split asunder out of the fear of Allah* (59: 21). Indeed, no treasure is more valuable and precious for you than the Qur'ān, as Allah says of His generosity: *O People! There has come to you an exhortation from your Lord, a healing for what is in the hearts, and a guidance, and a mercy for believers. Say: In* [this] *Bounty of Allah, and in His mercy – in it let them rejoice. It is better than whatever they amass* (10: 57–58).

Rejoice as you must, in the mercy, blessing and generosity of Allah. But the Qur'ān opens its doors only to those who knock with a depth of yearning, sincerity of purpose and exclusiveness of attention that befits its importance and majesty. Only they are allowed to gather its treasures while they walk through it, who are prepared to abandon themselves completely to its guidance and do their utmost to absorb it. What a tragic misfortune it would be if you came to the Qur'ān and went away empty-handed – soul untouched, heart unmoved, life unchanged – 'they went out as they came in'. You may recite its words and turn its pages endlessly and laboriously, yet fail to make an encounter with it that enriches and transforms your whole person. The Qur'ān's blessings are limitless, but the measure of your fill depends entirely upon the capacity and the suitability of the receptacle you bring to it. Nine months spent in the womb of your mother have transformed a drop of water into 'you' – hearing, seeing and thinking. Can you imagine what a lifetime spent with the Qur'ān – seeking, hearing, seeing, thinking, striving – can do for you? It can make you into an entirely new 'being' – before whom even angels will feel proud to kneel. So, at the very outset, make yourself more deeply aware of what the Qur'ān means to you and what it demands of you; and make a solemn determination to recite the Qur'ān in an appropriate manner, so that you may be counted among *Those whom We have given the Book, they recite it as it ought to be recited;* [it is only] *they who believe in it* (2: 121).

Tilāwah or recitation is an act in which your whole person – soul, heart, mind, tongue and body – should participate. To recite the Qur'ān, thus, as it deserves to be recited, is not a light task; neither is it difficult nor impossible. Otherwise the Qur'ān could not have been meant for a layman; nor could it be the mercy and the guidance that it surely is. But it does entail many a travail of heart and mind, soul and intellect, spirit and body; and requires that certain conditions be observed and obligations be fulfilled – some inwardly, some outwardly. You should know them all before you enter the glorious world of the Qur'ān.

ATTITUDES OF HEART AND MIND

There are certain basic attitudes of heart and mind, integrated deeply in the conscious soul and in action, which constitute the necessary pre-requisites to any fruitful study of the Qur'ān.

1. Firm Faith and Conviction

Come to the Qur'ān with the deep, firm faith and conviction that it is the revealed word of Allah. Such is the charm of the Qur'ān that even if a person takes it up and starts reading it as he would an ordinary book, he will still benefit from it, provided he reads it with an open mind. But, this is the Book of Allah; and you should always remain conscious that each word you are reading has been sent to you by Allah. This constant awareness is vital in developing the right attitude and strong determination required to reach the heart of the Qur'ān and assimilate its message. Think of His majesty, glory and power, and you will feel the awe and devotion and a longing for His Words. That is why the Qur'ān reminds you of this important Truth at the beginning of most *Sūrahs* and frequently in between.

2. Purpose of Recitation

Recite the Qur'ān with no other purpose than to come nearer to your Lord and to seek His guidance and good pleasure. You should seek guidance from the Qur'ān, for your total life, and only from the Qur'ān. It is the Word of Allah; and it requires as much exclusiveness as He does. One who desires worldly ends from the Qur'ān may get them, but he shall surely lose a whole ocean that could have filled his cup. One who has the Qur'ān with him and yet goes to other sources for guidance, is surely running after mirages.

3. Accept Truth, Knowledge and Guidance

Accept, without the slightest doubt or scepticism, every piece of truth, knowledge and guidance that the Qur'ān conveys to you. You have every right to enquire, reflect and understand what it contains; but what you cannot fully comprehend is not necessarily unreasonable. You have a right to reject that it is the Word of Allah; but once you have accepted it as His, you have no basis whatsoever to doubt even a single word of it. There must be a total surrender to the Qur'ān. Your own opinions, beliefs, notions, whims and caprices should not be allowed to override any part of it.

4. Readiness to Change Attitudes and Behaviour

Have the determination and readiness to change and mould your attitude and behaviour – inwardly and outwardly – in accordance with the teachings you come across in the Qur'ān. Unless you are prepared and begin to act, mere intellectual exercises will never bring you anywhere near the real treasures of the Qur'ān.

5. Seek Refuge with Allah

Remain aware, as you embark upon reciting the Qur'ān, that the possibilities and the potentials of your advancement are so great that Satan will, on this occasion, make greater efforts to deprive you of the fruits of your labour. He may pollute your intention; make you unmindful of its meaning and message; create doubt in your mind; create barriers between your soul and the Words of Allah; or tempt you away from obeying the Qur'ān. It is with the full consciousness of these perils and dangers that your tongue should, in obedience to the Qur'ān – *When you recite the Qur'ān, seek refuge with Allah from Satan, the rejected* (16: 98) – say *A'ūdhubillāhi min al-Shaiṭān al-Rajīm.*

6. Allah's Infinite Mercy

Realise that, just as it has been Allah's infinite mercy that has brought His words to you in the Qur'ān, so it can only be His Mercy that can lead you to the full rewards of its reading. Your desire and effort are the necessary means; but His will and support are the only guarantees, so approach the Qur'ān with humility, with a sense of utter dependence upon Him, with trust in Him and with supplication and devotion to Him at every step.

7. Constant Praise and Gratitude

Make yourself pulsate constantly with intense praise and gratitude to your Lord for having blessed you with His greatest gift – the Qur'ān, and for having guided you to its reading and study. It is but natural for your heart to beat with joy and murmur: *Thankful praise be to Allah, who has guided us to this;* [otherwise] *never could we have found guidance, had Allah not guided us* (7: 43). The more you are grateful, the more Allah will give you from the riches of the Qur'ān.

In this spirit of dependence, trust, praise and gratitude, let your heart and tongue, in mutual harmony, begin the recitation: *In the name of Allah, Most Gracious, Most Merciful* – the verse which appears at the head of all but one of the 114 *Sūrahs* of the Qur'ān. And also pray: *'Our Lord! Let not our hearts swerve* [from the Truth] *after You have guided us; and bestow upon us Your grace, indeed You alone are the bestower'* (3: 8).

PRESENCE OF HEART

Before starting to recite the Qur'ān, you should ensure that so long as you are with the Qur'ān, your 'heart' remains with you; not merely a piece of flesh, but the centre of all your attention, remembrance, emotions, aspirations and activities; or, your whole inner 'person'. Only then will you have the capability to receive the great gifts of Allah and respond with humble devotion. The seven pre-requisites discussed earlier lay the foundations for the communion of the Qur'ān with your heart. In addition to these, the observance of a few more rules will greatly increase the intensity and quality of this presence of heart.

1. In the Presence of Allah

Always keep yourself alive to the reality that, while you are reciting the Qur'ān, you are in the very presence of Him who has sent these words to you. *He is with you wherever you are* (57: 4). *We are nearer to him than his jugular vein* (50: 16). *You recite not the Qur'ān . . . but We are witness to you when you are engaged in it* (10:61). *Remember Me and I will remember you* (2: 152). You may not see Him, but He certainly sees you.

2. Listening to the Qur'ān from Allah Himself

Feel, as a part of your effort to 'remain' in the presence of Allah, as if you are listening to the Qur'ān from Allah Himself. Al-Ghazālī tells, in *Iḥyā' 'Ulūmuddīn* (Revival of the Sciences of Religion), of a person who could move nearer to the Qur'ān and could taste more of its sweetness by feeling; first, as if he was listening to it from the Prophet, then, as if from the Angel Gabriel; and lastly, as if from Allah Himself.

3. Direct Addressee of the Qur'ān

Consider that you, individually and personally, are the direct addressee of the Qur'ān. Though the Qur'ān has been received by you indirectly through persons, time and space, let all these intermediaries recede and disappear for some moments and allow yourself to receive the Qur'ān as if it is talking directly to you, penetrating your heart and intellect. The very thought of such direct reception will keep your heart seized by what you are reading.

4. Let your Posture Reflect your Inner Submission

Make your outward posture reflect your inner awe, respect, devotion and submission for the words of your Lord. There is a deep connection between the outward and the inward manifestations of a person. The 'presence' of the body will keep the 'heart' present. There should be a difference in your posture while reading the Qur'ān in comparison to an ordinary book.

5. Purify Yourself

Purify yourself as much as you can. You know that only the 'pure' are entitled even to touch the Qur'ān. You know that your body, dress and place should be clean. You also know about the purity of intention. But you should also realise that the purity of 'heart' and body from sins is equally important. No one can be completely free from sins; but try to avoid as much as you can. And if you happen to commit some, try to turn to Allah in repentance and ask for His forgiveness, as soon as you can. Also take care that, while reading the Qur'ān, you are not eating that which is *ḥarām*, wearing that which is *ḥarām* or living in a *ḥarām* situation, in other words through means not permitted by Allah. The purer you are, the more your heart will remain with you, and the more it will open itself to the Qur'ān.

UNDERSTANDING AND REFLECTING

It is vital that you should understand what Allah is saying to you and reflect over it as much as you can. If you read the Qur'ān without understanding, you may derive some reward because of your sense of devotion and your desire to read this Book. But this would not, in the least, fulfil the purpose for which it has been revealed. It has come to vitalise you, mould you and lead you to a new life and existence. It is not merely a source of blessing, a sacred ritual, a revered relic or a piece of holy magic. The Qur'ān is full of exhortations asking you as to why you 'hear not', 'see not', 'think not', 'reason not' and 'ponder not'. It says that, *When they are reminded of the verses of their Lord, they fall not deaf and blind thereat* (25: 73); and that, *Do they not ponder over the Qur'ān, or are there locks on the hearts?* (47: 24).

You will find elsewhere better guidance on how to understand and ponder over the Qur'ān, but there are some important principles you should keep in mind.

1. Understand and reflect over the Qur'ān as if it was being revealed today, as each word of it is as living and relevant today as it was when it was first revealed. In this light, you should try to relate and apply it to your own life, concerns, experiences and levels of knowledge and technology. Do not consider any verse of the Qur'ān as merely a thing of the past.

2. Read the whole of the Qur'ān, from beginning to end, with the help of a translation. This will give you an overall idea of the Book, its style and message.

3. Initially, read only short but good commentaries and do not delve into long and detailed *tafsīrs*.

4. Try to learn at least as much Arabic as will enable you to understand the meaning of the Qur'ān without the help of a translation. It may seem an arduous task, but I have known semi-illiterate people accomplish this within a few months, once they took it seriously and devotedly.

5. Ponder and think deeply over the various parts of what you read. This requires reciting a particular verse or portion thereof slowly (with *tartīl*) or even repeatedly. The more you think and reflect, you will have a greater share of its rich and unlimited meanings. It is in this sense that Ibn ʿUmar spent eight years on *Sūrah al-Baqarah* (Chapter 2) alone. The Prophet and many others used to spend whole nights repeating just one verse.

INNER PARTICIPATION

The Qur'ān was first sent down to the 'heart' or the inner person of the Prophet. You will, therefore, reap its full joys only when you are able to involve your inner self in your recitation. This will not prove difficult if you are mindful that you are reading the words of Allah, in His presence, and if you understand and reflect over what you read. Such a state of involvement may be achieved and intensified in certain other ways too.

1. Receiving the Qur'ān with Your Heart

Always keep reminding yourself of what the Qur'ān itself tells of those who receive it with their hearts, and of how the Prophet, his Companions and others used to involve themselves in it. *When Allah is mentioned, their hearts quake; and when His verses are recited to them, it increases them in faith* (8: 2). *Whereat shiver the skins of those who fear their Lord; then their skins and hearts soften to the remembrance of Allah* (39: 23). *When it is recited to them, they fall down upon their faces, prostrating, and say: 'Glory be to our Lord! Our Lord's Promise is fulfilled.' And they fall down upon their faces, weeping; and it increases them in humility* (17: 107–109). *And when they hear what has been sent down to the Messenger, you see their eyes overflow with tears because of what they recognise of Truth. They cry, 'Our Lord! We believe; so do write us down among the witnesses* [to the Truth]' (5: 86).

2. Consider it Personally

You have already prepared yourself to receive the Qur'ān as being addressed to you from Allah, and as being fully relevant to your own times. Now consider that the message in each verse is meant for you personally, whether it be a norm or value, a statement or piece of knowledge, a promise or a warning, a command or a prohibition.

3. Sincere Response

Your heart should then come alive and respond to the various notes and themes that are struck in it by different verses. Make it pass through the various states of adoration and praise, awe and wonder, hope and despair, assurance and anxiety, love and fear, happiness and sorrow, devotion and submission.

4. Sincere Expression

These states of heart should find expression through your tongue. That is how the Prophet used to recite the Qur'ān in his night prayers. He used to say *Subḥānallāh* after verses telling of the majesty and glory of Allah, and *Alḥamdulillāh* after verses describing His bounties and graces. He sought forgiveness and refuge with Allah and asked for His favours and bounties after verses containing corresponding themes.

5. Sincere Involvement

The heart should also overflow through the eyes to express its involvement. Often the Prophet, his Companions and others, 'who had a real encounter with the Qur'ān', would weep when they recited it. You may even make yourself cry, if you think of the heavy responsibilities, the warnings and the joys that the Qur'ān brings to you.

LIVING BY THE QUR'ĀN

The whole purpose of the Qur'ān is to guide you and to change you by bringing you into submission to Allah. As you read it, also try to live by what it invites you to. If it does not have any impact upon your actions and if you do not observe what it enjoins and avoid what it prohibits, then you are not getting anywhere nearer the Qur'ān. In fact, one who reads the Qur'ān and does not try to act upon it may be more likely to be cursed and punished by Allah. The Prophet said: 'Many of the hypocrites in my *Ummah* will be from among the reciters' (*Aḥmad*); and 'He is not a believer in the Qur'ān who makes *ḥalāl* (permissible) what it has made *ḥarām* (prohibited)' (*Tirmidhī*). It is narrated that, Companions like ʿUthmān and ʿAbdullāh ibn Masʿūd, once they learnt ten verses from the Prophet, did not move further unless they had 'learnt' it fully – both in understanding and in action; that is how they sometimes spent years in learning only one *Sūrah* of the Qur'ān.

If you sincerely start changing your life according to the Qur'ān, Allah will certainly help you and make the path easy for you.

RULES OF RECITATION

There are a few additional obligations regarding the recitation of the Qur'ān which you should keep in mind.

1. Daily Reading

Read the Qur'ān every day; in fact do not consider a day complete without it. It is better to read regularly, even if it be a small portion, than to read large sections, but only occasionally.

2. Memorise

Memorise as much of the Qur'ān as you can. You can start with small *sūrahs* and short passages, and then move on to longer portions.

3. Recite the Qur'ān in Prayer

Read as much of the Qur'ān in prayer as you can, especially during the night, after the *ʿIshā'*, before the *Fajr* and during the *Fajr* prayers, as nothing is more effective in making you attuned to the Qur'ān and ensuring you absorb it than reading it in the night or in the morning.

4. Melodious Voice

Read the Qur'ān in a good voice, as we have been told: 'Beautify the Qur'ān with your voices'; but also remember that 'the one whose voice reflects the fear of Allah is the one who reads the Qur'ān well.'

5. Read with Concentration and Understanding

Do not read hastily without proper concentration and understanding. The Prophet told Ibn ʿUmar not to finish reading the Qur'ān in less than a week, and also said that one who finished it in less than three days did not understand any of it. One Companion said that he preferred to read a short *sūrah* like *al-Qāriʿah* with proper understanding than to hastily finish long ones like *al-Baqarah* and *Āl-ʿImrān*.

THE LIFE OF THE PROPHET

To absorb the Qur'ān, you must move as close as you can to the Prophet who received it first from Allah. His whole life is a 'living Qur'ān'. If you want to 'read' the Qur'ān in action, observe the Prophet in his deeds, as ʿĀ'ishah said: 'His conduct was nothing but the Qur'ān' (*Muslim*). To move closer to the Prophet, you should read his sayings (*aḥādīth*) and His life (*sīrah*) as much as you can.

Let us, in conclusion, pray to Allah to enable us to recite the Qur'ān as it ought to be recited and not to make us like those, *to whom the Book was given before, but with the lapse of time, their hearts became hard* (57: 16); or *who were given the burden of the Torah, then they did not carry it, they are like a donkey carrying books* (62: 5); or about whom the Prophet will, on the Day of Judgement, complain *'O my Lord! These my people have abandoned the Qur'ān'* (25: 30).

Our Lord! Enable us to imbibe the meaning of the Qur'ān and guide us to and lead us along the Straight Path.

FAVOURITE RECITATIONS OF THE PROPHET

There are certain *sūrahs* which the Prophet, peace be upon him, used to recite more often in prayers or at other particular times, or about which he said something special. You should know them also. In *Fajr*, he used to recite *Qāf* and other similar *sūrahs* (*Muslim*); he also recited *al-Takwīr* (*Muslim*); on a Friday morning he preferred to recite *al-Sajdah* and *al-Dahr*; sometimes he even recited shorter *sūrahs* like *al-Falaq* and *al-Nās* (*Bukhārī* and *Muslim*), or *al-Kāfirūn* and *al-Ikhlāṣ* (*Muslim*), or verses 136 and 64 from *al-Baqarah* and *Āl-Imrān* respectively (*Muslim*). The last two he recited in *Fajr Sunnah* also (*Nawawī*). In *'Ishā'* he recited *al-Tīn*, and once asked Mu'ādh to recite *sūrahs* like *al-A'lā*, *al-Layl* and *al-Ḍuḥā* (*Bukhārī* and *Muslim*). In Friday and *'Īd* Prayers he recited *al-A'lā* and *al-Ghāshiyah*, or *al-Jumu'ah* and *al-Munāfiqūn*, or *Qāf* and *al-Qamar* (*Muslim*).

Before going to sleep, regularly or at one time or other, according to various *aḥādīth*, he recited verses 285–286 and 255 from *al-Baqarah* (*Bukhārī* and *Muslim*); *al-Ikhlāṣ*, *al-Falaq* and *al-Nās* (*Bukhārī* and *Muslim*); *al-Kāfirūn* (*Abū Dāwūd*); *al-Sajdah* (*Muslim*); *al-Mulk* (*Tirmidhī*); *sūrahs* starting with *tasbiḥ* (*Nasā'ī*); or *sūrahs* starting with *Ḥā-Mīm*, *al-Isrā'* and *al-Zumar* (*Tirmidhī*). After rising for *Tahajjud*, he very often recited the last eleven verses of *Āl-'Imrān*.

There are other *aḥādīth* regarding the excellent qualities of certain *sūrahs* and verses of the Qur'ān. *Sūrah al-Fātiḥah* is the greatest in the Qur'ān (*Bukhārī*). *Al-Baqarah* and *Āl-'Imrān* will plead for those who recite them (*Muslim*). Satan flees away from the house in which *al-Baqarah* is recited (*Muslim*). *Āyatul Kursī* is the greatest verse of the Qur'ān (*Muslim*). *Al-Fātiḥah* and the last verses of *al-Baqarah* are two lights, the like of which has not been brought to any Prophet (*Muslim*). One who recites the last two verses of *al-Baqarah* at night will avert harm from him (*Bukhārī* and *Muslim*). One who holds onto ten verses of *al-Kahf* will protect himself from Dajjāl. *Al-Zilzāl* equals half of the Qur'ān; *al-Ikhlāṣ* equals one-third, and *al-Kāfirūn* equals one-fourth (*Bukhārī*, *Muslim* and *Tirmidhī*). *Al-Mulk* will continue to intercede on behalf of the one who recites it, unless his sins are forgiven (*Abū Dāwūd*). *Yā-Sīn* is the heart of the Qur'ān (*Tirmidhī*). No *sūrahs* like *al-Falaq* and *al-Nās* have ever been revealed (*Muslim*).

These *aḥādīth* are not meant to prove the superiority of one part of the Qur'ān over another. But they give us an added incentive to memorise and recite certain parts of the Qur'ān. The Prophet himself used to recite the whole of the Qur'ān at least once during the month of Ramaḍān. He also recited long portions in the *Tahajjud* prayers.

II

Living in the Shade of the Qur'ān

Sayyid Qutb

To live 'in the shade of the Qur'ān' is a great blessing which can only be fully appreciated by those who experience it. It is a rich experience that gives meaning to life and makes it worth living. I am deeply thankful to God Almighty for blessing me with this uplifting experience for a considerable time, which was the happiest and most fruitful period of my life – a privilege for which I am eternally grateful.

COMMUNICATING WITH GOD

It is a great honour to feel that God Almighty should be addressing me, a humble and insignificant human being, with the blessed and inspiring words of the Qur'ān. They lifted my spirits, and I was raised to a unique vantage point from where I could observe the tumult of human life. I was able to gain a new perspective into man's endless quest for the trivial and the mundane, and the clamour for ephemeral and childish pursuits. I was astounded by the extent of our ignorance and our neglect of the Qur'ān's sublime and Divine message which has the power to uplift and entirely transform human perception, experience and history on this earth.

I had the opportunity to study the Qur'ān at length and ponder over its clear and full conception of creation and existence, and their purpose. I could compare the impact of those ideas with that of others put forward by people throughout history. And I wondered: how has life been allowed to degenerate into such darkness and despair, while this rich treasure of guidance and enlightenment is readily available?

I lived in the shade of the Qur'ān, filled with appreciation of that perfect harmony and balance inherent in God's creation, between a human being's actions and the movement of the universe around him. I was able to see clearly, the dire consequences of the conflict between the two. I could see the folly, indeed the catastrophe, to which humanity is being driven by wicked and ungodly miscreants. Pity the human race, indeed!

In the shade of the Qur'ān, I saw this world of ours expanding far outside what we can see or define. Beyond the visible world lies an unseen dimension which encompasses this life and the life hereafter. A human being's origins extend back into the dim and distant past, and death is not the end of our perennial journey but a passing phase of a long journey that stretches to infinity. What we earn in the temporal world is but a small portion of what is our due; the rewards or punishments we miss or escape here we shall duly meet in the life to come, and justice shall be done.

Nevertheless, our brief life on this earth is real. The world we live in is essentially friendly and hospitable, and its spirit interacts fully with ours. It, like us, turns to the One Creator in total submission and reverence. *All that is in the heavens and the earth, and their own shadows, prostrate themselves before God, willingly and unwillingly morning and evening* (13: 15). *The seven heavens, the earth, and all that is in them, glorify Him; there is nothing but celebrates His praises* (17: 44). Such a powerful, outward-looking, all-embracing and optimistic vision inspires utter confidence within the human heart and fills the soul with total inner peace and security.

I lived in the shade of the Qur'ān to see the human being given the respect and reverence never accorded him by any other philosophy or ideology before or since. The human being's *raison d'être* emanates from the Divine spirit God breathed into him. The Qur'ān tells us that during the creation of the human being, God said to the angels, *When I have fashioned him* [a human being] *and breathed into him of My Spirit, prostrate yourselves before him* (15: 29; 58: 72).

By virtue of this Divine breath, the human being was destined and commissioned to be God's representative on earth, where he was given access to, and authority and control over, everything. As a consequence of the high esteem in which the human being is held, God has ordained that ties of belief and faith are the only worthy and legitimate ties that can bring people together. They override all other incidental ties of nationality, race or ancestry.

The Qur'ān has also taught me that the believer of the One God is the descendant of a long and noble line of faithful ancestors that include great figures such as Noah, Abraham, Ishmael, Isaac, Jacob, Joseph, Moses, Jesus and Muḥammad, may peace and God's blessings be upon them all. The Qur'ān tells God's messengers, *This community of yours is one single community and I am your Lord; therefore fear Me alone* (23: 52; see also 21: 92).

The Qur'ān makes it clear that in this long procession which began at the very moment people appeared on the earth, all believers have had to face similar challenges and ordeals: oppression, persecution and threats of annihilation and dispersion. Nevertheless, the procession continues along its well-defined path with a steady step and a calm heart, ever confident that God's will shall prevail and His promise be fulfilled. *The unbelievers said to their messengers, 'Return to our religion, or we will banish you from our land.' But their Lord revealed His will to them* [the messengers], *saying, 'We shall destroy the transgressors and let you settle in the land after they had gone. This is for those who stand in awe of My presence and dread My warning'* (14: 14).

Throughout human history believers have upheld similar convictions and ideals, faced similar enemies and threats, undergone similar experiences and enjoyed similar triumphs and rewards.

ORDER IN ALLAH'S CREATION

In the shade of the Qur'ān, I learned that in this existence there is no room for blind coincidence or haphazard events: *We have created everything according to a measure* (54: 49). *He has created all things and assigned everything its appropriate measure* (25: 2). Everything is there for a purpose, but the true and deep wisdom underlying our existence may not always be apparent to the limited human mind. The Qur'ān says: *It may well be that you hate something in which God may yet make a source of abundant good* (4: 19). *It may well be that you hate something although it is good for you, or love something although it is bad for you. God knows, whereas you do not* (2: 216).

Causes, as known to a human being, may or may not lead to their usual 'logical' effects. Assumptions perceived as essentially inevitable may or may not lead to their conventionally expected consequences. This is so because causes and assumptions do not, in or by themselves, determine actions and events, since cause and effect are both determined by God's absolute will. The Qur'ān says: *You never know; it may be that God will after that bring something new to pass* (65: 1). *Yet you cannot will except by the will of God* (76: 30).

In performing any deed, the believer must prepare and carry out his actions, and leave God to determine the results and consequences of those actions. To trust in God's mercy, justice, wisdom and knowledge is the only safeguard against uncertainty and fear of the future. The Qur'ān says: *Satan promises you poverty and bids you to commit indecency whereas God Promises you His Forgiveness and Bounty. God is Munificent, all-Knowing* (2: 268).

In the shade of the Qur'ān I have, therefore, felt totally contented and reassured. I could see God's hand in every event and everything. I lived in God's care and custody and His attributes, as given in the Qur'ān, came alive before my eyes.

Who else would answer the constrained when he cries out to Him and alleviates affliction? (27: 62).

He is Omnipotent over His servants. He Alone is Wise and all-Knowing (6: 18).

God prevails in His purpose, though most people do not know (12: 21).

Know well that God stands between a person and his heart and that unto Him you shall all be gathered (8: 24).

[God] *is the doer of what He wills* (85: 16).

Whoever fears God, He will find a way out for him, and He will provide for him in a way he had never reckoned on. He who puts his trust in God, God will suffice for him. God is sure to bring about whatever He decrees (65: 2).

There is no living creature which He does not hold by its forelock (11: 56).

Is God not enough for His servant [Muḥammad]? Yet they [the unbelievers] would frighten you with those [they worship] instead of Him! (39: 36).

He who God wishes to disgrace will have none else to honour him (22: 18).

Whoever God lets go astray shall have none else to guide him (13: 33).

The destiny of the universe is not left to the mercy of some blind laws. Behind the physical laws there is an active will, the absolute power of God that creates and decides.

I also learned that God's hand acts in all things in a manner that is unique to Him. We humans have no power to either force God, rush His Actions or anticipate His will.

The Divine scheme, as outlined in the Qur'ān, is designed to operate equally well under all circumstances and at all stages of human development, on the macrocosmic as well as the microcosmic scale. It makes full allowance for a human being's own abilities and potential for improvement and gives careful consideration to his strengths and weaknesses. It neither devalues a person's role on earth nor denigrates his status as an individual or as a member of society.

In its view of the human being, God's scheme is neither idealistic, raising the human being far above his deserved position, nor does it describe a human being as worthless or dispensable.

A human being is a unique creature who can, through his natural talents and innate abilities, adapt himself to the Divine order of life and so rise to the highest levels of progress and achievement. The Divine order is a universal plan for the long term. It is neither oppressive nor arbitrary. Its perspectives and prospects are broad and not restricted to the life or interests of one individual: it looks far into the future. Human ideologies, on the other hand, are usually limited to the lifespan of their proponents, who are bent on achieving all their ambitions and settling all their scores within a single generation. This inevitably comes into conflict with human nature, resulting in oppression, conflict, bloodshed, and the destruction of human values and civilisation.

Islam adopts a very gentle approach towards human nature, encouraging, prodding, pampering, cajoling, reprimanding and, where necessary, disciplining and restraining. It prefers the patient, caring attitude, confident of the eventual outcome. It is a continuous process of growth and development that can only get better as time goes on. Islam, like the oak tree, starts slowly and grows gradually, steadily overcoming all difficulties, vicissitudes and adversities. There is no need for compromises, half-hearted solutions, or arbitrary or foolish measures. In God's scheme, things must be allowed to take their natural course. *No change will you ever find in God's way* (35: 43).

Another feature of the universal Divine order is that it is inherently built on a universal Truth (*al-Ḥaqq*). This, again, has not come about by pure chance or as a result of coincidence. God Himself is *al-Ḥaqq*, and from Him, as the Qur'ān affirms, emanates all existence: *It is because God is the Truth and all that they* [the unbelievers] *evoke beside Him is false. He is most High, Supreme* (22: 62).

The Universe was created in Truth: *God has not created all this* [the world] *save with the Truth* (10: 5). Believers confirm this, saying: *'Our Lord, You have not created all this in vain. Glory be to You'* (3: 191).

Truth is the mainstay of all existence and should the world deviate from the Truth, it would decay and fall apart: *Had God* [*al-Ḥaqq*] *followed their* [the unbelievers] *caprice, the heavens, the earth, and all that lives in them would have surely been corrupted* (23: 71).

Hence, regardless of how things may seem, Truth will eventually become manifest. The Qur'ān asserts: *We hurl the Truth against falsehood and it crushes it, and falsehood withers away* (21: 18).

Likewise, goodness and righteousness are inherent and permanent in the cosmic superstructure. The Qur'ān alludes to this fact in saying:

> *He sends down water from the sky and riverbeds flow, each according to its measure, and the torrent bears a swelling foam. Likewise from what people melt in the fire to make ornaments and utensils rise similar foam. Thus does God illustrate Truth and falsehood. The scum is cast away while that which is of benefit to mankind remains behind on earth. Thus God does set forth His parables* (13:17).

It also says:

> *Do you not see how God compares a good word to a good tree? Its roots are firm and its branches reach to the sky; it yields its fruit at all times by its Lord's leave. Thus does God set parables for people so that they may reflect. And an evil word is like a bad tree, up rooted from the face of the earth. It cannot have a stable position. God will strengthen the believers through the true unshakeable word in both this life and the hereafter. God lets the wrongdoers go astray. God does whatever He wills* (14: 24–7).

This clear and forceful belief brings infinite reassurance and fills the human heart and soul with peace and tranquillity. It reinforces a human being's trust in truth, goodness and righteousness, and gives the human conscience the dignity and the confidence to transcend the limits of its environment.

My study of the Qur'ān has led me to the firm conviction that humanity will see no tranquillity or accord, no peace, progress or material and spiritual advances without total recourse to God. This, from the Qur'ānic point of view, can mean only one thing: the organisation of all aspects of human life in accordance with the precepts and directions of the Divine order as outlined in the Qur'ān. The alternative would be corruption, regression and misery. The Qur'ān puts it thus: *If they do not respond to you* [Muḥammad], *know that they only follow their vain desires. And who is in greater error than he who follows his own vain desires and has no guidance from God? God does not guide the transgressors* (28: 50).

Adopting the Divine order is an inevitable obligation on a human being, without which he would have no faith. The Qur'ān says: *It is not for any believer male or female, to have any choice in a matter once God and His Messenger pass judgement on it* (33: 36). *Now We have set you* [Muḥammad] *on a Path which you should follow and do not yield to the desires of the ignorant ones. They can avail you nothing against God. Transgressors are patrons one to another while the believers have God for a patron* (45: 18–19).

It is, then, an extremely serious matter that concerns the very foundations of faith in God and the happiness and well-being of mankind.

The secret of a human being's talent and potential can only be unlocked by God, his Creator, and He alone can prescribe the cure for a human being's ills. The key to a person's happiness is in God's Hands. God says: *And We reveal of the Qur'ān that which is a panacea and a mercy for the believers* (17: 82). *This Qur'ān leads to what is most upright* (17: 9).

However, a human being tends not to follow the logical and sensible course of action, which is to refer matters concerning his guidance and direction to God, who knows the secrets and the limitations of a person's being.

This fundamental error of judgement on a human being's part is the cause of all the misery and confusion humanity has seen. The isolation of Islam from the active leadership of mankind has been a watershed in human history, and by far the worst setback humanity has suffered.

Islam assumed the leadership of humanity at a time of grave decline, when corruption and decadence were rife and injustice rampant. The revelation of the Qur'ān and the advent of Islam, which was based on it, marked a rebirth of a human being far more significant than even his first one.

Islam gained that leadership by virtue of the original concepts and laws outlined in the Qur'ān, which introduced a fresh understanding of life and its values, and of the whole world order. These concepts brought about new and exciting realities hitherto unknown in human society, characterised by purity and beauty, and a healthy and positive attitude towards life and the world.

Then came the tragedy that removed Islam from its position of leadership, which then fell into the hands of various man-made ideologies, dominated in the main by materialism.

There have always been cynics who claim that humanity has to choose between the adoption of either a God-given system which negates all the material achievements of a human being, or a system based entirely on a human being's own intellectual abilities and accomplishments which has no room for Divine intervention whatsoever.

This is a most vile and cynical view. The choice is never as stark or as cruel as that. The Divine order (*minhāj* or *Sharīʿah*) is not antagonistic to human innovation and achievement. It is, in fact, the progenitor and patron of the very spirit of that creativity which is the driving force behind a human being's fulfilment of his role as God's representative on earth. God has endowed a human being with all the necessary faculties, talents and skills to carry out that most noble role, and He has harnessed for his benefit all the natural laws and forces that can help him in fulfilling that task. God has ensured a certain harmony and co-ordination between a human being and his environment that can enhance a man's performance and creativity and raise the quality of his life. A person's own achievement, material or otherwise, thus becomes itself an expression of gratitude to God, and a spur to further constructive activity.

The argument that a God-given way of life and a human being's ability to advance and improve are mutually exclusive, stems from evil motives and bad faith. It can only add to a person's confusion, bewilderment and misery.

However, the argument is sometimes advanced in response to people's fascination with the astonishing achievements made by human beings, especially in the fields of science and material progress, rather than as a consequence of ignorance or bad faith. Being so much in awe of human achievement, some are easily tempted to separate natural forces and religious values, claiming that they are mutually exclusive and operate in totally separate spheres. This basically flawed argument leads to the distorted concept that material progress can be achieved without the need for religious values, and that the consequences of the interaction of natural laws are inevitable regardless of whether people believe in God or not, and whether they have adopted the imperatives of a God-given system or a man-made one.

This is what we may call the 'Grand Illusion'. Religious values and natural laws are, in fact, inseparable. They interact all the time and coalesce at several points, and they are both ultimately controlled by the Power of God. There is, therefore, no justification for separating these two sets of forces in a person's consciousness. This is the rational and intelligent understanding that the Qur'ān tries to instil in a person's mind when it says:

> *Had the people of the Book believed and been God-fearing, We would have pardoned them and admitted them to gardens of bliss. Had they truly observed the Torah and the Injīl and what was revealed to them from their Lord, they would have enjoyed abundance from above and from beneath them* (5: 66). *I* [Noah] *said, 'Seek forgiveness of your Lord; He is ever ready to forgive. He will send abundant water from the sky for you and bestow upon you wealth and offspring. He will provide you with gardens and flowing rivers'* (71: 10–12). *God does not change a people's lot unless they change what is in their hearts* (13: 11).

To believe in God, and to worship Him with full sincerity, and to implement His prescribed order in society, are all manifestations of submission to God's universal order. The laws governing this order have a positive effect on human life and relate back to the same origin of all the natural, human and physical laws that we observe and experience every day.

It is true that at times we are confused by certain paradoxes we observe in nature as well as in society. Sometimes it seems that discarding religious values and relying solely on materialistic laws leads to success. But this is a very shortsighted view, because the outcome in the long term is quite the opposite. This is true even in the case of the Muslim civilisation. It grew and prospered when religious values and materialistic principles were brought together, while its decline began exactly at the moment when they began to diverge. Muslim civilisation has yet to recover from that catastrophic reversal in its history.

In contrast, we have today's materialistic civilisation which is like an albatross flying with only one wing. The huge advances it registers on the material scale are undermined by its reverses on the humanitarian, psychological and spiritual one.

God's *Sharīʿah* forms only part of His overall universal order, and the implementation of the Divine law in society acts as a catalyst in bringing harmony and balance into a person's relationship with the world around. But the *Sharīʿah* must be built on faith in God. It is designed for application within an Islamic society; to whose building and progress it in turn contributes.

Islamic law is complementary to Islam's overall view of the human being, nature and the world. This view is based on a comprehensive and integrated concept that unites such elements as fear of God, conscientiousness, purity of feeling, broadness of concern, high moral standards and upright behaviour. Within such a view, compatibility is easily achieved between the so-called 'natural laws' and 'human values', which are perceived as different aspects of a single universal structure.

A human being is seen as an active force in this structure. His will and his actions, his faith and his well-being, his submission to God and his contribution are all forces that exercise a positive influence on life and the world. They also are influenced and controlled by the principles and precepts of God's universal scheme. These forces produce results and multiply when they act in harmony, but they can result in suffering, corruption and strife when they do not: *God will not withdraw a grace He has bestowed on people unless they change what is in their hearts* (8: 53).

The link between a human being's actions and his feelings on the one hand, and God's universal order on the other, is real and constant. No one would wish for this relationship to be broken or undermined, unless they wish ill for a person and his future.

These are but a few general observations that living 'in the shade of the Qur'ān' has inspired within me. I humbly pray to God that they may be of benefit to you.

12

The Unique Qur'ānic Generation

Sayyid Qutb

The callers to Islam in every country and in every period should give thought to one particular aspect of the history of Islam, and they should ponder over it deeply. This is related to the method of inviting people to Islam and its ways of training.

At one time this message created a generation without any parallel in the history of Islam, even in the entire history of humankind, the generation of the Companions of the Prophet (may Allah bless them). After this, no other generation of this calibre was ever again to be found. It is true that we do find some individuals of this calibre here and there in history, but never again did a great number of such people exist in one region, as was the case during the first period of Islam.

This is an obvious truth and a fact of history, and we ought to ponder over it deeply to fathom its innermost secrets.

The Qur'ān which enshrines this Message is still in our hands, and the *aḥādīth* of the Messenger of Allah, peace be on him, his guidance in practical affairs, and the history of his sacred life are also intact, as they were in the hands of the first Muslim community whose likes history could never again produce. The only difference is the absence of the Messenger of Allah, peace be on him; but is this the secret? Had the person of the Prophet, peace be on him, been absolutely essential for the establishment and fruition of this Message, Allah would not have made Islam a universal Message, ordained it as the Religion for the whole of humankind, given it the status of the last Divine Message for humanity, and made it to be the guide for all inhabitants of this planet, in all their affairs until the end of time.

Allah has taken the responsibility for preserving the Noble Qur'ān on Himself because he knows that Islam can be established and can benefit humankind even after the time of the Prophet. Hence he called his Prophet back to His Mercy after twenty-three years of messengership and declared this Religion to be valid until the end of time. The absence of the Messenger of Allah is not the real cause or explanation of this phenomenon.

We must look therefore for some other reason to explain the uniqueness of this first generation, and for this purpose we must look at that clear spring from which the first generation of the Muslims quenched their thirst. Perhaps something has been mixed with that clear spring. We should look at the manner in which they received their training. Perhaps some changes have found their way into it.

PURE TEACHINGS OF THE QUR'ĀN

The spring from which the Companions of the Prophet drank was the noble Qur'ān; only the Qur'ān, since the *ḥadīth* of the Prophet, peace be on him, and his teachings were an offshoot of this fountainhead. When someone asked the Mother of the Faithful, ʿĀ'ishah, may Allah be pleased with her, about the character of the Prophet, she answered, 'his character was the Qur'ān' (*Muslim*). The Noble Qur'ān was the only source from which they quenched their thirst, and this was the only mould after which they modelled their lives. This was the only guidance for them, not because there was no civilisation or culture or science or books or schools. Indeed, there was Roman culture, its civilisation, its books and its laws, which even today is considered to be the foundation of European culture. There was the heritage of Greek culture – its logic, its philosophy and its art, which are still a source of inspiration for Western thought. There was the Persian civilisation, its art, its poetry and its legends, and its religion and system of government. There were many other civilisations, near or far, such as the Indian and Chinese cultures. The Roman and Persian cultures were established to the north and to the south of the Arabian Peninsula, while the Jews and the Christians were settled in the heart of Arabia. Thus we believe that this generation did not place sole reliance on the Book of Allah for the understanding of their religion because of any ignorance civilisation and culture, but it was all according to a well thought out plan and method. An example of this method is found in the displeasure expressed by the Messenger of Allah when ʿUmar, may Allah be pleased with him, brought some pages from the Torah. The messenger of Allah said, 'By Allah, even if Mūsā had been alive among you today, he would have no recourse except to follow me.' It is clear from this incident that the Messenger of Allah deliberately limited the first generation of Muslims, which was undergoing the initial stages of training, to only one source of guidance. This was the Book of Allah. His intention was that this group should dedicate itself purely to the Book of Allah and arrange its lives solely according to its teaching. That is why the Messenger of Allah was displeased when ʿUmar turned to a source different from the Qur'ān.

The Messenger of Allah intended to prepare a generation pure in heart, pure in mind and pure in understanding. Its training was to be based on the method prescribed by Allah who gave the Noble Qur'ān, which was protected from the influence of all other sources.

This generation drank solely from this spring and thus attained a unique distinction in history. In later times, other sources mingled with it. Other sources used by later generations, included Greek philosophy and logic, ancient Persian legends and ideas, Jewish scriptures and traditions, Christian theology and fragments of other religions and civilisations. These mingled with the commentaries on the Qur'ān and with scholastic theology, with jurisprudence and its principles. Later generations after this generation were brought up and trained with this mixed source, and hence the like of this generation was never witnessed again.

Thus we may say without any reservation that the main reason for the difference between the first unique and distinguished group of Muslims and later Muslims is the loss of purity of the first source of Islamic guidance that was mixed with various alien sources.

LEARNING TO PRACTICE

Another basic cause contributing to this vast difference between the early Muslims and their subsequent generations is their method of learning.

Those of the first generation did not approach the Qur'ān for the purpose of acquiring culture and information, nor for the purpose of taste or enjoyment. None of them came to the Qur'ān to increase his knowledge for the sake of knowledge itself or to solve some scientific or legal problems, or to improve his understanding. Rather he turned to the Qur'ān to find out what the Almighty Creator has prescribed for him and for the group in which he lived, for his life, and for the life of the group. He approached it to act on what he heard immediately, as a soldier on the battlefield reads 'Today's Bulletin' so that he may know what is to be done. He did not read many verses of the Qur'ān in one session, as he understood that this would lay an unbearable burden of duties and responsibilities on his shoulders. At most he would read ten verses, memorise them, and then act upon them. We know this from a *ḥadīth* reported by ʿAbdullāh ibn Masʿūd.

This understanding – the understanding that instruction is for action – opened for them the doors to spiritual fulfilment and to knowledge. If they had read the Qur'ān only for the sake of discussion, learning and information, these doors would not have opened. Moreover, as action became easy the weight of responsibilities became light, and the Qur'ān became part of their personalities, mingling with their lives and characters so that they become living examples of faith – a faith not hidden in intellects or books, but expressing itself in a dynamic movement which changed condition and events and the course of life.

Indeed, this Qur'ān does not open its treasure except to the one who accepts it with this sprit, i.e. the sprit of knowing with the sprit of acting upon it. It was not revealed in order to be a book of literature, or to be considered as a book of stories or history, although it has all these facets. It was revealed to become a way of life, a way dedicated to Allah. Thus, Allah the exalted imparted it to the early Muslims in a gradual manner, to be read at intervals: *We have revealed this Qur'ān little by little so that you may recite it to people at intervals, and we have revealed it gradually* (17: 106).

The Qur'ān did not appear all at once; rather it came down according to the needs of the Islamic society in facing new problems according to the growth of ideas and concepts, according to the progress of general social life, and according to new challenges faced by the Muslim community in its practical life. One verse or a few verses would be revealed according to the special circumstances and events, these verses would answer questions that arose in the minds of people, or explain the nature of a particular situation, and prescribe a way of dealing with it. These verses would correct their mistakes, either of understanding or of practice, bring them closer to Allah, and would explain to them the wisdom of the various aspects of the universe in the light of Allah's attributes. Thus, they clearly realised that every moment of their lives was under the continuous guidance and direction of the Almighty Creator and that they were traversing the path of life under the wings of Allah's Mercy. Because of this sense of constant relationship with Allah, their lives were moulded in the sacred pattern that he himself had chosen for them.

Thus, instruction to be translated into action was the method of the first group of Muslims. The method of later generations was instruction for academic discussion and enjoyment. And without doubt this is the second major factor that made later generations different from the first unique generation of Islam.

DISCARDING JĀHILĪYAH PRACTICES

A third cause is also evident in the history of Muslims. When a person embraced Islam in the time of the Prophet he would detach himself from *jāhilīyah*. When he stepped into the circle of Islam, he would start a new life, separating himself off from his past life under influence of Divine Law. He would look upon the deeds of his life of ignorance with a feeling that these were impure and could not be countenanced in Islam! With this feeling, he would turn towards Islam for new guidance; and if at any time temptations overpowered him, or the old habits attracted him, or if he were amiss in any way, he would not rest until he had made amends for it and purified himself. He always turned to the Qur'ān for guidance, and to live by it.

Thus, there would be a complete break between the Muslim's present Islam and his past *jāhilīyah*, and this after a well thought out decision, as a result of which all his relationships with *jāhilīyah* would be cut off and he would be joined completely to Islam, although there would be give and take in commercial activity and daily business; yet relationships of faith are one thing and daily business is something else.

This renunciation of the *jāhilī* environment, its customs and traditions, and its ideas and concepts, proceeded from the replacement of polytheism by the concept of the Oneness of Allah. The *jāhilī* view of life, and the world was replaced by the Islamic view. Free from *jāhilīyah*, the new Muslims were absorbed into the new Islamic community under a new leadership, to which all their loyalties and commitments were dedicated.

This was the parting of the ways and the starting of a new journey, free from pressure of values, concepts and traditions of the *jāhilī* society. The Muslims encountered nothing burdensome except the torture and oppression of those who rejected Islam. But he has already decided in the depth of his heart that he would face the future with equanimity. Therefore no pressure from the *jāhilī* society could have any effect on his firm resolve.

RETURNING TO THE QUR'ĀN

This is why in the early stages of our training and education for the Islamic movement we must move ourselves from all the influences of the *jāhilīyah* in which we live and from which we derive benefits. We must return to that pure source from which the first generation derived its guidance, free from any mixing or pollution. Only from it can we reliably derive our concepts of the nature of the universe, the nature of human existence, and the relationship of these two with the perfect, the Real Being, Allah the Most High. From the Qur'ān we must also derive our concepts of life, and our principles of government, politics, economics and all other aspects of life.

We must return to this source in order to learn obedience and gain inspiration for action, and not for academic discussion and enjoyment. Each one of us should return to it to find out what kind of person Allah asks us to be, and then we should become that person. During this process we also discover the artistic beauty in the Qur'ān, the marvellous stories in the Qur'ān, the scenes of the Day of Judgement, the intuitive logic of the Qur'ān, and all the other such benefits that are sought in the Qur'ān by academic and literate people. We will enjoy all these other aspects, but these are not the main object of our study. Our primary purpose is to know which way of life is demanded of us by the Qur'ān, the total view of the universe that the Qur'ān wants us to have, the nature of Allah, taught to us by the Qur'ān, the kind of morals and manners enjoined by it, and the kind of legal and constitutional system it asks to establish in the world.

It is therefore desirable that we should be aware at all times of the nature of our course of action and the nature of our position. We should know the nature of the road that we must traverse to escape ignorance, as did the distinguished and unique generation of the Companions of the Prophet.

C. THE PROPHET MUḤAMMAD

Who is Muḥammad?
Khurram Murad

The Way of the Prophet
Muhammad Qutb

The *Ḥadīth*: Its Relevance to Contemporary Society
Sayyid Abul Hasan Ali Nadwi

Knowing Allah through Muḥammad
Muhammad al-Ghazali

The Prophet's Technique
Khurshid Ahmad

13

Who is Muḥammad?

Khurram Murad

THE PROPHET TODAY

One in every five persons on this earth firmly believes that the Prophet Muḥammad, the peace and blessings of God be upon him, is the last Messenger of God. He was a Muslim and there are more than 1.3 billion Muslims today.

Not only individuals but entire countries take pride in declaring their allegiance to him. There are 54 such Muslim states today, ranging from those as large as Indonesia and Bangladesh, with populations of 200 and 125 million respectively, to those as tiny as the Maldives or Brunei with populations of 230,000 and 260,000 respectively. Even in non-Muslim countries, large Muslim populations constitute significant minorities; as much as 120 million in India and 20 million in China. Indeed, within the last half century, Islam, the religion brought by the Prophet Muḥammad, has become the second largest religion in most European countries, as well as in America and Canada.

Black and white, red and yellow, followers of the Prophet Muḥammad come from all human races. Whether in Asia or Europe, Africa or America, in every nook and cranny of this globe, you are sure to find Muslims. They live in the most advanced, sprawling megalopolis as well as in the most primitive nomadic tent, village, hamlet, and even in the bush.

Down the centuries, across the planet, from end to end, billions and billions of men and women have lived all their lives, loving the Prophet and trying to follow in his footsteps, as no one else has been so loved and followed. They have lived and died, believed and acted, married and raised families, worshipped and ruled, made war and peace, even eaten and dressed, walked and slept, just as he did or taught them to do.

Indeed, never in history has a human being influenced mankind, even beyond his death, so deeply and so pervasively as he has. He brings light and peace to countless hearts and lives. They love him more dearly than their own selves. In him they find their greatest source of inspiration and guidance. He is the ultimate norm and the perfect example for them. Faith in him is their mainstay, and he is their chief source of support and comfort in all personal vicissitudes and tribulations. To him they also look to lead them through social and political turmoil. He has always inspired them to greater and greater heights of spiritual and moral upliftment and civilisational achievements. And still does.

In short, they believe that through him, a human like themselves, God has spoken to them, and guided him to live amongst them, setting an example and a model for all times to come. Even today he motivates and induces whole populations to yearn and strive to shape their private lives, politics and policies according to his teachings.

Who, then, is this man Muḥammad?

EARLY LIFE IN MAKKAH

It was in the year 570, after Jesus, that Muḥammad was born in Makkah, in what is now Saudi Arabia. Arabia, by all accounts, is the cradle of the human race. All the oldest human remains so far found come from the area of its location.

Hemmed in by red, black and brown volcanic hills about 80 kilometres to the east of the Red Sea, stands the city of Makkah. It was then a small merchant town on the ancient 'incense' route through which passed the great trade caravans between the south and north.

However, Makkah was, and remains, important for an altogether different reason. For here lies the Ka'bah, the 'first House' ever set up for mankind to worship their only God. More than 1,000 years before the Prophet Solomon built the Temple in Jerusalem, his ancestor, the Prophet Abraham, aided by his elder son the Prophet Ishmael, raised its walls on very ancient foundations.

Close by the Ka'bah lies the well called Zam-Zam. Its origin, too, goes back to the Prophet Abraham's time. It was this well which sprang up miraculously to save the life of the infant Ishmael.

Makkah never had, nor does it have now, any worldly inducement to offer for settlement. It is a barren, desolate place, where even grass does not grow! There were springs and wells of abundant water nearby in Ṭā'if, and a short distance away in Madinah. But it was the first House of God, architecturally an unremarkable cube, but spiritually and civilisationally the most remarkable fountain and spring of life – which made it supremely important, a place of attraction for people from all over the world. Forever, therefore, Makkah is a great centre of pilgrimage.

By the time Muḥammad was born, the Kaʿbah's then guardians, the tribe of the Quraysh, had more than 300 idols installed in and around the Kaʿbah to be worshipped as lords, gods and intercessors besides the One God. Muḥammad was a direct descendant of the Prophet Abraham through the Prophet Ishmael. He belonged to the financially poor but politically strong and noble clan of Banū Ḥāshim from the tribe of Quraysh. As guardians of the Kaʿbah, the House of God and the centre of pilgrimage for all Arabia, the Quraysh ranked higher in dignity and power than any other tribe. Ḥāshim held the high office of levying taxes and of providing pilgrims with food and water.

Soon after Muḥammad was born he became an orphan. His father, ʿAbdullāh, died before he was born. His mother, Āminah, passed away when he was only six years old. Thereafter his grandfather, ʿAbd al-Muṭṭalib, took him into his care. Only two years later, however, the orphaned boy was bereaved of his grandfather as well, leaving him in the care of his uncle, Abū Ṭālib.

After his birth, the infant child was sent to the desert to be suckled and weaned and to spend part of his childhood among one of the bedouin tribes, Banū Saʿd ibn Bakr, who lived in the south-east of Makkah. This was the usual custom of all the great families in Makkah.

As Muḥammad grew up, he earned his livelihood pasturing sheep and goats, as have done most Prophets. His uncle and guardian, Abū Ṭālib, also took him along with him on his travels with the trade caravans to greater Syria. He, thus, gained experience in trading. Because of his great honesty and diligence and the business acumen he showed in trading, he was soon sought after to take charge of other people's merchandise, i.e. for those who could not travel themselves, and to trade on their behalf.

At the age of 25, Muḥammad married a lady named Khadījah. A widow, Khadījah was 15 years older than Muḥammad. She was a rich Makkan merchant, and Muḥammad had managed some of her trade affairs. It was she who proposed marriage. Khadījah remained Muḥammad's wife and his closest friend and companion all her life till her death 25 years later. She bore him six children, of whom four daughters survived.

Until he was 40, Muḥammad led a very uneventful life, until he became a Prophet. What set him apart from his compatriots were his absolute truthfulness, trustworthiness and integrity, his sense of justice and compassion for the poor, oppressed and downtrodden, as well as his total refusal to worship any idol or do anything immoral. He was popularly acclaimed for these qualities. *Al-Amīn*, the trustworthy, the honest, *al-Ṣādiq*, the truthful, were the titles on everybody's lips for Muḥammad, which itself means the praised one.

At a very young age, Muḥammad enthusiastically joined a pact of chivalry for the establishment of justice and the protection of the weak and the oppressed made by certain chiefs of the Quraysh. He took part in the oath when they all vowed that henceforth they would stand together as one people on the side of the oppressed against the oppressor until justice was done, whether the oppressed was from among the Quraysh or one who had come from abroad.

In later years, at Madinah, Muḥammad used to say: 'I was present in the house of ʿAbdullāh ibn Judʿān at so excellent a pact that I would not exchange my part in it for a herd of red camels, and if now, in Islam, I were summoned to a similar pact, I would gladly respond.'

A testimony to Muḥammad's character was given by his wife Khadījah as she comforted him at the time when the first revelation came to him. He said later: 'I fear for my life.' She replied: 'By no means! I swear by God that God will never lose you. You join ties of relationship, you speak the truth, you bear people's burdens, you earn for the poor, you entertain guests, and you help against the vicissitudes which affect people's rights.'

Muḥammad's wisdom was also acknowledged by all. Once, while repairing the Kaʿbah, various clans of the Quraysh disputed violently as to who should have the honour of placing the Black Stone in its place. As they were about to unsheathe their swords and go to war, they made the Prophet their arbitrator and he brought them peace. He placed the Black Stone on his cloak and asked all the clan chiefs to hold its edges and raise it, and then he placed the Black Stone in its appointed spot with his own hands.

THE PROPHET IN MAKKAH

Muḥammad was not only a wise, just, compassionate, honoured and respected human being, but also a profoundly contemplative and spiritual person. As he approached the age of 40, increasingly he came to spend more and more of his time in retreat, in contemplation, worship, prayer, in the Cave of Ḥirāʾ in Jabal al-Nūr, sometimes for several days at a time.

It was here that one night before dawn, in the last part of the month of Ramaḍān, the holy month of fasting for Muslims, the Angel Gabriel appeared before him in the form of a human being, and said to him: 'Read', and the

Prophet said: 'I am not a reader.' Thereupon, as he himself told it, 'the Angel Gabriel overwhelmed me in his embrace until I reached the limit of my endurance. Then he returned me and said: "Read". Again I said: "I am not a reader". Thrice the same thing happened. The third time, after releasing me from his embrace, the Angel finally said:

> *Read in the name of your Lord who has created. He has created the human being from a clinging* [fertilised ovum]. *Read, and your Lord is the Most Bountiful: He Who has taught by the pen, taught the human being what he knew not* (96: 1–5).'

He recited these words after the Angel. And, then, the Angel said to him: 'You are the Messenger of God.'

Overawed by the unique experience of the Divine and overwhelmed by the huge burden of the Truth and the message, he came out of the cave, his body trembling and his heart quaking. The Prophet returned home. 'Cover me! Cover me!', he said to his wife Khadījah. She quickly covered him with a cloak. Wrapped in the cloak, he told her what had happened in the Cave of Ḥirā', how he had come to be appointed as God's Messenger.

The event in Ḥirā', as narrated by Muḥammad, was the supreme and most crucial event of his life. All that happened later has been happening over the centuries, and all the positions that he enjoys in the eyes of his followers, or his detractors, hinges on the veracity, truthfulness, authenticity and nature of this event in Ḥirā'.

Yet the only thing to support his claim in this respect was and remains his own word. Was he truly a Messenger of God? Was what he saw real and true? Or, was it a hallucination? Was he a man possessed? Did he just compose in words as poets do, the ideas he found in his heart?

These questions are raised today, as they were raised by his compatriots then. Of these, his wife of 15 years was to be the first judge. She knew him too well to doubt even for a moment that he could say anything but the truth. She also knew his character. So, she believed in him without a moment's hesitation.

As with his wife Khadījah, so his closest friend Abū Bakr, his adopted son Zayd, his cousin ʿAlī who lived with him, in short, all who knew the Prophet most intimately, believed in his truthfulness most spontaneously.

Khadījah took the Prophet to her cousin Waraqah, who had converted to Christianity, and acquired great knowledge in Christian scriptures. Both the Jews and Christians had been expecting the coming of the last Prophet as foretold in their scriptures. Had not Moses, just before he died, been told: 'I will raise up for them a Prophet like you from among their brethren; and I will put my words in his mouth?' (Deuteronomy 18: 18). Who could be the brethren of the sons of Israel except the sons of Ishmael?

Who could be the mysterious *Shiloh* but the Prophet Muḥammad, about whom Jacob prophesied immediately before his death, that to him would be transferred the Divine mission in 'the latter days': 'And Jacob called his sons and said, gather yourselves together, that I may tell you that which shall befall you in the last days. The sceptre shall not depart from Judah, nor a lawgiver from between his feet, until Shiloh comes; and unto him the gathering of the people be' (Genesis 49: 1, 10).

And, whom did Jesus mean other than Muḥammad when he said: 'If I do not go away, the helper will not come to you . . . he will not speak on his own authority, but whatever he hears he will speak?' (John 16: 7–14).

Waraqah therefore had no doubts that the last Prophet had come; so, he, too, believed in him.

But most of the people of Makkah who had acclaimed him as the trustworthy (*al-Amīn*) and the truthful (*al-Ṣādiq*) could not bring themselves to believe in him. Nor could most of the Jews and Christians who had for so long been living in expectation of his arrival. Not that they doubted his truthfulness or integrity but they were not prepared to turn their whole established way of life upside down by submitting to his simple but radical message:

> When I recite the Qur'ān, I find the following clear instructions: *God is He who has created you, and the heavens and the earth, He is your only Lord and Master. Surrender your beings and your lives totally to Him Alone, and worship and serve no one but Him. Let God be the Only God.*
> The words I speak, He places in my mouth, and I speak on His authority. Obey me and forsake all false claimants to human obedience. Everything in the heavens and on earth belongs to God; no person has a right to be master of another person, to spread oppression and corruption on earth. An eternal life beyond awaits you; where you will meet God face to face, and your life will be judged; for that you must prepare.

This simple message shook the very foundations of the Makkan society as well as the seventh-century world. That world, as today, lived under the yoke of many false gods: kings and emperors, priests and monks, feudal lords and rich businessmen, soothsayers and spell-binders who claimed to know what others knew not, and who all lorded over human beings. Not only that, people made gods of their own desires, their tribal loyalties, their ancestors, and the powers of nature, like the nations, cultures, science and technology today all lorded over human beings.

The Prophet's message challenged them all, exposed them all, and threatened them all. His immediate opponents in Makkah could do no better than brand him unconvincingly as a liar, a poet, and a soothsayer, a man possessed. But how could he who was illiterate, he who had never composed a single verse, he who had shown no inclination to lead people, suddenly, have words flowing from his lips, so full of wisdom and light, morally so uplifting, specifically so enlivening, so beautiful and powerful, that they began to change the hearts and minds and lives of the hearers? His detractors and opponents had no answer. When challenged to produce anything even remotely similar to the words Muḥammad claimed he was receiving from God, they could not match God's words.

First privately, then publicly, the Prophet continued to proclaim his message. He himself had an intense, living relationship with God, totally committed to the message and mission entrusted to him. Slowly and gradually, people came forward and embraced Islam. They came from all walks of life – chiefs and slaves, businessmen and artisans, men and women – most of them young.

Some simply heard the Qur'ān, and that was enough to transform them. Some saw the Prophet, and were immediately captivated by the light of mercy, generosity and humanity that was visible in his manners and morals, in his words and works and also in his face.

The opposition continued to harden and sharpen. It grew furious and ferocious. Those who joined the Prophet were tortured in innumerable ways: they were mocked, abused, beaten, flogged, imprisoned, and boycotted. Some were subjected to much more inhuman tortures: made to lie on burning coal fires until the melting body fat extinguished them, or were dragged over burning sand and rocks. Yet such was the strength of their faith that none of them gave it up in the face of such trials and tribulations.

However, as the persecutions became unbearable, the Prophet said to them: 'If you go to Abyssinia, you will find there a king, a Christian, under whom no one suffers wrong.' About 80 of his followers, therefore, forsook their homes and emigrated to Abyssinia, where the Christian king gave them full protection despite the pleadings and machinations of the emissaries sent by the Quraysh chiefs. This was the first emigration of Islam.

In the meantime, the Prophet and his Companions continued to nourish their souls and intellects and strengthen their character and resolve for the great task that lay ahead. They met regularly, especially at a house near the Kaʿbah called Dār al-Arqam, to read and study the Qur'ān, to worship and pray, and to forge the ties of brotherhood.

Ten years passed, but the people of Makkah would not give their allegiance to the Prophet's message nor showed any signs of mitigating their persecution. At the same time, the Prophet lost his closest companion, his wife Khadījah, as well as his uncle Abū Ṭālib, his chief protector in the tribal world of Makkah.

The Prophet now decided to carry his message to the people of the nearby town of Ṭā'if, known for its wealth. In Ṭā'if, too, the tribal leaders mocked and ridiculed him and rejected his message. They also stirred up their slaves and the street urchins to insult him, mock him, and throw stones at him. Thus, he was stoned until he bled and was driven out of Ṭā'if. And yet when his companion, Zayd, requested him to curse the people of Ṭā'if, and when God placed at his command the Angel of Mountains to crush the Valley of Ṭā'if if he so wished, he only prayed for their being guided. Such was the mercy and compassion of the one who is the 'mercy for all the worlds'.

The Ṭā'if episode was one of the hardest moments in the Prophet's life. It signalled the advent of a new era for him, when his mission was to find a secure base, and he was to ascend higher and higher in the coming days until the end of time.

To mark that, one night the Prophet was awakened and taken, in the company of the Angel Gabriel, first to Jerusalem. There he was met by all the Prophets, who gathered together behind him as he prayed on the Rock in the centre of the site of the Temple, the spot where the Dome of the Rock stands today. From the Rock, led by the Archangel, he ascended through the seven heavens and beyond. Thus he saw whatever God made him see, the heavenly worlds which no human eye can see, and which were the focus of his message and mission.

During this journey, the five daily prayers were ordained for his people. Furthermore, it was then that the Prophet was given the charter for the new society and state soon to be born, which, had also been prophesied and described in *Sūrah al-Isrā'* (Chapter 17) of the Qur'ān.

THE PROPHET IN MADINAH

The message that Makkah and Ṭā'if rejected, found responsive hearts in Yathrib, a small oasis about 400 kilometres to the north of Makkah. Now known as Madīnatun Nabī, the city of the Prophet, or Madīnah Munawwarah, the radiant city, it was destined to be the centre of the Divine light that was to spread to all parts of the world for all times to come.

In quick succession, the Prophet suffered the terrible loss of Khadījah, his intimate and beloved companion for 25 years, and of Abū Ṭālib, his guardian and protector against the bloodthirsty Makkan foes, and encountered the worst ever rejection, humiliation and persecution at nearby Ṭā'if. As the Prophet reached the lowest point in his vocation, God brought him comfort and solace. On the one hand, spiritually, He took him during the Night of the Ascension to the Highest of Highs, realities and Divinities, face to face with the Unseen. And on the other, materially, he opened the hearts of the people of Yathrib to the message and mission of Muḥammad.

Soon after Muḥammad's return from Ṭā'if and the Night Journey, at the time of the pilgrimage, six men from Yathrib embraced Islam. They delivered the message of Islam to as many as they could, and at the time of the next pilgrimage in the year 621 CE, 12 people came. They pledged themselves to the Prophet, that they would make no god beside God, that they would neither steal nor commit fornication, nor slay their infants, nor utter slanders, nor disobey him in that which is right. The Prophet said: 'If you fulfil this pledge, then Paradise is yours.' This time the Prophet sent Muṣʿab ibn ʿUmayr with them to teach them the Qur'ān and Islam and to spread the message of Islam.

More and more people over the course of a year – tribal leaders, men and women – became Muslims. At the time of the next pilgrimage, they decided to send a delegation to the Prophet, make a pledge to him, and invited him and all Muslims in Makkah to Yathrib as a sanctuary and as a base for spreading the Divine message of Islam.

In all, 73 men and two women came. They met the Prophet at Aqabah. They pledged to protect the Prophet as they would protect their own women and children, and to fight against all men, red and black, even if their nobles were killed and they suffered the loss of all their possessions. When asked what would be theirs if they fulfilled their pledge, the Prophet said: 'Paradise'. Thus, the beginning was made, the foundations of the Islamic society, state and civilisation were set.

The road was now open for the persecuted and tortured followers of the Prophet to come to the House of Islam, that was to be Madinah. He, therefore, instructed them to emigrate, and gradually most of them found their way to Yathrib.

Their Makkan foes could not bear to see the Muslims living in peace. They knew the power of the Prophet's message, they knew the strength of those dedicated believers who cared nothing for the age-old Arab customs and ties of kinship, and who if they had to, would fight for their faith. The Makkans sensed the danger that the Muslims' presence in Madinah posed for their northern trade caravan routes. They saw no other way to stop all this but to kill the Prophet.

Hence they hatched a conspiracy: one strong and well-connected young man was to be nominated by each clan, and all of them were to pounce upon and kill the Prophet one morning as he came out of his house, so that his blood would be on all the clans' hands. Thus, the Prophet's clan would have to accept blood money in place of revenge.

Informed of the plot by the Angel Gabriel, and instructed to leave Makkah for Madinah, the Prophet went to Abū Bakr's house to finalise the travel arrangements. Abū Bakr was overjoyed at having been chosen for the honour and blessing of being the Prophet's companion on this blessed, momentous, sacred and epoch-making journey. He offered his she-camel to the Prophet, but the Prophet insisted on paying its price.

On the fateful night, as darkness fell, the youths selected by the Quraysh leaders to kill the Prophet surrounded his house. They decided to pounce on him when he came out of his house for the dawn prayer.

Meanwhile, the Prophet handed over all the money left by the Makkans with him for safe-keeping to ʿAlī. ʿAlī offered to lie in the Prophet's bed. The Prophet slipped out of his house, threw a little dust in their direction, and walked past his enemies, whose eyes were still on the house.

He met Abū Bakr at his house, and they both travelled to a nearby cave, the Jabal al-Nūr. When the Quraysh realised that the Prophet had evaded them, they were furious. They looked for him everywhere and on all roads; they also offered a reward of 100 she-camels for anybody who would bring them the Prophet, dead or alive.

A tribal chief, Surāqah, sighted the Prophet and followed him, hoping to earn the reward. The Prophet, with bloodthirsty foes in pursuit and an uncertain future ahead of him in Madinah, told Surāqah: 'A day will soon come when Kisra's golden hand bracelet will be in Surāqah's hands.' Thereafter, Surāqah retreated, and the Prophet proceeded towards Madinah.

This was *Hijrah*, the emigration – a small distance in space, a mighty leap in history, an event that was to become a threshold in the shaping of the Islamic *Ummah*. This is why the Muslims date their calendar from *Hijrah*, and not from Ḥirā' or from the birth of the Prophet.

In Qubah, 10 kilometres outside Madinah, the Prophet made his first sojourn. Here he built the first *Masjid*. Here he also made his first public address: 'Spread peace among yourselves, give away food to the needy, pray while people sleep – and you enter Paradise, the house of peace.'

Three days later, the Prophet entered Madinah. Men, women, children, the entire populace came out on the streets and jubilantly welcomed him. Never was there a day of greater rejoicing and happiness. 'The Prophet has come! The Prophet has come!', sang the little children.

The first thing the Prophet did after arriving in Madinah was to weld the Muhājirs or Emigrants and the hosts, called the Anṣār or Helpers into one brotherhood. Still today this brotherhood remains the hallmark of the Muslims. One person from the Emigrants was made the brother of one from amongst the Helpers. The Helpers offered to share equally all that they possessed with the Emigrants.

So the Muslims were forged into a close-knit community of faith and brotherhood, and the structure of their society and polity was being built. The first structure was also raised. This was the *Masjid*, the building dedicated to the worship of One God – called *Masjid al-Nabawī*, the Prophet's *Masjid*. Since then the *masjid* has also remained the hallmark of the Muslims' collective and social life, the convenient space for the integration of the religious and political dimensions of Islam, a source of identification, a witness to Muslim existence.

At the same time, steps were taken and the required institutions built to integrate the entire social life around the centre and pivot of the worship of One God. For this purpose, five daily prayers in congregation were established.

Ramaḍān, fasting every day from dawn to sunset for an entire month, was also prescribed. Similarly, to establish 'giving' as the way of life, *Zakāh*, a percentage of one's wealth to be given in the way of God, was made obligatory.

As long as there was no different instruction from God, the Muslims followed the practices observed by the Jews and Christians. Hence, they used to pray with their faces turned towards Jerusalem. But soon this direction to which the Muslims faced in Prayer was changed from Jerusalem to Makkah. This historic episode signalled the formation of a new Muslim community, charged with Divine trust and the mission of God's guidance, replacing the earlier Jews and Christians, and following the most ancient message of Abraham, turning towards the most ancient House of God, built by him.

ATTACKS BY THE MAKKANS

The Prophet, after arriving in Madinah, first formed an alliance with the Jews. Next, he approached all the nearby tribes and tried to persuade them to make an alliance or at least enter into a no-war pact. Many did. Thus the small group evicted from Makkah assumed strategic importance.

The Makkans who had earlier planned to kill the Prophet, were now determined to annihilate this nascent community of Islam. Having failed in all other ways they decided on a military solution.

A heavily armed Makkan force marched towards Madinah in the second year after *Hijrah*, on the pretext of protecting their trade caravan. The Prophet, despite his community's small number and lack of arms, decided to face their threat boldly. On the 17th of Ramaḍān, at Badr, the two forces met and fought a battle in which 313 Muslims defeated the 1,000-strong Makkan army.

Seventy of the Makkan chiefs who had been most active and vehement in persecuting the Muslims were killed; many others were taken prisoner, later to be released for ransom. For the first time, prisoners of war were treated humanely and kindly; they were fed and housed in the same way as their captors ate and lived.

In the third year after *Hijrah*, a 3,000–strong Makkan force again marched on Madinah, both to avenge the defeat at Badr and to make another attempt to defeat the Muslims; 700 of them were mailed and 200 mounted. The Muslims numbered only 700. The two sides met just outside Madinah near Mount Uḥud. The initial Muslim victory was, however, reversed; the Muslim contingent posted to protect the rear, violated the Prophet's instructions and abandoned its position. The Quraysh attacked from behind, and victory was turned into defeat, resulting in the deaths of about 65 Muslims. The Makkans, however, failed to pursue their advantage and clinch victory.

The Makkans planned to make a final assault on Madinah to settle the matter once and for all. All bedouin tribes, Jews, and hypocrites within Madinah joined forces with them. In the fifth year after *Hijrah*, 24,000 of them advanced on Madinah. It was impossible to fight them on the open battlefield, or defend Madinah which was without walls. The Muslims, therefore, defended themselves by digging ditches all round Madinah. After laying siege to Madinah for 25 days, due to inner dissension, lack of supplies, cold weather and high winds, the Makkan army was forced to withdraw. This was the turning point in the history of confrontation with the Makkans. Madinah was never to be attacked again.

From the beginning, the Jews were given full rights of citizenship, yet still they committed acts of treason and treachery. Some had to be expelled; some were killed as a result of judgements given by an arbitrator appointed by them. However, subsequent generations of Jews were never held responsible for the misdeeds of the Jews of Madinah, as they were in Christendom for 2,000 years, for the crucifixion of Jesus. Instead, the Muslims always treated them justly and kindly.

The next year, the sixth after *Hijrah*, the Prophet and 1,400 Companions journeyed to Makkah to perform *ʿUmrah*, the lesser pilgrimage, in accordance with several traditions of the time. They were unarmed. The Quraysh chiefs, against all established and accepted traditions, refused them admission. However, the Quraysh were now so low in morale and strength that they had to sign a peace treaty with the Prophet, the Hudaybiyyah Treaty.

Though the terms appeared highly unfavourable, even humiliating, for the Muslims, they made tremendous gains by virtue of this treaty. They, who were driven out of Makkah and attacked thrice, were now recognised as an equal force, to be treated respectfully, taken seriously. Peace provided an opportunity for the wavering and the neutral, even the hostile, to witness Islam at first hand, and many sensed the imminent victory of Islam. The result was that many Makkans and Arab tribes either embraced Islam or made peace with the Prophet.

As soon as the Hudaybiyyah Treaty was signed, the Prophet sent letters to various neighbouring Arab and non-Arab rulers, including Khosroes of Iran and Heraclius of the Byzantine Empire. He invited them to Islam, and assured them that he did not covet their kingdoms or riches. They could retain both.

The Quraysh, however, soon broke the Treaty of Hudaybiyya. It was, thus, time to deal with their continuing hostility. The Prophet marched to Makkah, and captured the town. The fall of Makkah witnessed unparalleled acts of mercy, forgiveness and generosity. Not a single drop of blood was shed. Everybody who remained indoors was granted security of life and property. The Prophet forgave all who had been his bitterest foes all his life, who had persecuted him and planned to kill him, who had driven him out of Makkah, and who had marched thrice to Madinah to defeat the Muslims.

The neighbouring Byzantine Empire now prepared to attack and destroy the Muslim community in Madinah. However, when the Prophet marched to Tabūk on the northern border, his determination, courage and timely response made the enemy lose heart and withdraw.

SOCIETY BUILDING

Throughout those years, when the Prophet was surrounded by hostile forces and ultimately triumphed over them, he continued to purify the souls, uplift the morals of his followers and lay the foundations of a just and compassionate family, society and state. His mission was now complete: he had created a new generation, and changed the lives of multitudes of men and women by bringing them in total surrender to their Creator. He had created a new society: one based on justice. In his own life example, and in the Qur'ān, mankind was given the light and way of a Godly life.

It is remarkable that this entire epoch-making revolution which transformed not only Arabia but all of mankind for all time to come and which heralded the birth of the most brilliant civilisation in the world cost no more than 750 lives, mostly opponents, in the various battles. Yet the Prophet is sometimes maligned as a man of violence by those who have exterminated thousands of people in pursuit of their civilisational ideals.

The Prophet performed his only *Ḥajj* in the tenth year after migration to Madinah. In the Plain of 'Arafah, he gave a sermon of unsurpassable beauty and lasting value: 'No human being has any right to lord over other people; all human beings are equal, whatever their origin, colour or nationality.'

A few months later, in the eleventh year after *Hijrah*, the Prophet Muḥammad died. He was buried in the house in which he had lived in Madinah.

The Prophet possessed a character of exquisite beauty and charm. He was merciful, kind and compassionate. He loved children and taught kindness to animals. He spoke softly, never abused anyone, and forgave even his worst enemies. He lived a very simple life. He repaired his own shoes and clothes. He lived frugally, sometimes for days no food was cooked in his household.

Such is Muḥammad. According to every standard by which human greatness can be measured he was matchless; no person was ever greater!

14

The Way of the Prophet

Muhammad Qutb

It may be easy to say that the Prophet Muḥammad, may God bless him and grant him peace, is the greatest personality humanity has ever known in its extended history. But analysing the different aspects of this greatness is not so easy.

Great? Yes! But how was he greater than everybody else? How was he so highly adored and revered by his adherents throughout all those centuries since he was chosen by Allah, until this present moment?

There is something outstanding about his personality, about his career, about his message, about his role in the history of mankind that attracts the attention of all who try to know him. To say he is a Prophet is not enough to interpret that outstanding feature. Even to say he is *the* Prophet, or the 'Seal of the Prophets' is not enough.

CHARACTERISTICS OF THE PROPHET'S PERSONALITY

One of the most outstanding features of the Prophet's greatness is that his personality is a combination of a vast variety of great personalities. He was the great statesman, the great military leader, the great educator, the great believer, the great worshipper, the great household master and the great lover of humanity.

Let us try, through a process of simplification, to comprehend some aspects of this great personality.

1. The Great Statesman

When we hear in history about a human being who found his nation scattered and dissected by different factors, unable to unite itself in one consolidated nation, who then tried his best to bring them together – with all the resolution and insistence possible, giving the matter his whole energy, sacrificing his own interests for the sake of his nation and able finally to realise the dream and bring out from that scattered nation, not only a consolidated one, but one that has a specified message and a specified role in the history of mankind – what can we call such a person, who ever existed in the true sense of the word?

No doubt we shall call him a great human being – even if he did nothing at all through his life other than fulfilling this single, albeit complicated task. What then can we call the man who fulfilled that same task, not on the ordinary level, but on such a level that is unique in history, this task being at the same time only one of his great achievements during his limited human life?

2. The Great Military Leader

When we hear in history about a military leader who found his country not only weak but also occupied in part by foreign powers, never dreaming of liberating the occupied parts, of overcoming the great powers around them, then through his outstanding personality, his long perseverance, his strong resolution, he built up an army that not only liberated the country but became in a few years the greatest army in the region – always victorious, always pressing its enemies, never conquered by them – what shall we call such a leader?

Undoubtedly, we shall call him a great person. Caesar, Napoleon and other such figures of history are called great people, although they lived and died for their limited task and even though some of them failed to realise their goals.

What then shall we call the man who built an army that aimed, not at liberating some occupied lands of a certain country, but at liberating the whole of mankind? And liberating it, moreover, not from physical submissiveness to material factors, but from the submissiveness of the soul to any sovereignty other than the Sovereignty of Allah, Almighty. An army oriented not to conquer countries or to annex lands, but to conquer human despotism and human humiliation before the devil. And to offer people the real liberty that is worth obtaining because it fulfils the welfare of this world and the World-to-Come: the army of creed, the army of principles, the army that sprang out from the Heavenly message and lived and liberated for its cause. And when we bear in mind that this great task of building up such a unique army was only part of the Prophet's job and not his sole achievement, in what words or in what terms shall we qualify this greatness?

3. The Great Educator

Any educator, great or ordinary, must have some qualifications. To begin with, he must be of a higher level than those who receive his instruction, or else they will not feel the need to listen or the need to follow. He also must have something to say to his adherents, or else they will not gather round him. He must be able to notice the different types and different conditions of his disciples, or else he will not be able to give them – and give to each of them – suitable instructions. He must have the ability to follow up, step by step, the process of education or else the development of his disciple's personalities will stop before reaching the stage of ripening and full maturity. He must have the ability to love those whom he is educating – with that love which can convince them that his instructions are meant for their own good – or else the process of education will not give its desired effect.

In all of these aspects the Prophet was greater than any known educator in history whom we may describe as great, with the repeated addition that any one of those so-called great educators had only that job as their sole career, while the Prophet had that job only as one of his different tasks, and he fulfilled it on a higher level than anyone of them.

Let us consider here two examples of his greatness as an educator. Firstly, take the term used by the Prophet to call his followers *Ṣaḥabah* or 'Companions'. To what extent did it affect his adherents to call them 'companions' rather than 'disciples', or simply 'followers'? It was certainly an intended process to raise those adherents to the high standard of their Prophet and it produced the desired results. Secondly, consider what those Companions related about the behaviour of the Prophet towards them. They all said that the Prophet treated them with such love that each of them thought that he was the Prophet's favoured one, the nearest to his heart. To estimate this behaviour, let every one of us try to treat his friends – indeed, his family members – such that everyone of them may feel that he or she is the most favoured.

4. The Great Believer

The personality of the great believer within the wide-dimensioned personality of the Prophet is outstanding. Every one of us must have experienced, at least once in his lifetime, the feeling that he is near to Allah. That he is worshipping Him sincerely. That his love of Him is illuminating his heart. That His Almighty presence and existence is filling his soul.

How great is this experience! What loftiness and greatness one feels in one's self while experiencing this rare moment! But for how long can the ordinary person maintain a high level amidst his continuous occupations, leading his attention and his energy here and there?

Now let us come to the Prophet and try to imagine that state of mind, or rather that state of soul, that is continuously and deeply attached to Allah, the beloved God, which was filled all the time with His Existence, His Magnitude, His Mercy, His Sovereignty and His Overwhelming Power.

5. The Great Worshipper

It was only natural that the great believer should become the great worshipper, for knowledge of the True Divinity begets true feelings of worship – sincerity and devotion to Allah. The Qur'ān says: *Of all His servants only those who know fear Allah* (35: 28). The outstanding feature of the Prophet in this regard is the depth of that feeling: the continuous feeling of the presence of Allah, and the continuous remembrance of this presence, either through devoted Prayer, prolonged *duʿā'* or supplication, or in continuously reminding his Companions of that presence whenever anything happens – rain falls, the crescent appears, the sun rises or sets, a plant grows, a child is born, a creature dies.

In contemporary times, this feature of the Prophet's personality is quite important. For we live in a world that rarely feels the existence of Allah, and rarely remembers Him in this stunning turmoil of the materialistic life led by people of the so-called modern civilisation. No wonder if this false civilisation is beginning to go asunder, despite all the wonderful progress it possesses in the fields of science and technology. Useful as this progress might be it cannot be a substitute for the spiritual life so necessary for mankind. Indeed, deep in the inner heart of human nature, there is a place for worship in everybody's heart. It is either filled by the worship of Allah or the worship of something else.

Indeed it is in Islam and only in Islam that scientific and technological progress is not put as a substitute for the worship of Allah, but rather as part of that worship orientated and controlled by spiritual worship and, thus, giving the balance and equilibrium so necessary in life.

Let us have a quick glance at the great worshipper, on him be peace, to learn from him how to worship Allah. He went on praying during the night until his honourable feet swelled. *Bukhārī* records that ʿĀ'ishah, his loving wife, may Allah be pleased with her, was in pain at seeing the swollen feet of the Prophet. She tried to do something to relieve him. 'Not so hard, O Messenger of Allah,' she said to him. 'Allah has forgiven all your sins, antecedent and forthcoming.' But the great worshipper answered, 'Should I not be a thankful slave of Allah.'

6. The Great Domestic Leader

The Prophet's household consisted of several wives and daughters, and had its problems as does any human household. Although his wives were the Prophet's wives and were expected to lead a sort of life and behaviour different from any other wives; yet human nature is human nature. The jealousy of one wife from another is a concrete fact, even in the Prophet's household. But what a great domestic leader he was. Under the leadership of the great husband, peace was the eminent feature of life and strife the exception. It was the Prophet who said, 'The most perfect in faith among the believers are those who possess the best morals, and the best among you are those who are kindest to their wives' (*Tirmidhī*). This statement is indeed very significant for it gives a profound criterion through which humanity may measure its elevation or its failure.

Women are always treated unjustly during ages of ignorance because of their physical weakness. Yet the Prophet of Islam gives this human touch and makes the criterion of good behaviour the way a man treats his wife.

7. The Great Lover of Humanity

The man destined to be the Messenger to all humanity and the leader of all humanity was endowed by Allah with a great love for all people, black or white, red or yellow – a love for people without discrimination. In his farewell sermon to the Muslim community, Muḥammad, peace be upon him declared: 'All of you descend from Adam and Adam was made of earth. There is no superiority for an Arab over a non-Arab nor a non-Arab over an Arab; neither for a white person over a black person nor a black person over a white person except the superiority gained through God-consciousness (*taqwā*). Indeed the noblest among you is the one who is most deeply conscious of God.' This great love was indispensable for such a great task as his. Without this great love for humanity, he could not have led people upon the prolonged and patient path towards the great Truth, towards the liberation of mankind from the worship of false deities to the worship of Allah, the True Divinity.

Some so-called great people in history were led to their task by hatred, wrath, or malignity. Of course, they fulfilled some near or temporary goals because they employed the full strength of their energy to fulfil them. But when their lives came to an end, as all lives come to their ends, nothing, or indeed very little, was left after their departure. But not so the Prophet Muḥammad. For though he left this world over fourteen centuries ago, his message is still alive and his heritage still exists.

As an insight on this point, recall a rare situation the Prophet faced. When he was abandoned in Makkah by his near relatives through hatred and enmity to his cause, when he was persecuted under the violation and the tyranny of

Quraysh, what did he do? He said to his Lord, 'O Allah! May you forgive my people, for they are ignorant, they do not know the Truth.'

8. A Well-Integrated Personality

We have been demonstrating one fact about the Prophet, on him be peace, that is, the wide scope of his personality that comprises within it a combination of great personalities of different dynamics. If this by itself is a sign of greatness, it is not, however, the real core of his greatness. For supposing these different personalities were detached one from the other they could not make up a great personality. Integration of the personality is very important and such integration was outstanding in the Prophet's personality.

One never feels that the Prophet's statesmanship or his military leadership is detached from his strong belief in Allah or his devoted worship to Him or his companionship with his followers or his love for humanity. If we add to all of this a rare equilibrium that gives every dimension the necessary attention at the suitable moment then we can be near enough to attempt a contemplative glance at the great personality of the Prophet and to comprehend to any extent possible, how it is that this personality throughout the ages has been so loved and so revered.

Yet everything about that outstanding personality was the natural thing regarding the message this Prophet was sent to declare. It was Allah who moulded his personality in the shape it was moulded, and for a certain reason, to fulfil a specific task.

Islam is a religion designed for all of humanity. It is the blessing Allah wishes to bestow upon all humanity. *This day have I perfected your religion for you, and I have completed my blessings upon you, and I have chosen for you Islam as your religion* (5: 3).

Islam is also the complete way of life that comprises faith, morality, politics, economics, social relations, the correct mode of thinking and the correct attitude toward Divinity, life, nature, and mankind. This comprehensive scope of Islam was though in need of a human being to exemplify it for mankind. For Allah, the all-Knowing, knows that revealing a book to human beings is not enough to make them believe and then adopt what they believe and implement it in the correct manner. He knows that there must be a human example to carry out the revelation in a concrete manner in order to show people how to do it. He knows also that such an example must have certain characteristics suitable for the task. As we know in educational methods, the example should be so finely complete that it can both give the most effective impression and moreover the full guidance to those who are called to follow the example.

This, in brief, was the Prophet, may God bless him and grant him peace. Now we come to the important question, how can we follow his example?

HOW TO FOLLOW THE PROPHET'S EXAMPLE

Allah says in the Qur'ān, *You have indeed, in the Messenger of God an excellent exemplar for whoever places his hopes in God and the Final Day, and who remembers Allah much* (33: 21).

What does this mean? Does this mean that everyone should become a carbon copy of the Prophet, on him be peace, in each dimension and every phase of life? This is simply impossible. Allah, the all-Merciful, knows the capacity of His creatures and does not commit them to the impossible. Allah emphatically states, *on no soul does He place a burden greater than it can bear* (7: 42).

But still, he wants us to follow the Prophet's example. Yes, follow the example within the limits of our human capacity – on one condition: that we should try our best. That we should make our attempt to follow this example the *jihād* of our lives, to which we must dictate the fullness of our energy, asking the Guidance of Allah, Who has promised to offer it to those who try: *Whoever strives hard in God's cause does so only for his own good: for, verily, God does not stand in need of anything in all the worlds!* (29: 69).

1. Islam as a Complete Way of Life

In today's world people often differentiate between politics and morality, economics and morality, technology and morality, art and morality. This is not in keeping with the example of the Prophet.

To follow the Prophetic model, we must take life as one whole, as it is in reality, and as it should be the behaviour of the one, integrated, whole, called the human being. There is no partition within the human being. For ever since Allah created the human being out of the earth's crust and breathed into him of His Spirit, the two elements became one and can never and should never be disintegrated.

When your Lord said to the Angels, Lo, I am about to create a mortal out of mud. And when I have fashioned him and breathed into him of My spirit, then fall down before him prostrate (15: 29).

2. Thought for the Hereafter

Sometimes we may become so absorbed with life's activities that we forget the Day of Resurrection. The Prophet, however, was always in remembrance of that Day and was always reminding his Companions to prepare themselves for that Day through every deed they did, every word they said, and every feeling they experienced, even in the secrecy of their inner hearts. For Allah knows our secrets, and even what is more obscure than our secrets. *He knows the secret thought and that which is yet, more hidden* (20: 7).

In educating our children, we are usually keen to teach them everything that makes out of them successful personalities in this life, which is of course very important. But paying attention to this side only is against the example of the Prophet. To follow his example, we must strive for success in this life and success in the hereafter, the latter, being at least as important as the first. And the former is only achieved by sticking to the instructions of the Qur'ān and *Sunnah* alike.

The example of the Prophet was not, and is not, a temporary one, nor is it confined to a certain nation. This example was set by Allah for all nations, for all time, until the Day of Judgement.

It is He who has sent forth His Messenger with the guidance and the way of the Truth, so that he makes it prevail over all other ways of life; and God suffices as a witness (48: 28).

Remember we cannot propagate Islam to mankind until we ourselves follow the Prophet's way and became worthy examples of Islam. This is the greatest challenge before us, the challenge unto which we must direct all of our *jihād* . . . and then ask Allah for assistance and orientation.

15

The *Ḥadīth*: Its Relevance to Contemporary Society

Sayyid Abul Hasan Ali Nadwi

The sayings and doings of the Prophet not only complement the Qur'ān but being the authentic record of the Prophet's life, they lead his followers to the source of revelation and provide them access to the inner, spiritual dimension of the Prophet's teachings. Every religion which seeks to build an ideal pattern for society prescribes certain ethical rules and devotional observances for achieving that end. These are, nevertheless, only the outward manifestations of that system. Life in complete harmony with the spirit of such rules and laws, can be realized only by forming and moulding the life of the followers of that religion after the perfect model of that system. In the case of Islam, this model is obviously the life of the Prophet of Islam. His sayings and doings, the minute details of his everyday life, provide us with the means of realizing the inner reality, the gist and spirit of the Islamic system of beliefs and observances.'

THE MISSION OF THE PROPHET

Let us begin with the aims and effects of the mission of Prophet Muḥammad. These, according to the Qur'ān, consist of the following:

1. Recitation of the revealed verses;
2. Teaching of the Book;
3. Teaching of Wisdom; and
4. Cleansing and Purification.

He it is who sent among the unlettered ones a messenger of their own, to recite unto them His revelations and to make them clean, and to teach them the Scripture and Wisdom, though heretofore they were indeed in error manifest (62: 2).

Even as We have sent unto you a Messenger from among you, who recites unto you Our Revelations and makes you clean, and teaches you the Scripture and Wisdom, and teaches you that which you knew not (2: 151).

Indeed, the mission of Prophet Muḥammad comprehends the four above-mentioned objectives. Just as the blessed Prophet gave to humanity a new Scripture and bestowed upon it new knowledge, in the same way he granted to it new moral virtues and sentiments, a new belief and faith, a new devotion and eagerness, a new magnanimity and high-mindedness, a new spirit of self-effacement and solicitude for the Hereafter, a new ideal of contentment and contemptuous disregard of worldly goods and glory, a new concept of love and affection, compassion and kindliness, and a new joy of worship and a wealth of divine fear, repentance and supplication.

Upon these very characteristics was founded the entire structure of Islamic Society and from them originated the religious environment commonly known as the Era of the Prophet and the *ṣaḥābah*. The Companions were the finest result and symbols of the efforts of the Prophet as the Apostle of God. One has only to look at this august body of men for the manifestation of the various aspects of Prophethood in everyday life.

The mission of the Prophet and his teachings were the fountainhead of these blessings and the whole of Islamic life and social design of the first century of Islam stemmed from them. But if an in-depth study was made of how it all came about and its ways and means were analysed it would appear that the marvellous revolution sprang from these formative factors which worked in the new society and *Ummah:*

i. The personality of the sacred Prophet – his life and character;
ii. The Qur'ān; and
iii. The sayings and sermons, teachings and precepts, and exhortations and admonitions of the Prophet.

The three factors, as a little thought will show, lie behind the perfect materialization of the aims and effects of the mission of Prophet Muḥammad. They have played a decisive role in the making and moulding of the new *Ummah*. A complete society, a perfect life and a collective design in which beliefs and actions, moral virtues and emotions, aptitudes and inclinations and kinship and mutual relations find their due expression cannot come into existence apart from them. Life springs from life.

In our world, a lamp is lighted by another lamp. The true Islamic morality, which along with belief and action, is seen in the lives of the Companions and their faithful successors, and their lofty idealism and deep religious feeling, are not merely due to the recitation of the Book but have also been instilled by the most inspiring and lovable personality that was before them all the time.

These are the effects of the life and character as well which the Holy Companions could see and observe during all the hours of day and night and of the company, discourses and exhortations from which they used to profit continually during the lifetime of the Prophet. The special temperament of Islam evolved as a result of the assemblage of all these factors in which there was not only the habitual obedience to commands and injunctions but a growth of the true spirit was characterized by the urge to act on them. Side by side with compliance with rules and regulations and the rendering of rights, this spirit also possessed the ability to conceive the subtleties of tender emotions and refined feelings.

EFFECT OF THE PROPHET'S COMPANY

The Companions had received the command from the Qur'ān *to establish worship* (2: 83) and also heard the commendation *who are humble in their prayers* (23: 2). But it was only when they had offered *ṣalāh* with the Prophet and observed the state of his *rukūʿ* which they have described in these words: 'We used to hear sounds coming from his bosom as if something was being cooked in a pot on the stove' (*Abū Dāwūd, Tirmidhī*), that they realized the true significance of it. They had learnt from the Qur'ān that *ṣalāh* was the favourite occupation of a truthful believer but until they had heard the Prophet say, 'The coolness of my eyes lies in *ṣalāh*' (*Nasā'ī*) and, 'O Bilāl! Give the call to *ṣalāh* and bring comfort to my heart,' (*Abū Dāwūd*) they had no clear idea of the intensity of the attachment. They had repeatedly read in the Qur'ān the exhortation to supplicate God and had also heard that He is displeased with those who do not beseech Him humbly for their needs. They were not unaware of the meaning of 'humbling one's self', 'perseverance' and 'crying' but the reality of it dawned upon them only when they saw the Prophet placing his forehead on the ground, in the Battle of Badr, and crying out to the Almighty from the depth of his heart: 'O Lord! I beg You in the name of Your Promise and Your Covenant. O Lord! If You decide [to destroy these handful of men] then You shall not be worshipped' (*Bukhārī*).

They noticed the extreme anguish of Abū Bakr which forced him to cry out 'O Messenger of God! It is enough.' They knew that the essence of supplication lay in humbleness and submission and an entreaty was precious to the extent to which it possessed these attributes, but the real import of 'humbleness' and 'submission' was perceived by them only when they heard the Prophet making this prayer at ʿArafah:

> O Lord! You hear what I say and see where I am and in whatever state. You know what is secret and what is manifest in me, and nothing concerning me is hidden from You. I am in distress, a beggar. I beg You for protection and succour. You fear is gripping me. I confess my sins. I entreat You like a poor, helpless supplicant. I beseech Thee like a wretched sinner. I implore Thee like an afflicted, awe-stricken slave – a slave whose head is bowed before You, whose tears are flowing in Your presence, and whose body is bent [in utter submission] – a slave who is lying prostrate on the ground begging and imploring and crying his heart out. O Lord! Do not reject my prayer. Have mercy on me. O You, the Best and Most Excellent of Givers, and the Noblest of Helpers (*Kanz al-ʿAmal* on the authority of Ibn ʿAbbās).

QUR'ĀNIC ETHICS

They had read in the Qur'ān about the worthlessness of this world and the permanence of the Hereafter. They knew by heart the *āyah*, *The life of the world is but a pastime and a game. Lo! The home of the Hereafter – that is Life* (30: 64). But they could comprehend its fundamental significance and be acquainted with its practical interpretation solely from the life of the Prophet. It was only by observing his way of living and the painfully low level of material comfort that prevailed in his household that they felt what was meant by considering the life after death to be the real existence. His day-to-day life reflected the motto: 'O Lord! There is no joy other than the joy to come' (*Bukhari*).

When from this brief exhortation and practical life-pattern they came to know about the details of the cloudless joys and comforts of Paradise and endless torture of Hell from the Prophet, they were seized with the mixed feelings of fear and eagerness and the picture of both the ultimate resting places remained constantly alive before their eyes.

Likewise, they were well-acquainted with the meanings of moral virtues like compassion, humility, affability and gentleness but they realized the full scope of their implication, their application in real life and the proper ways and occasions of putting them into practice only when they had an experience of the behaviour of the Prophet towards the weak and the indigent, and towards his own friends and companions, family members and domestic servants, and heard his exhortations and admonitions in that regard. They had received the command from the Qur'ān to fulfil the rights of the general body of Muslims but its numerous forms like visiting the sick, attending the funeral and making a prayer for the welfare of anyone who sneezed were such that most of the people could, perhaps, not think of them on their own. Similarly, the Qur'ān has enjoined kindness to parents and to others who have a claim, but how many moral teachers have dreamt of the lofty standard held out in the following Tradition:

> The highest grade of the loyalty and kindliness of a son towards his parents is that, after their death, he showed affection to their friends and behaved with them in a benevolent and obliging manner (*Muslim*).

Few have attained the level of gentlemanliness in social conduct shown in this *ḥadīth*:

> When a goat was slaughtered in the Prophet's house he would often get it cut into pieces and send the pieces of meat to ladies who were the friends of his deceased wife, Khadījah (*Bukhārī*).

From these few examples drawn from the *ḥadīth* of the Prophet's sayings and doings one can imagine the guidance the traditions furnish in different branches of life, what new knowledge they impart and what a treasure-house they constitute for humanity.

THE ATMOSPHERE REQUIRED FOR VIRTUOUS BEHAVIOUR

On the other hand, the history of religions and communities bears witness to the fact that mere legislation is not enough to bring about a deed in its true spirit and to create the atmosphere that is needed to make it effective and purposeful. For instance, the brief command to establish prayers cannot produce the inner feeling that helps in the preservation of its form and spirit, encourages its regular observance and leads to the attainment of the desired moral, spiritual and collective results. For it, rules and principles, guidance and proprieties are needed that lend grandeur and effectiveness to the act.

The essential conditions of ablution, cleanliness, understanding, humility, peace and calmness have been laid in the Qur'ān for this very reason. It should not be hard to appreciate that the proper climate in which the fruits of *ṣalāh* are borne forth and its moral, spiritual and collective benefits accrue, will be generated in proportion to the attention paid to these requisites and formalities.

Students of the *ḥadīth* of the Prophet will be aware that his precepts and sayings have made the *ṣalāh* a most efficacious means of inner purification, moral uplift and God-consciousness as well as a means for training and instruction of the *Ummah* and for the promotion of discipline and solidarity in it. From him we have learned the virtues of ablution and precise formulation of intention, the importance of going to the mosque, the prayer of the way, the correct manner of entering the mosque and the formula of remembrance of God, the salutation of the mosque (meaning practices firmly established by the conduct of the Holy Prophet), the virtue of waiting in the mosque for *ṣalāh,* the reward of congregation, the reward of *adhān* and *iqāmah* (second call to prayer uttered immediately before the commencement of the *farḍ* prayer), the office of *Imāmah* and the requirement to follow the *Imam* implicitly, the arrangement of rows, the excellence of people sitting together for the recitation of the Names, Praises and Attributes of the Lord and for religious education and instruction, the correct way of coming out of the mosque and the special prayer for the occasion, etc. Add to it the condition of the Prophet's *ṣalāh,* his enthusiasm for the supererogatory prayers and the description of his absorption in prayer and lamentation during the recitation of the Qur'ān (which have been described in detail in the Traditions) and you will see what a high degree of excellence the *ṣalāh* of the *Ummah* acquired and how wonderful is the intellectual and emotional atmosphere that is generated by it. On the same basis, think of the other obligatory duties of *ṣawm*, *zakāh* and *ḥajj* and judge for yourself how far they can retain their effectiveness and the ability to stir the deepest feelings of the devotees, and prove helpful in the building up of a new society, if these acts of worship are shorn of the virtues and formalities mentioned in the Traditions and isolated from the atmosphere we have just indicated.

The life, precepts and sayings of the Prophet, in reality, provide the climate for faith in which it thrives and bears fruit. Religion is not the name of a soulless dogma or wooden ethical code. It cannot endure without genuine emotions, solid facts and practical examples.

The best and most reliable collection of these feelings, events and instances is the one related to the personality of the sacred Prophet and derived from the record of his life. Many faiths became crippled so soon because they did not possess an authentic record of the precepts and practices of their Prophets. The atmosphere in which adherents prosper morally and spiritually and withstand successfully the onslaughts of godlessness and materialism was not available to them. They, ultimately, tried to fill the void with the accounts of the lives and attainments of saints and holy men and their discourses and utterances, but succeeded only in reducing religion to a package of innovations, rituals and ingenious interpretations. The hollowness of these faiths and communities, as regards reliable life-records of their Prophets, is a historical fact upon which a great deal has been written already.

One of the proofs of Islam being the last and eternal religion is that it was never overtaken by such a disaster. The intellectual and spiritual environment in which the Companions of the Prophet spent their lives has been preserved in its pristine purity for all time to come through the *ḥadīth*. Thanks to them, it is quite possible for anyone belonging to the succeeding generations to break away instantly from his own surroundings and begin to live in the environment in which the Prophet himself is present – he is speaking to the Companions and the Companions are listening to him intently. Forms of action are seen side by side with precepts, and episodes of feeling along with forms of action – an environment in which an idea can be formed of the kind of deeds and morals that originate from faith and the design of life that is determined by belief in the Hereafter. It is a window through which the family life of the Prophet, the house where he lived, the usual way in which he spent his nights, and the level of material comforts enjoyed by the members of his household can be distinctly viewed. The state of his genuflexion can be seen with the eyes, and the melody of his hymns and prayers can be heard with the ears. How, then, can anyone be guilty of negligence who sees the Prophet's eyes overflowing with tears and feet swollen, and hears him protesting earnestly, 'Should I not be a thankful slave?' (*Bukhārī*).

How can they be in two minds about the worthlessness of this world? And how can they remain unmoved by the call of asceticism when they can 'see' that fire was not lighted in the Prophet's house for as many as two months on end or when they observe the stone tied to his stomach to banish hunger, the marks of the mat on his back, the remainder of the gold meant for charity being spent anxiously in the path of God before retiring to bed and the oil for the lamp being borrowed from the neighbour during the last illness? Where would one go for a lesson in nobility of mind and character who has seen the Prophet attending upon the members of his family, showing affection to his children, leniency to his servants, kindness towards the Companions and forbearance and compassion towards the enemies?

In fact, not only is the door of the Prophet's dwelling open in this atmosphere through which all this is seen by the viewers but also the doors of the dwellings of the blessed Companions, as is everything else – their style of living, the burning of their hearts, the ardour of their nights, their activity and occupation in the market and ease and tranquillity in the mosque, their devoutedness and self-surrender, the ceaseless attacks of the carnal desires on them, their whole-hearted submission to the Almighty and their human weakness – is visible. Here the glorious self-denial of Abū Ṭalḥah Anṣārī when he put off the candle and made out as though he was eating until his guest had taken his own meal meets the eye (*Bukhārī*), as well as, the unique incident of Kaʿab bin Mālik's staying away from the Battle of Tabūk and how he acknowledged that his own indolence was the only reason for not making necessary preparations to join the expedition (*Bukhārī*).

In brief, it is a natural environment in which life is present in its true colours and the manifold facets of human personality are on display, and the *aḥādīth* of the Prophet have been made safe for eternity by painting a vivid picture of the Era of the Apostle in its minutest details.

The preservation of the historical portrait of the Era of the Prophet along with that of the Companions is an achievement of the Muslims of which they can justly be proud. It is unequalled in the annals of religions and communities. A faith that has to endure till the end of time and provide proper incentive to action and wholesome nourishment to the heart and mind cannot remain alive and active without the environment that is peculiar to it. This environment has been preserved till Doomsday by means of the *ḥadīth*. The history of the collection and compilation of the *ḥadīth* emphatically shows that it was not a chance occurrence. The attention of the Companions was drawn towards writing down the *ḥadīth* even during the Prophet's lifetime and a large part of the sayings was preserved by them. Then, the compilation and arrangement of the Hadith narratives was the task of their immediate successors. Thousands of scholars and researchers studied and worked all the way to Iran, Khurasan and Turkestan. Their phenomenal memory, resoluteness and dedication, the birth of the masters of *Asmā' al-Rijāl* (the study of narrators, a most important branch of *ḥadīth* literature which was created as an aid to the formal criticism of the *ḥadīth*) and the science of narration, and, finally, the enduring interest of the *Ummah* in the subject and its popularity and propagation in the whole of the Islamic World – all these facts go to prove that like the preservation of the Qur'ān, the preservation of the *ḥadīth*, too, was willed by God. In his infinite wisdom, the Lord had decided that the reports of the sayings and practices of the Prophet be collected and made safe forever. It was due to it that the continuity of the Glorious Life was maintained and the moral, spiritual and academic legacy the Companions had inherited directly went on reaching the *Ummah* during all the stages of its history. In this way, the process of 'succession' continued not only in respect of beliefs and injunctions but in the emotional and temperamental fields as well. The mental and emotional disposition of the age of the Companions was duly transmitted from one generation and class to another because of the *ḥadīth*.

CONTINUITY OF RELIGIOUS OUTLOOK

In the long and chequered history of the *Ummah* this quality and temperament never left it altogether – it did not become wholly extinct at any time – and there were always found in it people who could be said to possess the nature and disposition of the Companions. The same passion for worship, the same piety and devoutness, the same constancy and steadfastness, the same humility and introspection of the self, the same ardour for the Hereafter, the same detachment from the material world, the same fervour for sanctioning what was lawful and prohibiting what was forbidden, the same revulsion for innovations and the same keenness to follow the doings and practices of the Prophet which are the fruits of the study of the Traditions and of keeping company with those who have received illumination from the bosom of the sacred Apostle are evident in them. The mental and emotional disposition of the *Ummah* has endured from the first century of Islam to the modern materialistic times. From Sufyān Thawrī, ʿAbdullāh bin Mubārak and Imām Aḥmad bin Hanbal to Mawlānā Faẓlur Raḥmān Ganj Moradabādī, Mawlānā Rashīd Aḥmad Gangohī and Mawlānā Syed ʿAbdullāh Ghaznavī we have an unbroken chain of its glowing symbols. As long as the matchless stock of the *ḥadīth* remains and the process of benefiting from it continues, the true disposition and temperament of the *Ummah* in which solicitude for the Hereafter is dominant over attachment to the present world, the confirmed practice of the Prophet over custom, and spiritualism over materialism will endure. It will never be that the Muslims, as a whole, fall a victim to gross materialism or get immersed altogether in innovations, worldliness and rejection of the life to come. On the contrary, under its influence, reformative movements will always be at work and the process of renovation will continue in the *Ummah* and one group or another will at all time be striving in it for the promotion of *Sunnah* and *Sharīʿah*.

Those who want to deprive the *Ummah* of this priceless source of life, vitality and guidance, and seek to undermine faith in its genuineness and reliability do not realise what a grievous disservice they are doing to the Muslims. They do not know that their efforts can end up only in making the *Ummah* rootless and wayward exactly in the same way as the enemies of other faiths and the vicissitudes of time have played havoc with great religions. If they are doing it deliberately, no one can be a greater antagonist of Islam for there is no other way of reviving and recreating the temperament and fundamental inclination that was the grand peculiarity of the Companions. It can either be produced directly from the company of the Prophet or indirectly through the *aḥādīth* which are a living portrait of that era and an eloquent record of the life of the Prophet.

16

Knowing Allah Through Muḥammad

Muhammad al-Ghazali

I am one of the many thousands of people who believe in Allah, recite His praises, avow His glory and majesty, and are strengthened by His bounty and support. I have come to know the Almighty through the Prophet Muḥammad, upon him be peace. I read the Qur'ān and I studied the Prophet's biography; then I discovered my inner self harmonising with his message. My heart and mind were refreshed by his call. Thus, I became one of the vast multitude who have accepted Allah as their Lord, Islam as their way of life, and Muḥammad as their guide and Prophet.

There were people who knew nothing about Allah at all but Muḥammad illumined the way for them, and led them through their own hearts to their true Master. And those who knew Him, but did so mistakenly, thinking that He had a partner, to them also Muḥammad came and re-established the belief in Absolute Oneness, refuting once and for all the supposition that Allah could have a son, or daughter, or a partner, or an opposite, or an analogue in majesty.

Or have they taken protectors apart from Him? Allah – He is the only Protector; He revives the dead, and He is capable of everything. No matter how you have differed on anything, the Judgement is still with Allah. [Say, therefore:] *'Such is Allah, my Lord;*

on Him have I relied, and to Him do I turn.' Originator of heaven and earth, He has granted you spouses from among yourselves as well as pairs of livestock by which He multiplies you. There is nothing like Him! He is the Alert, the Observant. He holds the key to heaven and earth; He extends sustenance and measures it out to whom He wills. Surely He is aware of everything (42: 9–12).

THE PROPHET'S KNOWLEDGE OF ALLAH

No one, past or present, knew their Lord the way that Muḥammad knew Allah. Indeed, his knowledge sprang from *shuhūd*, or witnessing. The Muslim who is keen to emulate the example of the Prophet will be able to discern certain special characteristics of Muḥammad's knowledge and awareness, in the penetrating and emotionally charged words he used when speaking to, or about, Allah. Clearly, there was nothing either doubtful or contrived about his utterance. Whoever reads or hears the words which Muḥammad used when addressing his Lord will immediately sense a quickening of his pulse to the flow of those words, and a corresponding rise in the intensity of his emotions. In the end he will have no alternative but to be humble and to submit to the Lord of all the worlds.

I remember on one occasion trying to follow the distances mentioned in a study of astronomy, distances so great that they raced beyond my ability even to imagine them. Indeed, I felt myself growing ever smaller until I looked down to the earth at my feet and thought of what lay hidden beneath its surface. I realised then that I was capable neither of comprehending nor even of perceiving anything. Have we any idea of the number of things there are in this world about which we know nothing at all?

Then, as I was reflecting on these thoughts, I recalled how Allah, Exalted is He, has described Himself in the Qur'ān:

The Merciful is established on the Throne: to Him belongs all that is in heaven and earth and all that is between them, and all that is beneath the surface. If you speak aloud [or not, it is all the same to Him], *for surely He knows the concealed and what is even more hidden. Allah, there is no god but He. To Him belong the Glorious Names* (20: 4–8).

The sublime radiance of the lote-tree in the seventh heaven and the tiniest seed in the darkest recesses of the earth are as one in His Knowledge, may His Name be praised! I found myself so filled with awe for the Great Creator that I was at a loss to put it into words. But by His Will I did discover the words to express what I felt. These were words used by the Prophet in his *ṣalāh*. In the *ḥadīth*, ʿAlī ibn Abī Ṭālib related: 'And when he assumed the *rukūʿ* or the bowing position, he would say: 'O My Lord, for You I have bowed down, and in You I have placed my faith, and to You I have committed myself. My ears, my eyes, my marrow, my bones, and my sinews have humbled themselves before You.' When he raised his head from the *rukūʿ* position he would say: 'May Allah listen to those who praise Him. Our Lord, may Your praises fill the heavens, and fill the earth, and fill everything between them, and fill whatever else remains to be filled after that.' When he assumed the *sajdah* or prostrating position he would say: 'Our Lord, for You I have made *sajdah*, and in You I have placed my faith, and to You I have committed myself. My face lies prostrated before the One who created it, and fashioned it, and opened within it its sense of hearing and its sight. Blessed be Allah, the Best of Creators.'

In *rukūʿ* and *sajdah* before the Creator of heaven and earth, an inspired servant kneels and whispers exemplary words – what every being should utter by way of greeting to the Possessor of the perfect attributes – for in this supplication, one may discern perfect Divinity and perfect servanthood.

Without a doubt, the first Muslim – and that is the station of Muḥammad among the Prophets, the believers, martyrs, and righteous – was an expert in the art of *dhikr* and *duʿā'*, without equal in giving thanks or seeking forgiveness. We shall endeavour to clarify this truth by examining something of what has been preserved of the *duʿā'* of the Prophet Muḥammad, upon him be peace.

Recently I looked again through the sacred scriptures of the other religions, and found none of them the equal of the Qur'ān in its glorification of Allah, and its exposition of His splendour and majesty. In the Qur'ān, the exquisite names of Allah are mentioned hundreds of times in the course of its narration of the stories of the Prophets, in its verses of legislation, in its description of the wonders of nature, and in its description of the events of Judgement Day and what is to come thereafter. Furthermore, the Qur'ān refuses to allow its glorification of Allah to be merely abstract, without the energy to stir a heart or project a way of life. Indeed, the Prophet Muḥammad, upon him be peace, translated the way of the Qur'ān in every aspect of his daily life, and became the ideal – 'a man of God', focusing his attention on Allah alone, and doing everything that he did in this world in His Name.

The person to whom Allah has granted spiritual strength and richness will not be shaken by fear or desire, nor by considerations of numerical inferiority or superiority. The spiritually observant person will be equally at home whether alone or at a wedding feast. If his only concern is the life to come he will never be daunted by the setbacks and obstacles of the present life.

The heart of Muḥammad, upon him be peace, was constantly occupied with his Lord, immersed in the sense of His Majesty. Indeed, this profound awareness was the basis for his relationship with both God and people. Follow closely his thoughts in this *duʿā'*:

> Our Lord, by Your Knowledge of the Unseen, and by Your power over Your creation, grant me life so long as You know life to hold good for me, and grant me death when You know death to hold good for me! Our Lord, I ask You for the fear of You in public and in private, and I ask You for [the ability to speak] the word of truth in tranquillity and in anger, and I ask You for frugality in wealth and in poverty, and I ask You for happiness which is never exhausted, and I ask You for pleasure which is never ending, and I ask You for contentment with Your decisions, and I ask You for the finer life after death, and I ask You for the pleasure of looking upon Your Face, and meeting You without ever having undergone great suffering, and without ever having been subjected to misleading temptation.
> Our Lord, adorn us with the adornment of faith, and make of us guides who are rightly guided.

And still there are those who claim that Muḥammad was a pretender to Prophethood! How they regard the Truth! From the beginning of time to the present, no human being ever addressed Allah with words nobler than his words, nor ever devoted himself to Allah with greater ardour than he. Who then can be accounted truthful if Muḥammad was a fraud?

17

The Prophet's Technique

Khurshid Ahmad

The personality of the Prophet Muḥammad is a myriad one. All colours shine there. You can study him as a human being moving about in the ordinary routine of life, behaving as a father, as a husband, as a member of the family. You can study his attitude to the elders, to the youngsters; his role as a statesman, a general, a commander and as a ruler. Common in all these aspects is that he was a *dāʿī il'al-Ḥaqq* (a caller to the Truth), a *dāʿī il'Allāh* (a caller to God). It is this central theme – the Prophet as the *dāʿī il'al-Ḥaqq* – which provides the key to his personality. It is this aspect of the Prophet which is emphasised over and above others in the Qur'ān.

Perhaps the most significant and all-embracing expression of this is that the Prophet has been called a *shahīd* (or *shāhid*) – a witness unto Truth: *The Messenger of God is a witness (shahīd) over you, so be you witnesses (shuhadā') over mankind* (22: 78).

For us what is really important is that on the one hand, the Prophet has been called *shahīd* or witness and on the other, the entire Muslim *Ummah* has been called *shuhadā'* or witnesses. Therefore it is possible to see that the chief characteristics of the Prophet's life are also the distinctive characteristics of the *Ummah*.

It is because of this we find that a solitary voice is heard in the wilderness and soon there are echoes from here, there and everywhere. We find that this one man ignites a new faith, produces a new generation of people, canalises them into a new movement and launches a struggle against the forces of evil. This struggle continues and produces a new society – a society which is distinct from the overall society in which it takes place and eventually prevails over it. It enters history and then gives a new direction to history. This transformation emanates from the Prophet's distinctive characteristic of being the *dāʿī il'al-Ḥaqq*.

The importance of studying the *sīrah* or life history of the Prophet from this viewpoint lies not so much in the content but in trying to suggest an attitude and approach. It is the responsibility of each one of us as the followers of the Prophet to study his life from this angle and to see what light it sheds for us in our own times and on the problems which beset us. Then you will find a newly discovered similarity between your situation and his situation, between your conditions and the conditions which you find portrayed in the *sīrah*. Then you will discover the meaning of the verse: *You have indeed, in the Messenger of God an excellent exemplar for whoever places his hopes in God and the Final Day, and who remembers Allah much* (33: 21).

In stressing this approach, let us cast a quick look at the entire life perspective of the noble Prophet.

THE *PRE-NUBUWWAH* PERIOD

The *Pre-Nubuwwah* period or period before Prophethood is very important, in that it is the period of preparation. What strikes us most is the pure, simple, clean and uncorrupted life of the Prophet. It is distinct. It shines like a diamond among stones. It is the clear and pure life which gives us a clue to the making of the man with a mission. The person with a mission must keep this in view. Not merely the words he speaks, the high ideas he expresses, the fascinating speeches he can make, but the silent impact of his personality, and the example he sets for the people, which is to be his greatest aid in this mission – leaving apart the personal importance for him here and in the hereafter. Perhaps the greatest testimony to this in the Prophet's life came from his wife – a person who knew his weakness and against whom no facades could be built up – when he came back from the cave of Ḥirā' after the first *waḥī* or revelation. Then in the seventh year of the *Hijrah* comes the testimony of the greatest enemy of the Prophet – Abū Sufyān, the leader of the Quraysh, when he was summoned to the court of the Byzantine emperor Heraclius. There Abū Sufyān testified, as did the Prophet's wife Khadījah, to the completely honest, simple and humanitarian life of the Prophet. And what more can be said about the life of the Prophet than the testimony of the Qur'ān? In *Sūrah Yūnus*, Allah presents a testimony to the Truth and veracity of the Qur'ān and to the life of the Prophet by describing him as *a human being who has lived amongst you* (10: 3). Here the entire life of the Prophet is being presented as a testimony to the Truth.

The second point which strikes me during this period is the Prophet's involvement and participation in society. Out of the many, there are three examples which can be quoted here.

Firstly, there was a virtuous agreement (Ḥilf al-Fuḍūl) between the best and the most virtuous in Arabian society to uphold five things, 'to establish peace and virtue, to help the poor, to help the wayfarer, to help the persecuted and finally to see that any *ẓālim* or persecutor is driven out of power'. By co-operating on these points, the Prophet showed his involvement and interest in that society, demonstrating a way out of the condition in which the society found itself.

Secondly, there is the incident of the Kaʿbah, when the roof was rebuilt and the walls raised up and the Black Stone was to be replaced. This was a very august and sacred moment but every tribe was eager to have the honour of replacing it. To settle all questions with honour, swords were taken out of their sheaths. Because of the Prophet's standing in society, he was accepted as the arbiter. He resolved the issue in a very simple and peaceful way. By placing the Black Stone on a sheet, all the leaders of the tribes lifted it together. In this symbolic way, all tribes who were torn apart by rivalries were put together by this simple act of goodness. The cloth was raised by all concerned and the Prophet himself put the Black Stone in the required place. This is involvement in society. This is solving a decisive problem.

Thirdly, the Prophet participated in trade. This represents economic involvement with society. In a society which was primarily concerned with commerce, the Prophet participated and showed a better example. It is because of this that he was called *as-Ṣādiq al-Amīn* or the truthful and the trustworthy.

So whether it be in the political, tribal or economic arena, we find involvement, we find a distinctive example and we find that the situation is created whereby people start looking towards the *dāʿī* as different from them and as one who can solve their difficulties.

During this period there was a great restlessness in the Prophet, and unending agony of the plight in which he found the people around him. He was moved to the last fibre of his being. It is this situation which took him to prayer, to contemplation and to meditation of Allah. And through the pain of this restlessness, this wandering for the Truth, this search for the Lord, the body becomes capable of receiving the message, understanding it and conveying it to others.

THE FIRST PHASE OF PROPHETHOOD

This extends to more or less three years. During this period, the distinctive characteristic is that the message is not conveyed publicly and openly. It is not a period of secret work but a period of silent persuasion. The scale of the work remains limited during this period. The people contacted are only those who are in direct touch with Muḥammad or those whom he himself contacts. The first converts to Islam – Khadījah, Abū Bakr, ʿAlī, Zayd ibn Ḥarīthah – were affected immediately after the beginning of the *waḥī* or revelations from God. And then through Abū Bakr, people like ʿUthmān and Zubayr come to the fold of Islam.

Perhaps the best understanding of this period can be had through a study of the early Makkan *Sūrahs* of the Qur'ān, particularly, *al-Muzzammil* (Chapter 73) and *al-Muddaththir* (Chapter 74). These *Sūrahs* give the strategy which is being taught to the Prophet and they foreshadow what is to happen to the movement, how opposition is to come. During this period *dhikr* (remembrance of Allah) and *ṣabr* (patience and perseverance) are the values emphasised.

During this period, the basic *daʿwah* or message is emphasised in clear terms, in words that penetrate the depths of the heart. The style is extremely simple, small sentences; just like cut diamonds. The emphasis again and again is on the concept of *tawḥīd*, life after death, the relationship between one person and another – a relationship of compassion and mercy – the destitute and the starved the oneness of the human being which comes naturally as a result of the Oneness of God. These are the basic themes.

Another striking theme is that with increased and repeated emphasis, the Prophet is commanded to prepare himself for the mission. Here comes the *tazkiyah* or purification aspect. Prayer, particularly *ṣalāt al-layl* (night prayer), as an instrument in this preparation is especially emphasised. Where it is said that, *And your garments purify* (74: 4), does not merely refer to the cleansing of bodily clothes but rather to the purification of the character. During this period the real strategy is built up in preparation for the great Call.

THE SECOND PHASE OF PROPHETHOOD

This is the phase of open declaration. From this time to the *Hijrah*, broadly speaking, there are three stages. Firstly, two years when the Prophet was charged to make a public pronouncement of the faith (*qum fa andhir,* arise and warn, as the Qur'ān declares). He makes it with no fear of any adversity, proclaiming it from the Mount of Ṣafā. Open persuasion and open dissemination of the message then begins.

These first two years are distinct because of the particular types of reaction to the message. The message is regarded as insignificant and irrelevant – just the cry of a human being which will die out in its own way. Then comes ridicule and an unending volley of allegations and objections: 'This is the speech of the madman, of the wizard and the sorcerer; what he says are just the stories of the bygone'. Then it is realised that whatever is being said is in the nature of a challenge to the status quo, to the people in authority and to the system as such. The attempt is then made to persecute and opposition in a different way begins.

This is, in a way, the next phase which starts from the fifth year of the *Nubuwwah*, approximately, and continues until the time of the *Hijrah*. During this period, the opponents are fully conscious of the great challenge which this message poses to them. They try to win over each one from this new group, especially the Prophet. They promise him sovereignty, women and wealth – on condition that he abandons the message.

Having failed in this method, they then sought to persecute, to harass, to beat and to torture. Stones were thrown, thorns were laid in the way of the Prophet, dirt and filth were flung upon him. He was beaten and made to bleed. The Muslims were persecuted, dragged across the burning sands of Arabia and suffocated. It is during this period that the first *Hijrah* or migration took place – to Abyssinia (now called Ethiopia). Then there was the boycott of Banū Ḥāshim, the clan of the Prophet. It was a boycott that lasted approximately three years. All supplies were cut off, so much so that the Muslims had to eat whatever they could find in the wild.

The last three years of the Makkan period in one way represents a continuation of the persecution and in another way, a departure from the same. The Quraysh realised that it was not possible for them in anyway to break the will of this man. This is also the period when the message seeped into new places – to tribes outside Makkah. The message of Islam had now found its way to Madinah.

The *Hijrah* then takes place. The Prophet comes to Madinah, a new society is established and a new state. Now we have the realisation of that movement in the society as faith and civilisation. The force of evil challenges this civilisation, this centre of the Islamic movement and it retaliates with force. The fight begins from the sixth month of the *Hijrah* and in the second year there is the Battle of Badr, the importance of which can be discerned from the Prophet's Prayer: 'O my Lord, if this handful of the believers are obliterated this day then You shall not be praised, O Allah, You shall not be worshipped, O Allah.' He succeeded and God is worshipped and God shall be worshipped.

Then from the Battle of Uḥud to the Treaty of Ḥudaybiyyah there is another period in the Prophet's life. Ḥudaybiyyah is again a turning point. Although *prima facie* it seemed as a kind of retreat, in fact, as the Qur'ān says, *it was a clear victory* (48: 1), since it was because of Ḥudaybiyyah that it was possible to connect with Makkah to consolidate the Islamic state, to conquer Khaybar, to safeguard the state from other dangers and to spread the message to the whole of Arabia and, indeed, far beyond.

In particular, what is striking in the Prophet's life is the vision of total change. The Prophet does not want merely to ameliorate this economic ill or that social evil or that political problem. All these are to be solved in the process of a complete transformation of the life of the individual and of the society. All this is on the basis of *tawḥīd* and God-given *hidāyah* or guidance. Sometimes this fact is not kept in view of the Makkan period. It is alleged that perhaps this breadth, this vastness of vision comes after the *Hijrah*. This is however, wrong. From the very beginning, this total concept of change and the vision of the victory of religion, the success and supremacy of this way is there. There are many instances to support this. This is the vision which inspires the *dā'ī* even in those early days. This faith, this perseverance, this steadfastness is really striking. It is not in the spirit of any arrogance, or superiority or aggressiveness. It is sweet sympathy, it is love, it is *raḥmah* or mercy, it is eagerness to save people from the Fire, to protect them, to show them the right path, to illumine and shed away the darkness. It is this spirit which permeates the entire life of the Prophet, from the first act of his mission to his last day. The Prophet's sense of responsibility is overwhelming. Study the prayers of the Prophet. It is a method through which you can approach the 'spirit' of the Prophet.

A CREATIVE RESPONSE

As regards how the Prophet worked amongst people, this is a vast topic on which you will find a wealth of information in the *sīrah*. One thing stands out – the creativity of the *dā'ī*, responding to specific situations, in adopting a method that suits the occasion. As far as the basic message is concerned it is unchanged. As far as the basic strategy of work is concerned, it, too, is unchanged. But the *dā'ī* is eager to use every opportunity as it presents itself and to find a way out of that situation through applying his creative genius.

Everyone who has to work for the cause of Truth in any age or in any circumstance has to learn a lot from this aspect of the example of the Holy Prophet – how the *dā'ī* is ever conscious, ever creative, ever vigilant; sticking to his message but devising new methods, new tactics to meet the situation.

This applies to the first three years and the continuing process of silent persuasion throughout the Makkan period. During the early period the Prophet had to offer prayers secretly in hidden places. This process continued until ʿUmar's embrace of Islam. But the Prophet used to offer the prayer which is offered after sunrise at the Kaʿbah. This prayer was an *ʿurf* or custom of the Arabs. He availed himself of this one opportunity to bring his practices out in the open.

Another example is the first open proclamation of the message. From the viewpoint of the Prophet's work technique it is highly significant. He selected for this purpose the raised platform, Ṣafā, a place which was used for important gatherings, the best that was available in that situation. He went there and called to the people in the manner recognised in any emergency, making them realise that they were being called to something significant and important. When the people came, he did not start by saying 'I am God's Prophet. Accept me.' Instead he asked in words like these: 'If I tell you that there is an aggressive force behind these mountains out to crush you would you believe that?' And they answered, 'Yes, we shall, because we have found you to be honest and truthful.'

A basis is thus built up for communication between them. He has also made them realise that if he were to warn them against a threat or penalty, they would accept this warning. And then the Prophet said, 'I want to invite you to the obedience of the One God and ask you to shun the worship of false gods.' The reaction, of course, was ridicule. But notice the technique of the *dāʿī*, how he approaches the problem, how he gradually develops his thesis and how he totally disarms his opponents, whatever be their reactions.

The method he used with his family members was, however, different. The Prophet called them to a feast – an Arab custom – to bring them together and used this occasion for the propagation of his message. And because it is the family, the appeal is personal and emotional: 'Who is going to be my helper in this cause?'

Then of course, the occasion of *ḥajj* was used by the Prophet. Even the festivals of the Arabs were used. He would go to those festivals not for the festivities, but to go round every camp conveying the message to the people. The conquest of Makkah also provides a very interesting example of his work technique. And on the personal plane we could look at the way the Prophet tackled the problem of disaffection created by the distribution of the booty after the Battle of Ḥunayn. His speech to the Anṣār is one of the best examples of applied psychology. All parts of the problem are considered; the incipient *fitnah* (temptation, tribulation) is not neglected but faced squarely and in a clear, straightforward and understanding manner.

As far as the technique is concerned, how the demands of pragmatism and gradualism are combined with the demands of an uncompromising ideology is a tricky point for some. If you study the Prophet's life from this viewpoint, you will find a unique balance between the two. For example, when the Banū Thaqīf, one of the most highly developed tribes in Arabia came to the Prophet saying that they were ready to accept Islam provided they were allowed to continue drinking wine, taking *ribā* or interest and practising adultery their demand was not accepted. On the other hand, some *Ṣaḥābah* or Companions presented a situation to the Prophet whereby some people said they would accept Islam but could not fulfil the duties of *ṣalāh, zakāh* or *jihād*. The Prophet told them not to worry but to call the new Muslims to *ṣalāh*. Then he continued, by way of explanation, in these golden words, that once they really accept and practise *ṣalāh*, they would eventually take to *zakāh* and other matters as well.

Now you can see the demands of these two apparently conflicting cases poised together. This is only one instance. You will find dozens of them in the life of the Prophet. This is the way in which the workers of the Islamic movement should try to learn that gradualism and the uncompromising nature of ideals can co-exist and work together harmoniously. A study of the *sīrah* from this angle brings home the realisation that this is an on-going struggle and it is wrong to think that there is any short cut to it. It demands arduous effort and continuous work. Unless we are prepared for this continuous struggle we will not be able to discharge the responsibility of being a *dāʿī il'al-Ḥaqq*.

What gives promise and confidence is that if a list is made of all those persons who embraced Islam in the early period in particular – the first ten years of the Makkan period – one is struck by the fact that almost all of them were below the age of thirty-five. Indeed, most of them were between the ages of twenty-five and thirty-five. This of course, is significant in that a new revolutionary movement which stands for change should have its appeal and attraction in the minds and souls of those persons who are young, who are enthusiastic, who have something to live for and who will contemplate over the problems and respond to the situation. By the grace of Allah, may the youths of today take up this message, respond to it in the way the early Companions responded and seek from the noble Prophet guidelines for their individual and collective lives.

D. WORSHIP, ETHICS AND LAW

The Islamic Concept of Worship
Mustafa Ahmad al-Zarqa

Foundations of Islamic Morality
Sayyid Abul Ala Mawdudi

Inner Dimensions of Worship
Ismail al-Faruqi

Principles of *Ḥalāl* and *Ḥarām*
Yusuf al-Qaradawi

The *Sharīʿah* – Islamic Law
Khurram Murad

Inner Dimensions of the *Sharīʿah*
Khurram Murad

Introduction to Fiqh
Sayyid Sabiq

Understanding Juristic Differences
Ahmad Zaki Hammad

The Ethics of *Daʿwah* and Dialogue
Yusuf al-Qaradawi

18

The Islamic Concept of Worship

Mustafa Ahmad al-Zarqa

Worship, according to Islam, is a means for the purification of a human being's soul and his practical life. The basis of *ʿibādah* or worship is the fact that human beings are creatures and thus slaves of God, their Creator and their Lord, to whom they are destined to return. Thus a person's turning towards God, in intimate communion, reverence, and in the spirit of devotion and humble submission, is termed *ʿibādah*.

Worship is an indispensable part of all religions. It is motivated, however, in each religion by different objectives, assumes different forms and is performed under a different set of rules.

In some religions worship is a means to develop the attitude of asceticism and isolation from life. In these religions it seeks to develop a mentality which anathematises the enjoyment of the pleasures of this world. Then, there are other religions which consecrate certain places for the sake of worship and prohibit its performance at any other place. There are also religions which are of the view that worship can be performed only under the leadership of a particular class of people – ordained priests. People may, therefore, perform worship under the leadership of priests and only at the places consecrated for it. Thus, the nature as well as the form of worship differ from one religion to the other.

As for Islam, its conception of worship is related to its fundamental view that the true foundations of a good life are soundness of belief and thinking, purity of soul, and righteousness of action.

Through belief in the Oneness of God, who is invested with all the attributes of perfection, Islam seeks to purge human intellect of idolatry and superstition. In fact, polytheism and idolatry, which are opposed by Islam, degrade a human being to a level which is incompatible with his dignity. Islam fights against idolatry and polytheism in whichever form and to whatever extent they might be found.

Islam takes notice even of imperceptible forms of idolatry. It takes notice even of those beliefs and practices which do not appear to their adherents as tainted with idolatry. One of the manifestations of this concern is that Islam does not permit the performance of *ṣalāh* or ritual Prayer in front of a tomb, nor does it permit a person to swear in the name of anyone except God. All this is owing to the uncompromising hostility of Islam to idolatry. When Caliph ʿUmar saw that people had begun to sanctify the tree beneath which the Companions of the Prophet pledged to lay down their lives in the way of God on the occasion of Ḥudaybiyyah, he feared that its sanctification might corrupt peoples' beliefs. He, therefore, had it cut down. By destroying everything which might blur the distinction between the creature and the Creator, Islam brought people out of the darkness of superstition and ignorance to the full daylight of reality.

DISTINGUISHING FEATURES

The characteristic features of worship as propounded by Islam may be stated as the following:

1. Freedom from Intermediaries

Islam has liberated 'worship' from the bondage of intermediaries between a human being and his Creator. Islam seeks to create a direct link between a person and his Lord, thus rendering the intercession of intermediaries unnecessary.

Religious scholars in Islam, it may be pointed out, are neither intermediaries between a human being and God nor are they entitled to accept or reject acts of worship on behalf of God. Instead, they are equal to ordinary human beings in the sight of God. Rather, they have been burdened with the additional duty of imparting knowledge to those who lack knowledge. They will be deemed guilty if they hold it back from the seekers after knowledge. In other words, the *Sharīʿah* or the Islamic legal code, does not impose the domination of religious scholars on the rest of the people. The function of these scholars is merely to guide people in the right direction. This is amply borne out by what Allah said to the Prophet: *Remind them, for you are but one who reminds; you are not at all a warder over them* (88: 21–22).

The Prophet, may God bless him and grant him peace, once addressed the following words to his own daughter Fāṭimah, which again shows that all human beings stand on a footing of complete equality before God: 'O Fāṭimah, daughter of Muḥammad: I shall be of no help to you before Allah.'

2. Worship is not Confined to Specific Places

Islam has not only liberated a human being's *ʿibādah* from the bondage of intermediaries; it has also liberated it from confinement to specific places. Islam regards every place – whether it is one's dwelling, the back of an animal, the board of a vessel on the surface of the sea, or a *masjid* specifically built for worship – as pure enough for the performance of worship. Wherever a person might be, he can turn towards his Lord and enter into communion with Him. The Prophet has expressed this idea beautifully: 'The [whole of the] earth has been rendered for me a mosque, pure and clean.'

3. Worship is All-Embracing

Islam has also considerably widened the scope of worship. In Islam, worship is not confined to specified prayers and litanies which are to be performed on particular occasions. Rather, Islam considers every virtuous action which has been sincerely performed and with a view to carrying out the commandments of God and in order to seek His pleasure, an act of worship for which a human being will be rewarded. Thus, eating, drinking, sleeping and enjoyment of innocent recreation, even those worldly actions which satisfy a human being's physical needs and yield sensuous pleasures, become acts of worship when they are performed with true religious motives.

It is also an act of worship to try to strengthen one's body by providing it with its due of nourishment and sleep; by making it undertake exertion as well as giving it rest and recreation so as to enable it to shoulder the responsibilities which have been placed on it by God. In fact, if one does all this with the above-mentioned intention, one's action will be in harmony with the following saying of the Prophet: 'A believer who is possessed of strength is better and dearer to God than a believer who is weak.' In short, it is simply by purification of motives, that the actions which are part of worldly life, become acts of devotion and worship.

Thus, it is possible that a human being can advance spiritually even while he is fully enjoying the pleasures of worldly life. The reason is that during all this enjoyment his heart will remain in communion with God by virtue of the purity of his intentions, and owing to his having attached himself completely to the service of God. It will enable him to remain perpetually in the state of submission, obedience and devotion to God even during his working pursuits – and this is the very essence of worship. For Islam, unlike other religions, does not anathematise gratification of a person's instinctive bodily appetites. Islam does not even consider abstention from the satisfaction of these desires to be in any way an act of greater piety and virtue than satisfying them. Islam wants us to enjoy the pleasures and good things of life provided we do not transgress the limits of legitimacy, the rights of others, or injure the larger interests of society.

There is a profound wisdom and an important reason for this extension of the scope of worship. The reason is that Islam wants our hearts to remain in perpetual communion with our Lord. Islam also wants that we should observe ceaseless vigilance over our desires so that our lives may become a source of welfare for the life to come, as the Qur'ān says: *Seek the abode of the hereafter in that which Allah has given to you and neglect not your portion of the world* (28: 77). When we realise that even our enjoyment and pleasure can become acts of worship merely by virtue of purity of intention and motive, it becomes easy for us to render obedience to God continually and to direct all our attention in seeking Divine pleasure. For we will be confident that our devotion to God will not necessarily mean abandonment of worldly life nor a life of misery and wretchedness.

Good intention, will also prevent a person from forgetting God because of excessive self-indulgence. The Prophet has said that even when a person affectionately puts a piece of food in the mouth of his wife in order to strengthen bonds of matrimonial love, he is rewarded for it. This is understandable for he is trying to fulfil the purpose of living together with love and affection, the purpose which, as the Qur'ān says is the *raison d'être* of family life: *And of His signs is this: He created for you your partners that you might find rest in them and He ordained between you love and mercy* (30: 21).

INTENTIONS AND MOTIVES

Muslim jurists and scholars have proclaimed that good intention changes acts of habit (*ʿādah*) into acts of worship (*ʿibādah*). Good intention creates a world of difference in human life. It is owing to an absence of purity of intention that there are people who eat and drink and satisfy their animal desires and while doing so simply live on the same plane as animals do. The reason for this is that their actions are actuated by no other motive than the gratification of their animal desires. Of such people the Qur'ān declares: *Those who disbelieve, take their comfort in this life and eat even as the cattle eat, and the Fire is their habitation* (47: 12).

Conversely, there are others, apparently similar to those mentioned above, in so far as they also satisfy their desires and enjoy the pleasures of life. Nevertheless, thanks to the noble intention which motivates their actions, even their physical self-fulfilment becomes an act of worship for which they merit reward. The reason is that the motive behind all their actions is to live in compliance with the will of God. Their sublimity of motive is manifest in their day-to-day conduct and reflects the fact that they distinguish between good and evil.

What a world of difference it makes when we decide to orientate our lives towards God and purify our intentions. For it is this, and only this, which can transform our pursuit of pleasure and enjoyment into acts of worship, earning the eternal rewards of the hereafter and the satisfying pleasure of God.

This, then, is the Islamic philosophy of worship. Without saying 'no' to any of a person's legitimate physical needs and desires, Islam seeks to elevate humanity to a place which befits its dignity and status.

POSITION OF SPECIFIC RITUALS

The wide jurisdiction of worship, its incorporation into all acts which are performed with the intention of complying with the will of God, is sometimes used as a pretext to support the erroneous view that the formal rituals of worship such as prayers, fasting, *zakāh* and pilgrimage can be dispensed with; or that they are not very important. The truth, however, is quite contrary to this. In Islam, they are the chief means for strengthening one's attachment with God. Thus the view of those who are given to laxity in religious matters with regard to obligatory acts of worship, and who imagine that true faith does not consist of *ṣalāh* and *ṣawm*, and who believe that the basis of true faith is merely purity of heart, goodness of intention and soundness of conduct is absolutely misconceived. This constitutes a fundamental misrepresentation of the Islamic teachings.

So far as the intention to live a life of righteousness is concerned, some take the view that this does not lend itself to external observation. But such intention to do good alone does not mark off true people of faith from the rest. Religion, after all, has an external aspect in the same way as it has an internal one.

This attitude of deliberate disregard for obligations is destructive of the very foundations of religion. For, were this viewpoint to be adopted, everyone, even those who are opposed to religion, could claim to be the most devout of all worshippers! Prayers, and all other prescribed forms of worship for that matter, serve to distinguish the ones who do really have faith and who wish sincerely to serve God from those who are content with lip service. So important is Prayer that the Prophet has said: '*ṣalāh* is the pillar of the Islamic religion and whosoever abandons it, demolishes the very pillar of religion.'

A PRACTICAL IDEAL

The real purpose of Islam in declaring that *ʿibādah* embraces the whole of life is to make faith play a practical and effective role in reforming our lives, in developing in us an attitude of dignified patience and fortitude in the face of hardship and in creating in us the urge to strive for the prevalence of good and the extirpation of evil.

All this makes it amply evident that Islam is opposed to those defeatist and isolationist philosophies which scholars have termed as asceticism. It is that erroneous kind of asceticism which is based on world-renunciation, on resignation from the resources of life, on withdrawal from the life of action and struggle, on sheer stagnation and decadence. These things have nothing to do with Islam. Rather, they are the symbols of defeatism and escape from the struggle of life. For life requires strength, material resources and active habits. The role of Islam in the struggle of life is a positive one. It is through this attitude that Islam ensures the channelling of a person's powers and resources in such a manner as to lead eventually to general good. The Islamic system of worship is a means to ensure this soundness of orientation.

An event may be narrated here to illustrate the Islamic attitude to asceticism, and to disabuse minds of wrong notions of spiritual life. It is reported that ʿĀ'ishah, the mother of the faithful, once saw a person walking with his body stooped down and his back bent with weakness, appearing as if he were not fully alive, attracting thereby the glances of those around him. She inquired about him and was informed that he was a saintly person. ʿĀ'ishah denounced this kind of saintliness and said: 'ʿUmar, son of Khaṭṭāb, was the saintliest of people. But when he said something, he made himself heard; when he walked, he walked fast; and when he hit, he caused pain.'

19

Foundations of Islamic Morality

Sayyid Abul Ala Mawdudi

What we characterise as Islamic morality contains, according to the Qur'ān and the *aḥādīth*, four aspects or grades:

- *Īmān* or faith in God
- *Islām* or surrender to God
- *Taqwā* or God-consciousness
- *Iḥsān* or Godliness

Each of these four concepts are mutually linked. Each grows out of the one on which it rests and simultaneously provides a base for the other to grow.

ĪMĀN

Īmān is the foundation of this edifice. Upon it is built the structure of *islām* and then *ṭaqwā* and *iḥsān*. Without *īmān*, none of the other three exist. Similarly, weak *īmān* means that the upper structure, if even somehow built, will be shaky. A limited *īmān* means limited *islām*, limited *ṭaqwā*, and *iḥsān*.

Īmān implies belief in the Oneness of God and the Prophethood of Muḥammad, blessings and peace be on him. Anyone who testifies to this belief fulfils the legal requirement for entry into the fold of Islam and is entitled to be treated as a Muslim.

But can this simple testimony be enough? Can it support the edifice of an Islamic morality? Is not understanding the nature and demand of one's commitment of fundamental importance? Some people think that verbal profession is enough; hastily they begin to build further. But, constructing *islām*, *taqwā* and *iḥsān* on a foundation which has not been fully and firmly laid will lead to the whole edifice being incomplete or collapsing at the first sign of stress.

Consider the belief in God, which comes first. It may mean different things to different people. Some know nothing beyond the fact that God is there, that He is the Creator of the universe and He is One. Others may not see God as more than the object of our devotions and as the One to be worshipped. For others again, the concept of God's attributes and His rights and authority may not extend beyond the notion that He has no partner in His claim to be the Knower of the Unseen, Hearer of prayers, Provider of people's needs and the object of people's worship, and that in matters 'religious' the final authority is the Book of God.

These different concepts are reflected in the kinds of lives people lead. The narrower the concept of God, the narrower will be the application of Islamic principles in a person's life and the narrower will be the base of his morality. Even where the concept of *īmān* is wider, but only in a 'religious' sense, Islamic life may end up as a compromise between Islam and *kufr*, at one and the same time, owing allegiance to God and rebelling against Him!

Similarly, the depth of belief in God varies. An individual, although believing in God, may not want to make even the smallest sacrifice for Islam. Another person may hold God very dear, but hold a few things even dearer. A third person may be prepared to sacrifice his life and possessions for God, if necessary, while at the same time trying not to give up his ideas, thoughts, or desires, though they may conflict with the belief in God. He may also not be prepared to get into a position where he thinks his reputation will suffer. We can work out the extent of *īmān* in a person's life by analysing his attitudes. In fact, one's Islamic morality betrays one at the very point where the foundation of *īmān* is weak.

The edifice of a complete Islamic life can only be built on a belief in God's Oneness (*tawḥīd*) that permeates a person's entire personal and social life, and which is so strong that he considers himself and all that he possesses as belonging to God; he accepts Him as the sole rightful Owner, Object of worship, Receiver of obedience and Law-giver for himself as well as the rest of the world; he considers Him the fountainhead of guidance, and is totally aware that disobedience to God, indifference to His guidance or an inclination to associate some other being as a partner with Him in His Being, constitute deviation from the Right Path.

That is to say, for the edifice of Islamic life to be firmly founded in an individual implies that he should declare that he, and all that he has, belong to God and are at His command. It also means that he is prepared to subordinate his personal likes and dislikes to the will of God, annihilating his ego and moulding his ideas, desires, passions and ways of thinking according to the knowledge that God has imparted through His Book; that he will abandon any loyalties to forces repugnant to God, accord the love of God the highest place in his heart and cast away from the recesses of his heart any idol that may demand to be held dearer than God. He will base his love and hate, friendship and enmity, likes and dislikes on what God approves of. This is real *īmān*. How can imperfect *īmān* be made up for by the length of a beard, the style of dress, recitation of the rosary or nightly worship?

Other beliefs that are part of the Faith may be considered in the same way. Belief in Prophethood (*risālah*) cannot be complete unless one accepts the Prophet, blessings and peace be on him, as one's guide in all the affairs of life and rejects all that is contrary to his guidance. Belief in the Qur'ān remains imperfect until the code of life it lays down is accepted in its entirety. Moreover, there should be no lack in longing to see one's life or the life of the rest of the world governed by the rules that God has prescribed.

Similarly, belief in the *ākhirah* or life hereafter cannot be complete until one is prepared to attach more importance to it than to the present life and to reject the values of this world for the values of the other world. It is equally important that the thought of one's accountability on the Day of Judgement should guide one at every step on life's road.

Where these beliefs are missing from a person's life, what foundations can there be on which to build the structures of Islamic life? It is ironic to see that people have taken the building of Islamic life for granted without seeing the need to extend, strengthen and complete its foundations, with the result that the door to the highest stages of *taqwā* and *iḥsān* has been opened for a judge who may make decisions in violation of the Qur'ān, for a lawyer who may argue on the basis of laws contrary to the *Sharīʿah*, for the administrator who may manage the affairs of life in accordance with a system based on *kufr*, for the leader and his followers who may work for the founding and building of life on the social and political principles of disbelievers – in short for everyone, provided they fashion their outward style of life after a certain pattern and observe the ceremonies of ritual worship and attach great importance to voluntary prayers.

ISLĀM

As we have seen, the edifices of *islām* can be built only on the deeply embedded and solid foundations of *īmān*. In fact, *islām* is the practical demonstration of *īmān*. The relationship between the two is the same as that between seed and plant. *Īmān* is the seed and *islām* represents its fruition. Examine the tree and you find what the seed contained. *Īmān*, if present, will manifest itself in a person's practical life, in his morality, in his conduct, in his relations with others, in his choice of activities, in the nature of his struggle, in the use of his time, energies and capabilities; in short, in every aspect of life.

If there is a sphere of a person's life where un-Islamic instead of Islamic behaviour is evident, it is there that *īmān* is absent or at most has only a fragile existence. If an individual's entire life follows an un-Islamic pattern, it is obvious that either *īmān* is lacking altogether or that the soil is too barren for the seed of *īmān* to grow. The Qur'ān and *Ḥadīth* show that it is impossible to have *īmān* in one's heart without it showing through in one's day-to-day life.

Let us forget for a moment the arguments of the jurists and philosophers about *īmān* and its ramifications and try to understand it in the light of the Qur'ān. It becomes obvious from the Qur'ān that the inner conviction of faith and the practice of Islam are essentially interdependent. God frequently mentions faith and righteous conduct together. All the promises of a blissful future that He has made to Muslims apply to those believers who really do submit to His will. In fact, wherever God castigates hypocrites in the Qur'ān, He cites the faults of their practises as evidence of imperfection in their faith and declares the practise of Islam as the sign of real faith.

Branding somebody a disbeliever, however, and excommunicating him from Islam demands extreme caution. It is not an issue which need concern us here. Our present concern is with the actual, not the legal, *īmān* and Islam, which are acceptable in the sight of God and which lead to rewards in the hereafter.

If we consider the essence of both facts we will find that where there is deficiency in submission to God, where one's desires differ from God's will, where loyalty to others co-exists with loyalty to God, where attention is being devoted to activities other than the struggle for the revival of God's guidance, where efforts are being made for causes other than the cause of God, *īmān* necessarily suffers from flaws and blemishes.

One can deceive oneself by wearing false appearances, but this will not carry any weight on the Day of Judgement. We must appreciate that real *ṭaqwā* and *iḥsān*, which are needed to bring glory to Islam in this world and to tilt the balance in favour of goodness on the Day of Judgement, can never be reached unless the foundation of *īmān* is firm and the proof of its strength is provided by a life lived according to *islām*.

TAQWĀ

What is *taqwā*? Let us understand first that *taqwā* does not merely imply any particular form, appearance or lifestyle. Rather, it is a state of inner self, which no doubt reflects itself in every part of life. *Taqwā* consists of a person's awe of God, consciousness of his duty towards Him and an awareness of his accountability to Him: that the world is a place of trial where God has sent a person for a specified period of time; that God's decisions on the Day of Judgement on an individual's future in the hereafter will depend on how he makes use of his energies and capabilities in the given period of time at his disposal in this world and how he deals with his fellow beings.

A conscience which is fired by consciousness of God becomes alive. A person's sensitivity becomes sharp under this influence and he avoids everything that is against God's Will. He starts examining his own thoughts and feelings to see what tendencies are being nurtured within him. He begins to scrutinise his life to find out on what activities he is spending his time and energy.

Not only does he scrupulously avoid things that are explicitly prohibited; he also hesitates from getting involved in affairs which are in any way dubious. His sense of duty makes him fulfil God's commands in a spirit of total submission. His fear of God causes a feeling of faintness whenever there is a possibility that he may be in danger of exceeding limits prescribed by God. Ensuring the discharge of his obligations towards God and towards his fellow-beings becomes his way of life; he shudders at the thought of doing anything unjust.

This state of consciousness does not appear in any one form or in one particular sphere; instead, it manifests itself in an individual's entire way of thinking and in all his actions. By contrast, where *taqwā* merely consists of putting on a certain mode of conduct and outwardly assuming some immediately recognisable, measurable appearance, one perceives two ways of life in conflict: meticulous conformity to outward detail along with a morality which has the least relationship with *īmān*. As Jesus said, the situation is similar to that of one who strains at a gnat but swallows a camel.

The difference between real and seeming *taqwā* can be understood by the following example of two different people: One has a deep sense of cleanliness and a concern for purity. He will abhor filth in whatever form it may appear, and will be clean in all essential manners, even if not in all outward forms. The other person, who has no innate sense of purity, carries with him a long list of prohibitions under the heading of cleanliness. This individual will avoid all the unclean things that he finds on his list, but he will be found indulging in many other loathsome acts, which are not included as such on the list and which may be far more revolting than those he is avoiding.

This is not a theoretical example. We can see it with our own eyes in the lives of those who often enjoy great fame for their *taqwā*. They are so particular about the minutest details of the *Sharīʿah* that someone having a beard shorter than a certain length is threatened with excommunication and someone with his trousers extending below the ankles is threatened with Hell Fire. Deviating from the secondary injunctions of their own juristic persuasions is, to them, tantamount to heresy. But their neglect of the fundamentals of Islam reaches such heights that they have turned the Muslim's entire life into a life of compromise and political expediency. They have found numerous ways of evading the struggle for the revival of Islam.

What is even more regrettable is that if someone places before them the real demands of Islam and draws their attention to the struggle required for the Islamic cause, they resort to ruses, tricks or stratagems to excuse both themselves and other Muslims from such a struggle. Still, their *taqwā* apparently remains unimpaired and none among the religious-minded spiritualists suspects any deficiency in it. Such paradoxes can be discerned only if we have a clear concept of *taqwā*.

None of this means that the importance of the precepts regarding etiquette, dress, conduct and deportment that are traceable to the *aḥādīth* should be belittled. The point to emphasise is that the essence of *taqwā* lies in an attitude of heart and mind rather than in its outward forms. The whole life of a person who develops real *taqwā* will be consistently Islamic. Islam with all its comprehensiveness will be increasingly reflected in such a person's thoughts, emotions and inclinations, frame of mind, allocation of time and spending of energies, in short, in all aspects of his worldly life. But without sowing the seed of *taqwā* no artificial measures will be fruitful.

Taqwā requires time and patience, develops gradually and bears fruit after a long time just as a tree takes long to grow from a seed and bloom. That is why people of superficial character avoid it. The second type of personality can be developed quickly and with as much ease as a stick may be dressed with leaves, blossoms and fruits to give it the appearance of a tree. That is why this method of cultivating *taqwā* is popular today. But it is obvious that the benefit expected from a real tree cannot be attained from an artificial one.

IḤSĀN

Iḥsān is the highest stage of Islam. It implies the deep attachment, profound love, genuine faithfulness and sacrifice which make a Muslim completely identify himself with Islam. The essence of *taqwā* is fear of God which may enable a person to escape God's anger. The essence of *iḥsān* is love of God, which tries to win God's pleasure.

The difference between the two may be illustrated by the following example: Among the employees of a government may be some who scrupulously discharge the functions entrusted to them, doing nothing to which one can take exception, but are not otherwise committed. Others, however, may be loyal, devoted and totally committed to the government. They do not just carry out the duties that have been assigned to them but are always zealously concerned to promote the interests of the government. They exert themselves beyond the call of duty, being prepared to sacrifice their lives, property and children in defence of their country. Any violation of the law hurts them personally, any sign of rebellion is enough to arouse them. Far from deliberately harming the government they will spare no effort to support it.

The first kind of people are *muttaqīn* of the government and the other are *muḥsinīn*. Though the *muttaqīn* are regarded as good servants, the honour and reward reserved for *muḥsinīn* is exclusively theirs. Though *muttaqīn* are valued and trustworthy people, *muḥsinīn* make up the real strength of Islam. The task that Islam has to accomplish can only be carried out by this group.

It is, therefore, impossible for people to be counted as *muḥsinīn* who stand passively by and see the Divine laws being at best neglected and at worst overturned, the reign of tyranny and oppression unleashed on God's earth, or who see that the ascendancy of disbelief is not only promoting moral and social ills in human society, but is also causing the Muslim community, itself, to turn from the Path of Righteousness, and do nothing.

How can anyone be regarded as *muḥsinīn* who can stand by and see this decline in Muslim society without feeling the urge to try and change this state of affairs. Can they attain *iḥsān* merely because they are found at Prayer in Mid-morning (*al-Ishrāq* and *al-Ḍuḥā*) and past midnight (*Tahajjud*), spending time in meditation and remembrance of God and lecturing on the Qur'ān and the *aḥādīth*? Or, because they devote time to observing the minutest but superficial details of *fiqh* or jurisprudence and *aḥādīth* and to teaching in the *masājid* such practices of self-purification which incorporate all the subtleties of *ḥadīth*, *fiqh* and *taṣawwuf*, but which lack that religiosity which inspires one to sacrifice one's life for the cause of justice rather than to accept an order not in accordance with God's commands.

Can one believe that God cannot recognise those who are truly loyal to Him? Can one imagine that He will be taken in by the length of a beard, the distance of the trousers above the ankles, the recitation of rosaries, devotions and prayers, worship and meditation and other outward signs when He comes to judge true loyalty and devotion?

20

Inner Dimensions of Worship

Ismail al-Faruqi

THE MEANING OF *'IBĀDAH*

In all the religions of the world, *'ibādah* or worship means a ritual consisting of *legomena* (things thought or recited) and *dromena* (things done or acted) performed by people, more often regularly rather than at random, by which people adore, thank or petition God, the Ultimate Reality. According to this definition, *'ibādah* in Islam refers to the 'Five Pillars' that is the *shahādah, ṣalāh, zakāh, ṣawm* and *ḥajj.*

There is yet another meaning to *'ibādah.* This meaning, however, is unique, and found only in Islam. *'Ibādah* means any and all actions entered into for the sake of God, and fulfilment of the general imperative of Islam regarding human life on earth. This general imperative flows from the essence of religious experience in Islam. Briefly expressed, this essence is *tawḥīd,* the affirmation that 'No god is God but God' or *Lā ilāha illa Allāh.* In both, its metaphysical sense, which regards Allah as the Ultimate Cause of all events, the Ultimate Source of all beings, the eternal Creator, and in its axiological sense, which regards Allah as the Ultimate End of all Ends, that which makes all good acceptable, the Master and Judge; the affirmation of *tawḥīd,* thus, implies that God is indeed the determinant of a person's whole life. A human being's reason to be, the meaning and purpose of his existence, is to serve God; i.e. to fulfil His will.

The Divine will, immutable and ubiquitous in space and time, consists of patterns of conduct (*sunan*) that are embedded in the world of nature (which are, hence, always, fulfilled with the necessity of natural laws), and of laws or commandments (*awāmir* or *Sharīʿah*), which were revealed for people to fulfil deliberately and in freedom. The human situation is indeed exactly as Allah has described, *I have not created jinn and mankind but to serve Me* (51: 56).

The content of this service, Islam teaches, is to affirm life, to live it to the full, to procreate, to learn, to grow, to have and to enjoy, doing so in loyalty to God, with a sense of justice and charity, with concern and responsibility, in one's personal life as well as within the family and society. That is why the Prophet told us that 'a day of learning is better than *ʿibādah* for 50 years'; that the pursuit of a livelihood for oneself and one's family is *ʿibādah*; that *jihād bi'l-māl* (spending of one's substance) and *jihād bi'l-nafs* (spending of one's life) are *ʿibādah*; that every act of self exertion in the cause of God is *ʿibādah*. Obviously, with this vision *ʿibādah* is the very substance of life, its sustenance and promotion, as well as the building of society, of social institutions, of culture and civilisation. What role does such *ʿibādah* play in the development of the Islamic personality?

ʿIbādah (in the more general sense of fulfilling one's *raison d'être*) makes of its seeker 'a person of *tawḥīd*', a person with a distinct personality. The *tawḥīdī* person is possessed, enchanted. Every movement of his wakefulness is filled with the presence of God, the ultimate cause and purpose. He seeks God's work in everything that is or happens around him. In his mind, *Subḥāna Allāh, Māshā Allah, Alḥamdu Lillāh, Lā ḥawla wa lā quwwata illā billāh, Innā lillāhi wa innā ilaihi rājiʿūn* reverberate constantly. His heart is always moved by the desire for good; but good is itself the desire or command of God. So that in his desiring, emoting and feeling, judging and expressing, Allah again is the only determinant. The difference that this fixation or possession by God makes is that the person affected by it is a person with a cause, a cause greater than himself and all others, greater than his own world and, indeed, the whole world. This makes him necessarily an idealist in the best sense of the term, a person of gravity, of seriousness, of commitment, a person for whom no act is haphazard and every action and inaction counts.

THE *SHAHĀDAH*

The *Shahādah* is the solemn affirmation that Allah is indeed Allah; that worship is due to Him alone; and that Muḥammad is His Prophet and Messenger, sent by Allah to teach the Divine message, the Qur'ān, whose essence is *tawḥīd*. The *Shahādah* is an official confession of the cause of Islam. It is a modality of existence raised to the level of consciousness; the moment in which commitment to the cause of Islam has become conscious of itself.

Its role in the development of the human personality lies in the moulding of the Muslim's personality into constant awareness of his Islamic commitment, the promulgation and proclamation of Islam, the *summum bonum* (absolute supreme good) which the Muslim appropriates anew through the *Shahādah*; is wished by the *Shahādah* itself to be known, shared and appropriated by other humans. The social dimension of the *Shahādah* is, therefore, *da'wah* to one's self and to others in its highest and most intense meaning.

ṢALĀH

Ṣalāh, as *'ibādah* in the technical sense which Islam shares with most other religions, is an act of obedience to God. It is the supreme act of worship in Islam. It is often incorrectly called prayer. Muslims, however, should insist on calling it by its Qur'ānic name, *ṣalāh*. Unlike *ṣalāh*, prayer, is an invocation addressed to God in any form, at any time, place or in any position, whose purpose may be adorational, proclamational, thanksgiving or petitional, singly or collectively, in any combination of these. Unlike prayer, *ṣalāh* is an act of worship in a specific form, at specific times, with specific postures, whose purpose and content can only be that which the Prophet has assigned to it.

Its role in the development of the Islamic personality distinguishes it further from prayer. Whereas prayer is a purely subjective affair concerned with the worshipper and his relation with God, *ṣalāh* fulfils a number of other functions. The *niyyah* or intention sets up the framework of consciousness required for communication with the Divine. The *wuḍū'* or ablution cleanse the exposed organs of the body of dirt and refreshes the whole 'self' as a consequence.

Regular observance of *ṣalāh* makes one clean and keeps one clean. It imposes upon a person a number of ablutions every day of the year and one whole-body bath at least once a week. *Ṣālāh* is, thus, a combination of spiritual refreshment and bodily exercise. These elements contribute to enhancing the general health and well-being of the body.

Finally, the moral benefits of *ṣalāh* are richer and more complex:

- *ṣalāh* teaches an awareness of the movement of time, and punctuates the day. Since it must be observed at its specific time, it disciplines a person in the habit of punctuality and in the proper utilisation of his time.

- *ṣalāh* cultivates in the Muslim a feeling of equality with his peers, as it must be performed in a straight line in which a person stands on a par with all others.
- *ṣalāh* creates in a Muslim a feeling of solidarity and unity, as it demands all Muslims to press together, shoulder to shoulder and foot to foot.
- *ṣalāh* teaches the Muslim the martial quality of pressing forward towards the front and of filling the gap in the front line.
- *ṣalāh* imparts self-confidence as it eliminates all middlemen in a person's contact with God, frankness and candidness, since it presumes the person can communicate directly with God, the Omniscient.
- *ṣalāh* teaches responsibility, since it reminds a person constantly of the reckoning he has with God by enacting this accountability every time it is performed.
- *ṣalāh* prohibits *al-faḥshā' wa al-munkar* or debauchery and evil (29: 45). For, by its direct communion with God, *ṣalāh* teaches both the fear and love of God, endearing His commandments and condemning His prohibitions. It is, thus, the source of virtue and piety, the preventive shield against corruption.
- *ṣalāh's* open communication with God uplifts a person's morale, deepens his commitment to things universal and draws him into a life of piety and virtue.

ZAKĀH

Zakāh is neither charity nor alms. Nor, is it the 'poor due'. These are formless acts of altruism, devoid of specification and modality other than that of being given freely. Unlike them, *zakāh* is a yearly levy at a specific rate of the *niṣāb* (two and a half percent of the total wealth appropriated to date, above a certain minimum) for distribution among categories specified in the Qur'ān. This is why it should be called by its Qur'ānic name whatever the language of discourse, like *shahādah*, *ṣalāh* and the entire set of Qur'ānic religious vocabulary.

Zakāh functions as a 'sweetener'; making innocent, legitimate and good the consumption of wealth earned by any lawful activity or means. It is indeed a sharing of one's wealth with the unfortunates who have no wealth.

To people, Allah made the whole universe an inheritance to master and to possess, to usufruct and to enjoy. He called the universe His bounty granted to people and He enjoined them to seek and enjoy every material and aesthetic value in it. Sharing it with the destitute, however, Allah declared tantamount to the whole of religion, not merely to the observance of the command of *zakāh*. In His wisdom, He instituted the *zakāh* as a means of forcing wealth to circulate, preventing economic sclerosis. He equated spending of one's substance with spending one's life; both being forms of the supreme struggle called *jihād*.

How does observance of *zakāh* as an *ʿibādah* affect the development of personality? Firstly, it is an act of obedience to Allah, requiring a person to give up for Allah's sake that which he cherishes and values most, the fruit of his labour. Therefore, it relates people to Allah, their Creator, or Master, and establishes between them a bond of loyalty, of love and esteem. *Zakāh* makes the observant a 'party' to Divine providence, a soldier–servant of Allah bearing His brand and raising His banner.

Secondly, *zakāh* establishes a bond of mutual affection and concern, of genuine brotherhood. Thus, it contributes the cohesive cement out of which society is made, marshalling the economic, cultural, moral and religious factors and combining them together in the service of the *Ummah*. There can be no firmer foundation for society, for social justice, for social welfare and solidarity. A group of humans sharing together their physical, psychic and linguistic characteristics is a *gemeinschaft* or community. One that shares together their history and culture and a will to a common future is a *gesellschaft* or society. But that society which observes the *ʿibādah* of Islam is an *Ummah*, a new being, a modality of existence higher than all the rest. The personality that is a full member of the *Ummah* in this sense is an *ummatic* or international personality.

ṢAWM

Lest it be misunderstood as an act of self-denial, and an act of asceticism and, therefore, a renunciation of the world and of life, as an act of self-mortification, let us not call *ṣawm* by the word fasting. Fasting in religions which practise it most, rests on a condemnation of this life and this world. In those religions, one fasts because life in the world is 'fallen', 'evil'. Fasting, to them, is real renunciation, an existential 'No!' addressed to life and the process of space and time. For it is assumed they are a change-for-the-worse which had occurred to the absolute, to the ideal.

Ṣawm, per contra, is none of that. This life and this world are God's creation, and are, therefore, good. He established them as people's destiny enjoined upon him to seek and promote them. His Prophet, Muḥammad, defined the good, the noble, the felicitous person as one whose career adds a real plus to the total value of the universe, who leaves the world a better place than that in which he was born. But, *ṣawm* is definitely an abstinence from food, drink and sex. What then is its meaning?

Besides constituting another act of obedience to Allah, hence realising all values appertaining to obedience to and a communion with the Divine, *ṣawm* is an exercise in self-mastery. The instincts for food and sex are the basic ingredients of which life is made. They are the strongest and ultimate urges a person possesses. For their sake as ultimate goals, normal human life and energy are spent. *Ṣawm* addresses them. It does not deny them continuously and perpetually, but only during the month of Ramaḍān, and does so only between dawn and sunset. That is precisely what self-mastery requires: to deny and to satisfy, to deny again and to satisfy again, and so on for every day of Ramaḍān. Had denial been the consequence of condemnation, it would have been commanded for continuous observance. That is why the Muslim rejoices and celebrates at every sunset in Ramaḍān. For the sunset signifies his victory over himself during the day! This is why Ramaḍān is the happiest month of the year.

Ṣawm is, furthermore, an act of 'retreat' and self-stock-taking; an occasion for *ḥisāb* or evaluation with oneself as to one's whence and whither; a remembrance of and commiseration with the poor and hungry, the destitute and deprived. It is the prime occasion for every noble act of *ṣadaqah* or charity, of altruistic concern which is the opposite of egotism, and ultimately for all ummatic values. Its effect on the development of the human personality is capital and decisive. It disciplines a person and enables him to master the strongest urges raging within him. It trains him to subdue them to the nobler ends of the ethics of religion. It orients him – in his physical and psychic being – towards the *Ummah*, and, thus, makes him an effective executor and actualiser of the Divine cause in history.

Indeed, it prepares him, *par excellence*, to enter the arena of history, and there to fulfil the pattern of God. The true observant of *ṣawm* is a person ready to be the subject of history, not its object.

ḤAJJ

The *ḥajj* is not a memorial pilgrimage to a place declared holy by its association with a Divine act, a Prophet, a saintly person or simply an historical event of great significance. Its purpose is not merely to remember. Hence, it would not be called 'pilgrimage'. Rather, it must be known by its Qur'ānic name alone, *ḥajj*. Certainly, it is an act by an individual worshipper; but it is not an individual act, affecting its subject-doer alone or primarily alone, on the religious level. Moreover, it may not be entered into in private, at random or at any time the subject chooses. It is a collective, rather ummatic, act which must be done at its proper time, and must include a specific sequence. There is no *ḥajj* without the *Ummah's* participation. Indeed, there is no Islam when there is only one Muslim at rest, as it were, with space and time.

Ḥajj is a re-enactment, a living or going-through once more of the experience of Abraham and of the *Hijrah* from Makkah of the Prophet Muḥammad and of his triumphant re-entry eight years later. It is at once the re-destruction of the idols of the Kaʿbah, the re-establishment of Islam as *al-Dīn* or the way of life, the primordial religion, the ultimate norm of a person's relation with Allah, the Absolute, as its motto indicates: *Labbayk Allāhumma Labbayk* – Here I am, O Allah, here I am. *Ḥajj* is the affirmative response of a human being to his Creator's call, a re-dedication and re-consecration of one's life to the Divine cause. It is a re-enactment on the deepest personal level, of the *miḥnah* or persecution of Abraham being called upon to give up his sole son, Ishmael; of the *miḥnah* of Muḥammad when oppression forced him to abandon the city of Abraham and seek refuge in Yathrib, as well as a base for launching the world movement of Islam, and of the path of Makkah and its reconsecration as a *bayt* or abode (city), and the *Ummah* fused together to represent and effectuate the Cause of God in history. To undertake the *ḥajj* is really to be and to feel oneself in the companionship of Abraham, Ishmael and Muḥammad as they lived out their ministry and mission; indeed to re-live their experience.

On the collective level, the *Ummah* level, *ḥajj* is the coming together of all parties, all races, and peoples, all nations and states, all schools and classes, groups of all colours – to the God of all creation. All subdue and suppress their differences in order to affirm their unity and communion. As bearers of the banner of Allah, in space and time, they assemble in order to redefine and reconfirm their mission as callers to God, as actualisers of His patterns in space-time. *Ḥajj* is, equally, an occasion for the *Ummah* as a whole to take and give account of itself before Allah; for its leaders, its teachers, thinkers and guardians to render account of themselves and their roles. It is the occasion for the *Ummah* as a whole to re-dedicate itself to Islam as the cause of Allah in history, to proclaim and to call the nations of the world to join ranks with them as would-be transformers of space-time, the would-be fulfillers of the Divine will in the world. It is, in short, for the universalism of Islam to reaffirm itself, to proclaim its plans for history, and to launch the actualisation of those plans.

As such, *ḥajj* is a unique religious, political, cultural and human event. It is spectacular, indeed the greatest of spectacles ever put on by human beings. No religion and no civilisation ever witnessed or sustained a similar event.

The effect of *ḥajj* on the participant is always radical. It shatters his personality by convincing him of its futility or vanity; and it reconstructs that personality and orients it towards Allah and His cause. It destroys every vestige of individualism, egotism, every trace of subjectivism and isolationism, every tendency to particularism and nationalism and finally, every touch of an inferiority or superiority complex. It restores and instils in the participant's mental health, emotional equilibrium, concern for humans across every boundary of race or colour, of culture, language and social classification. It makes or reinforces his consciousness of himself as an ummatic being endowed with a universal mission. With all this, *ḥajj* lifts the participant above the flow of space and time, and confirms him as the guide and leader of that flow.

CONCLUSION

No system of *ʿibādah* in any religion has ever come anywhere close to the *ʿibādah* of Islam. None has succeeded as did the *ʿibādah* of Islam. None has fit the purposes of its religion and ideology as did the *ʿibādah* of Islam. That is why no system has ever lasted as long, and none has been as universally and consistently, and identically observed, as the *ʿibādah* of Islam. Why? Because it is from Allah, the perfect, whose every work is perfect.

This magnificent system of *ʿibādah* is yours; yours to have free, to possess and appropriate and teach to your sons and daughters, your neighbours and strangers and the whole of humankind. Why? Because it is from God, the system which truly and certainly leads to Him, the Supreme Good.

Having given it to you as an act of mercy, a *raḥmatul li'l-ālamīn* or mercy to the worlds, having made the whole of creation subservient to you; having raised you with sagacity and wisdom above the angels whom He commanded to prostrate themselves before you; having made you His *khulafā'* or vicegerents on earth and having invited you to act as vortices, the real *aqṭāb* or axes, around which the world and history may or should be made, what is left for you to do but to acquiesce and to say with me: All praise is due to Allah, the Lord of the Worlds; Allah is the Greatest.

21

The Principles of *Ḥalāl* and *Ḥarām*

Yusuf al-Qaradawi

The question of what ought to be *ḥalāl* or lawful and *ḥarām* or unlawful was one of the things, prior to the advent of Islam, which utterly confused people. Basically, they had gone so far astray that they permitted many impure and harmful things and prohibited many things that were good and pure.

Thus, one of the Prophet's initial tasks was to establish certain legal principles and measures for rectifying this. These principles were then made the determining criteria on which the questions of what is *ḥalāl* and what is *ḥarām* were to be based. They were established on the overriding principle of justice. The Muslim *Ummah* or community thus became an *Ummah* occupying a position between extreme deviations, which Allah the Most Exalted describes as *the middle Ummah, the best Ummah that has ever been brought forth for mankind* (3: 110).

The following are the *uṣūl* or principles established by Islam for differentiating the lawful from the prohibited.

1. EVERYTHING IS *ḤALĀL* UNLESS EXPLICITLY FORBIDDEN

As long as there is no authentic statement from the Qur'ān or the *Sunnah* of the Prophet that a particular thing is forbidden, then it is considered *ḥalāl*. Muslim scholars found authority for this principle in these clear verses of the Qur'ān: *He has subjected to you, from Himself, all that is in the heavens and all that is on the earth* (45: 13) and *Do you not see that Allah has subjected to you whatever is in the heavens and what is on earth, and has showered upon you His favours, both apparent and unseen?* (31: 20).

If Allah has created things and harnessed them for people's use, then it cannot be true that Allah would deprive them of its use by making them unlawful. He has made unlawful certain things for good reasons, with great wisdom. Therefore, the forbidden area in the *Sharīʿah* is considerably small. In this regard, the Prophet said: 'What Allah has made lawful in His Book is *ḥalāl* and what He has forbidden is *ḥarām*, and that concerning which He is silent is allowed as His favour. So accept from Allah His favour, for Allah is not forgetful of anything. He then recited, *And your Lord is not forgetful* (19: 64)' (*al-Ḥākim*).

2. ONLY ALLAH HAS THE RIGHT TO LEGISLATE FOR PEOPLE

Islam declares that the only legislating authority is Allah. Islam, therefore, took the legislating authority away from the hands of human beings, regardless of their religious or worldly position. No one is allowed to forbid something that Allah has permitted. If he does so he would be exceeding the limit set by Allah and claiming for himself what is a Divine attribute. Moreover, those who accept and follow this human-made legislation will also be held responsible. Concerning the *mushrikīn* or idol worshippers, the Qur'ān says: *Do they have partners* [with Allah] *who have prescribed for them in religion that concerning which Allah has given no permission?* (42: 21).

The Qur'ān also took to task the People of the Book, that is, the Christians and Jews, for placing the power to make things lawful and unlawful into the hands of their rabbis and priests. ʿAdī bin Ḥātim, who was from the People of the Book before accepting Islam, once came to the Prophet. When he heard him reciting the verse of the Qur'ān, *They have taken their rabbis and priests as lords besides Allah, and the Messiah, son of Mary, although they were commanded to worship no one except the One Allah. There is no deity but He, Glory be to Him above what they associate with Him!* (9: 31), he, ʿAdī, then said: 'O Messenger of Allah, but they do not worship them.' The Prophet replied, 'Yes, they prohibit to the people what is *ḥalāl* and permit them what is *ḥarām*, and the people obey them. This is indeed like their worship of them.' (*al-Tirmidhī*).

The Qur'ān also took the polytheists to task for legislating and prohibiting things without any authority from Allah: *Do you see what Allah has sent down to you for sustenance and yet you have made some part of it ḥalāl and some part ḥarām?* (10: 59).

From these explicit verses of the Qur'ān and from the clear traditions of the Prophet, the jurists of Islam grasped with certainty that it is Allah alone who has the right to make something lawful or unlawful, either through His Book or through the tongue of His Messenger. They also understood that their task in *fiqh* or Islamic jurisprudence does not go beyond explaining what Allah has decreed to be *ḥalāl* or *ḥarām, when He has explained to you in detail what He has made ḥarām for you* (6: 119). Early Muslim scholars, therefore, used to be very cautious in passing judgement concerning *ḥalāl* and *ḥarām*. We should learn from them and never call something *ḥarām* unless we have definite authority for saying so.

3. PROHIBITING THE *ḤALĀL* AND PERMITTING THE *ḤARĀM* IS SYNONYMOUS WITH *SHIRK*

Islam opposed those who forbade what is good and lawful, as it carried the risk of making life difficult and thus depriving people of Allah's mercy. Islam does not approve of this attitude. The Prophet said in this regard, 'I have been sent with what is straight and easy' (*Aḥmad*).

The Qur'ān strongly condemned the pagans of Arabia for their *shirk* and for their forbidding lawful things like the eating of cattle. They used to declare the eating of some animals as *ḥarām* or to ride them or prevent them from water and pasture for various baseless reasons. The Qur'ān condemned this attitude when it declared: *Say: Who has forbidden the adornment of Allah which He has brought forth for His servants, and the good things of His providing? . . . Say: What my Lord has indeed prohibited are shameless deeds, whether open or secret, and sin and rebellion without just cause, and that you associate with Allah that for which He has sent down no authority, and that you say concerning Allah that about which you do not know* (7: 32–33).

4. *ḤARĀM* IS ASSOCIATED WITH WHAT IS BAD AND HARMFUL

Having created the human being and bestowed upon him immeasurable gifts, Allah has the right to declare what is permitted and what is forbidden. He, also, has the right to command upon man whatever acts of worship He desires. Man, being the creation and subject of Allah, has to obey. Allah, however, being the Most Merciful and the Most Compassionate, allowed only good things and forbade bad things for the benefit of people. It is true that Allah prohibited certain good things to the people before Islam.

Thus He says: *And to the Jews We forbade every animal with claws, and of cattle We have forbidden them their fat, except what is carried on their backs or entrails, or what is connected to the bone; thus did We recompense them for their rebelliousness, and indeed, We Speak the Truth* (6: 146).

When Allah sent His final Messenger with the eternal complete religion to humanity after it had developed to a state of maturity, He demonstrated His mercy by removing these prohibitions. They had, after all, been a temporary penalty for a rebellious, stubborn people. And the coming of the Prophet who would relieve them of this burden was foretold to the Jews and Christians, who, as the Qur'ān states: *they find described in their own Scriptures, in the Torah and the Injīl. He commands them what is right and forbids them what is evil; He makes lawful to them what is good and makes unlawful what is foul; He releases them from their burdens and from the yokes which were upon them* (7: 157).

In Islam, ways other than prohibiting the good things were prescribed by Allah for the eradication of sins: sincere repentance, which cleanses sins as water cleanses dirt; good deeds which compensate for evil ones; spending in charity which extinguishes the fire; and trials and sufferings which disperse sins as the autumn wind disperses dry leaves.

Accordingly, we know that in Islam things are prohibited only because they are impure or harmful. If something is entirely harmful it is *ḥarām*, and if it is entirely beneficial it is *ḥalāl*; if the harm of it outweighs its benefit it is *ḥarām*, while if its benefit outweighs its harm it is *ḥalāl*. This principle is explained in the Qur'ān in relation to wine and gambling: *They ask you concerning wine and gambling. Say* [O Prophet]: *In them is great sin and some benefit for people, but the sin is greater than the benefit* (2: 219).

By the same logic, if it is asked, what is *ḥalāl* in Islam, the answer is, the good things. Good things are those which moderate people acknowledge to be wholesome and which are approved of by people in general without relation to the habits of a particular group. Allah says: *They ask you what is lawful to them* [as food]. *Say: Whatever is good is lawful to you* (5: 4).

It is not essential for the Muslims to know in detail all the reasons why a certain thing is forbidden, as that which is unknown today may be clear tomorrow. What is required of Muslims is simply that they say: 'We have heard and we shall obey'. An example of this is in the Prophet's saying: 'Avoid three abominable acts: defecating in streams, defecating on roadways, and defecating in shaded places' (*Abū Dāwūd*). People of earlier times knew that these three acts were abhorrent to civilised taste, hygiene and public manners. With the advancement of science, however, we now know that these 'three abominable acts' are hazards to public health. As our knowledge increases so will our understanding of the merits of Islamic teachings regarding *ḥalāl* and *ḥarām* and, in fact, all aspects of the *Sharīʿah*.

5. IN *ḤALĀL*, THERE IS A BETTER SUBSTITUTE FOR *ḤARĀM*

One of the merits of Islam is that it shows mercy towards people in that whenever it forbids something it provides a better substitute with which to replace it. Islam forbids usury but allows profitable business. Islam forbids gambling, but allows winning prizes in contests of shooting, racing, wrestling, etc. Islam forbids adultery but urges Muslims to marry as soon as they can support a family. Islam forbids drinking alcohol but allows all other good and healthy drinks. Islam forbids what is bad in food but allows what is good and nourishing. The same principle can be traced through all the teachings of Islam. For assuredly, Allah has no desire to make peoples' lives difficult, narrow, and circumscribed; on the contrary; He desires ease, goodness, guidance, and mercy for them according to His saying: *Allah desires to make clear to you and to guide you to the ways of the* [righteous] *people before you and to turn to you in mercy; and Allah is all-Knowing, Wise. And Allah desires to lighten your burden, for the human being was created weak* (4: 26–28).

6. WHATEVER LEADS TO *ḤARĀM* IS *ḤARĀM*

Whenever Islam forbids something, it also forbids all the means that could lead to it. In this way, Islam intends to block all avenues leading to what is *ḥarām*. For example, as Islam has prohibited sex outside marriage, it has also prohibited anything which leads to it or makes it attractive, such as seductive clothing, private meetings and casual mixing between men and women, the depiction of nudity, pornographic literature, obscene songs, and so on.

Accordingly, Muslim jurists have established the criterion that whatever is conducive to or leads towards the *ḥarām* is itself *ḥarām*. A similar principle is that the sin of the *ḥarām* is not limited only to the person who engages in it but extends to others who have supported him in this, materially or morally; each is held accountable according to his share. For example, in the case of intoxicating drinks, the Prophet cursed not only the one who drinks them but also the one who produces them, the one who serves them, the one to whom they are served, the one to whom the price of them is paid, etc. Again, in the matter of usury, the Prophet cursed the one who pays it, the one to whom it is paid, the one who writes the contract, and the one who acts as a witness thereto. Accordingly, we derive the rule that anything which assists in the doing of what is *ḥarām* is itself *ḥarām*, and anyone who helps another person to do it shares in the sin of it.

7. FALSELY REPRESENTING THE *ḤARĀM* AS *ḤALĀL* IS PROHIBITED

Just as Islam has prohibited whatever leads towards the *ḥarām*, it has also prohibited resorting to technicalities and 'loop-holes' in order to do what is *ḥarām* by devious means or excuses inspired by Satan. Those who so resort to rationalisations and excuses to justify their actions are thus acting in the way of *ḥarām*.

Calling a *ḥarām* thing by a name other than its own or changing its form while retaining its essence is a devious tactic, since obviously a change of name or of form is of no consequence as long as the thing and its essence remain unchanged. Thus, when people invent new terms in order to deal in usury or to consume alcohol, the sin of dealing in usury or drinking remains. As we read in the collections of *aḥādīth*: 'A group of people will make peoples' intoxication *ḥalāl* by giving it other names' (Aḥmad). And again: 'A time will come when people will devour usury, calling it 'trade'' (*Bukhārī*). And among the strange phenomena of our time is that people sometimes term, for example, obscene dance as 'art' or have positively renamed liquor as 'spirits', and usury as 'interest'.

8. GOOD INTENTIONS DO NOT JUSTIFY COMMITTING *ḤARĀM*

In all its legislation and moral injunctions, Islam lays great stress on nobility of feelings, loftiness of aims, and purity of intentions. The Prophet said: 'Actions will be judged by intentions, and everyone will be recompensed according to what he intended' (*Bukhārī*).

Indeed, in Islam the routine matters of life and its mundane affairs are transformed into acts of worship and devotion to Allah by good intentions. Regarding *ḥarām*, however, the case is different. Whatever good intentions the doer might have and no matter how noble his objectives might be, Islam does not accept *ḥarām* methods being used as a means for achieving good ends. This is because Islam emphasises both the means and the ends to be noble, and never accepts the principle of 'ends justifying the means'. Thus, earning money through dealing in usury, gambling or any other illegal means to spend on building *masjids* or other charitable objects is not acceptable in Islam. The Prophet once said: 'Allah is good and does not accept anything but good, and Allah has commanded the believers, as He commanded His messengers, saying, *O you messengers! Eat of whatever is good and work righteousness. Indeed, I am aware of what you do* (35: 31). He also said, *O you who believe! Eat of the good things which We provide for you* (2: 172).

The Prophet then said, 'A person travels far, unkempt and dust-stained [for *ḥajj*, *ʿumrah*, or the like], raising his hands to the sky [and saying], "O Lord! O Lord!" while eating what was *ḥarām*, drinking what was *ḥarām*, wearing what was *ḥarām*, and nourishing himself through *ḥarām* means. How then could his Prayers be accepted?' (*Muslim*).

9. DOUBTFUL THINGS ARE TO BE AVOIDED

There is a grey area between the clearly *ḥalāl* and the clearly *ḥarām*. This concerns matters about which there is some doubt. Some people may not be able to decide whether a particular matter is permissible or forbidden; such confusion may be due to doubtful evidence or because of doubt concerning the applicability of the text to the particular circumstance or matter in question.

In relation to such matters, Islam considers it an act of piety for the Muslim to avoid doing what is doubtful in order to stay clear of doing something *ḥarām*. Such a cautious approach, moreover, trains the Muslim to be farsighted in planning and increases his knowledge of affairs and people. The root of this principle is the saying of the Prophet: 'The *ḥalāl* is clear and the haram is clear. Between the two there are doubtful matters concerning which people do not know whether they are *ḥalāl* or *ḥarām*. One who avoids them in order to safeguard his religion and his honour is safe, while if someone engages in a part of them he may be doing something *ḥarām*, like one who grazes his animals near the *ḥimā* (the grounds reserved for animals belonging to a king which are out of bounds for others' animals); it is thus quite likely that some of his animals will stray into it. Truly, every king has a *ḥimā*, and the *ḥimā* of Allah is what He has prohibited' (*Bukhārī*).

10. THE *ḤARĀM* IS PROHIBITED TO EVERYONE ALIKE

In Islam, what is *ḥarām* is *ḥarām* for all people and likewise what is *ḥalāl* is *ḥalāl* for everyone. There are no privileges enjoyed by a certain class or group enabling them to do whatever they like, be they kings or monks. Theft, for example, is *ḥarām*, whether the thief or his victim is a Muslim or a non-Muslim. The thief will face the charge and pay the penalty whatever his status. This is what the Prophet meant when he said, 'By Allah, if Fāṭimah, the daughter of Muḥammad, were to steal, I would punish her' (*Bukhārī*).

11. NECESSITY DICTATES EXCEPTIONS

Islam is not oblivious to the exigencies of life, to their magnitude, nor to human weakness and human capacity to face them. It permits the Muslim, under the compulsion of necessity to eat a prohibited food in quantities sufficient to remove the necessity and save himself from death. In this context, after listing the prohibited foods in the form of dead animals, blood, and pork, Allah says: *But if one is compelled by necessity, neither craving* [it] *nor transgressing, there is no sin on him; indeed, Allah is Forgiving, Merciful* (2: 173).

On the basis of this and other similar verses, Islamic jurists formulated an important principle, namely, that 'necessity removes restriction'. However, it is to be noted that the individual experiencing the necessity is permitted to eat the haram food with the stipulation that he is 'neither craving [it] nor transgressing'. A Muslim should not indulge in what is *ḥarām* unless he is forced to, and even then he should only partake of the minimum to justify his most urgent need. The spirit of Islam is that Allah desires to make life easy: *God desires ease for you, and desires not hardship for you* (2: 185). And again: *God desires to lighten things for you, for the human being was created weak* (4: 28).

22

The *Sharīʿah* – Islamic Law

Khurram Murad

To understand the essence of the *Sharīʿah*, one must understand the relationship between the human being and God that Islam lays down. 'There is no god but One God; Muḥammad is the Prophet of God': this simple sentence is the bedrock of the Islamic creed. God is the Creator; to Him Alone, therefore, belongs the Kingdom and He is the Only Sovereign:

Surely Your Only Lord is God who has created the heaven and the earth. Verily to Him belong the Creation and the Sovereignty (7: 54). And: *He has created the heavens and the earth with a purpose. He wraps night about day and He wraps day about night . . . He has created you from one being . . . That then is God, your Only Lord; His is the Kingdom. There is no god but He* (39: 5–6).

God is the Creator. To Him Alone, therefore, as his only Lord and Master, a person must submit his entire being: 'Your God is One God, so only to Him submit' (22: 34). *That then is God, your only Lord; there is no god but He, the Creator of Everything. So, Him Alone serve* (6: 102).

God is the only true Provider. It is He Who has bestowed on the human being such faculties and capabilities as seeing, hearing, thinking and articulating – attributes which he cannot live without, but which he cannot create for himself. It is He Who has made available the resources of the external world which people may discover, exploit and develop but, again, cannot create.

Yet surely a person's greatest need is to know how to live his life so as to fulfil successfully the purpose of his creation; how to relate himself to his Creator, to his own self, to his fellow human beings and to everything around him. To Him Alone he must, therefore, turn to seek guidance. For there is no one apart from or beside Him who can truly provide answers to a person's eternal questions or Who is capable of guiding him. All else can only be speculation and conjecture. And why should the One who has provided even for a person's most trivial material needs not also have provided for his more important moral and spiritual needs?

The Qur'ān says: *Say: Is there any of those you associate* [with God] *who guides to the Truth? Say: only God guides to the Truth. Does then, He Who guides to the Truth deserve more to be followed or he who can guide not unless he be guided? What ails you? How judge you? And most of them follow naught but speculation, and speculation can never take the place of Truth* (10: 35–6). And further: *Or, do they* [claim to] *have associates who have laid down for them the way for which God gave not leave?* (42: 21).

It was to provide for this greatest human need that God sent His Prophets from amongst people in all ages and to all nations, bringing them the Light of the Divine guidance revealed to them. Among them were Adam, Noah, Abraham, Moses and Jesus. And Muḥammad was the last of them, in no way different or new. May God bless all of them. *He has laid down for you the Way that He entrusted to Noah, and that We have revealed to you, and that We entrusted to Abraham, Moses and Jesus. Establish fully the Way and follow not different ways* (42: 13).

A person's relationship to God is expressed by the very word 'Islam' – submitting to Him by following His Will and guidance as brought by His Prophets. But this submission must be total and all-embracing. A Muslim submits his entire 'person' to his Creator as his only Lord and Master. No part of his life can be exempt from the need of Divine guidance or from the Writ of Divine Sovereignty. God and His Lordship and Sovereignty are indivisible; and so is a person's life in its submission to Him. It would, indeed, be an imperfect God who could only be experienced or related to in the realm of the Spirit or in the provision of material needs like one's daily bread – a God unconcerned, uncaring or incompetent to help a person in the more arduous and complex task of living his life. Him he worships; Him he invokes; Him he depends upon; Him he trusts; Him he seeks; and, equally important, Him he obeys. The human being has been given the freedom to reject God; but, once having accepted Him, he must follow His guidance. He is not free to follow one part of it and ignore another, nor to seek guidance from sources other than God. Denial of a part is denial of the whole.

What, believe you in part of the Book and deny part thereof? And what is the reward of those who do so except ignominy in the present life, and on the Day of Resurrection to be returned unto most grievous punishment (2: 85).

What, do they seek another way other than God's Way; whereas unto Him submits whosoever is in the heavens and the earth, willingly or unwillingly (3: 83), *And who seeks a way other than Islam, it shall not be accepted from him* (3: 85).

In its fullest sense, the *Sharīʿah* is, therefore, virtually synonymous, and can be used interchangeably, with the word *dīn*, which can only inadequately be translated as 'religion'. *Dīn* literally means 'Way of Life', 'submission', 'following' or the 'Way'. Though the word *Sharīʿah* in its various derivative forms is found in five places in the Qur'ān, its extensive use only came into vogue much later; for the words Islam and *dīn* were more commonly employed to express the same meaning in the early days of Islam.

The *Sharīʿah* includes both faith and practice. It embraces worship, individual attitude and conduct as well as social norms and laws, whether political, economic, familial, criminal or civil.

It may also sometimes be used to imply, in a more restricted sense, do's and don'ts – the rules and regulations for conduct and behaviour. Lastly, it is also used as the equivalent of the Islamic laws.

The *Sharīʿah* is, thus, nothing less than the Divinely Ordained Way of Life for people. To realise the Divine Will, people must follow the *Sharīʿah*. To live in Islam is to live according to the *Sharīʿah*. To give up the *Sharīʿah* or any part of it knowingly, wilfully or deliberately is to give up Islam. A Muslim must, therefore, do his utmost to observe and to implement the whole of it, wherever and in whatever situation he finds himself. Hence the Muslim insistence, persistence, commitment and passion for it.

HUMAN FREEDOM AND DIGNITY

The act of total submission to God in accordance with the *Sharīʿah* given by Him in no way diminishes human dignity, freedom and responsibility. The act of submission is the highest act of human volition and freedom, for it implies freedom to disobey God. Indeed, in submitting to God, all the chains and shackles of every form of serfdom, servility and bondage are broken, whether they be to other people, to ideas, to nature, to manmade objects or to institutions. For before the affirmation of One God must come the forsaking of every false god.

More importantly, total submission to God elevates a person to the state of *khilāfah* or vicegerency, whereby he is accorded the highest place on earth by being endowed with reason, articulation, volition, freedom and responsibility. The responsibility to follow the *Sharīʿah* according to the Qur'ān (33: 72), is the fulfilment of *amānah*, the trust, which even the heavens, the earth and the mountains dare not bear.

THE SOURCES

How do we know the *Sharī'ah*, the Will of God? There are four sources: the Qur'ān, the *Sunnah* of the Prophet Muḥammad, *ijmā'* and *ijtihād*.

1. The Qur'ān

The principal source of the *Sharī'ah* could only be the Word of God revealed to the Prophet Muḥammad. These revelations are compiled in the Qur'ān which – and nobody disputes this – has come down to us word for word as it was conveyed by the Prophet. Both the meaning and words of the Qur'ān are God's, as it clearly states in variously different ways. It uses extensively the word 'sending down' in preference to any other word to describe the process of revelation. The very first revelation was: 'Read'. The Prophet always clearly indicated when he was using his own words and when he was using words he had received.

The Qur'ān's main emphasis is unquestionably on faith and the moral conduct of people and nations; but it does lay down, both explicitly and implicitly, though with brevity, the principles, broad outlines and necessary rules and regulations which are essential for the formation of the community of Islam. For one cannot be realised without the other; the trust of the *Sharī'ah* cannot be fulfilled without the presence of moral fibre of the highest quality.

2. The *Sunnah*

The Prophet himself was not a mere postman who delivered the Book of God and then disappeared. Acting under Divine guidance, he not only delivered the message, but launched a movement. He changed the people and their society; founded a community; established a state; and spent every moment of his Prophethood in guiding, directing and leading his followers. His example of living by God's guidance, which consists of whatever he did or said or approved of, is the *Sunnah*, the second basic source of the *Sharī'ah*. The authority of the *Sunnah* is firmly rooted in the Qur'ān and in the historically continuous consensus of the Muslim *Ummah*.

The explicit statements in the Qur'ān in this respect are many. By way of paraphrasing, every Prophet was sent to be obeyed (4: 64). The Prophet Muḥammad is the last and perfect model (33: 21). To obey him is to obey God (4: 80). God and the Prophet are frequently coupled together, especially where obedience is enjoined, but the imperative 'obey' is also used separately for God and for His Prophet (4: 59). To follow and obey the Prophet is the only way one can love his God and be loved by Him and have one's sins forgiven (3: 31–2). All matters which cause differences or disputes are to be referred to God and His Prophet as the final authority (4: 59). No one can be truly a believer unless he accepts the Prophet as the final arbiter in all affairs and submits to his decisions, willingly and free from all misgivings (4: 65). The Prophet has the authority to permit and prohibit (on behalf of God) (7: 157). And, finally, whatever the Prophet gives, must be taken; whatever he forbids, must be eschewed (59: 7).

The historically continuous consensus and practice of the *Ummah* dates back to the moment when Abū Bakr, the first Caliph, assumed office and, in his inaugural address, explicitly accepted 'God and (the example of) His Prophet as deserving obedience and binding upon him'. There is also ample evidence that the first community of Islam invariably looked to the *Sunnah* for guidance in every sphere of life. Indeed, ever since that time the entire *Ummah* has almost always been agreed on the *Sunnah* as the second source of the *Sharī'ah*: the very few isolated voices that have been raised in disagreement from time to time have never enjoyed support.

The *Sunnah* is mostly recorded in books of *aḥādīth*. Initially, mainly because people were concerned that the reports of what the Prophet said or did or approved of would get confused with the actual text of the Qur'ān, they were not recorded on a large scale; many compilations were, however, written down privately by individuals, of which authentic evidence exists. As those who had known the Prophet began to die, the need to compile his life example became pressing, and tremendous efforts were made to do so. By the middle of the third century, the first comprehensive source books, those now in use, were completed by *Bukhārī* (d. 870 CE) and *Muslim* (d. 875 CE). More followed and are still extant. *Bukhārī* lists 2,762 Traditions and Muslim approximately 4,000 Traditions, without taking into account repetitions.

That some reports were forged by various political and theological factions was inevitable: the authority of the *Sunnah* was so widely accepted that to fabricate their own Traditions was the only course open to the unscrupulous to project their own opinions. But, first, fabrication itself constitutes strong evidence that the *Sunnah* was accepted as binding from the very earliest times; why otherwise bother to fabricate it? Second, the existence of historical records of forgery also proves that the problem was recognised and tackled as soon as it arose. Finally, and most importantly, to argue, as some have argued, that all the scholars of the *Ummah* for the first two hundred years of Islam were engaged in a carefully co-ordinated plot to do nothing but fabricate *aḥādīth* and put into the mouth of the Prophet their own opinions, is untenable. Such fabrication would have required a stupendous, superbly organised effort of a scope beyond even perhaps the most sophisticated means of communication available today. It is, too, difficult to believe that a single individual like Shāfiʿī, two centuries after the Prophet, when Muslims had spread far and wide, could force all the scholars and the entire *Ummah* against their will to accept the *Sunnah* as the source of the *Sharīʿah*.

3. *Ijmāʿ*

Ijmāʿ or the consensus of the *Ummah* in understanding, interpreting and applying the teachings of the Qur'ān and the *Sunnah* forms the third basic source of the *Sharīʿah*. This can be the only natural, feasible and wise course to determine the *Sharīʿah*.

Any consensus which has a historical continuity from the days of the four Caliphs and the Companions of the Prophet is accepted to be binding. Any other consensus serves as a strong precedent but one which is nonetheless replaceable by another.

Ijmāʿ (within the limits set by the Qur'ān and the *Sunnah*) provides a mechanism for the *Ummah* to undertake legislation collectively on issues and problems it may face in an ever-changing world, and even to venture fresh thinking on past interpretations.

The Shīʿahs would prefer to look to *Imāms* and *mujtahids* to meet this need. But the acceptance of any particular *Imām* or *mujtahid* will also finally depend on the acceptance and consensus of the followers. There are no Divine Signs to support any particular person; and the differences have been many among the Shīʿahs as to who really was the *Imām*.

4. *Ijtihād*

The exercise of reason and judgement to determine the *Sharīʿah* is called *ijtihād*. It subsumes various categories of endeavour such as opinion (*ra'y*), analogy (*qiyās*), equity (*istiḥsān*), public good (*istiṣlāḥ*) and so on. *Ijtihād* is a precursor to *ijmāʿ* and has to be exercised within the framework provided by the Qur'ān and the *Sunnah*. It is a key element in ensuring the dynamism of the *Sharīʿah*, but it is sometimes misunderstood, misrepresented and even misused.

23

Inner Dimensions of the *Sharīʿah*

Khurram Murad

One image of the *Sharīʿah* which has been assiduously cultivated, is that of a collection of laws enforceable only through political authority. This is not the case; all its laws are religious, but religion is not all law. Laws are, therefore, an important and integral part of the *Sharīʿah* and it admits of no distinction between its parts: 'to pray' is as valid, enforceable, obligatory and sacred as 'to consult in collective affairs' or to 'prohibit interest'. Yet the *Sharīʿah* overwhelmingly consists of morals, norms, manners and rules, from worship to statecraft, which depend for compliance entirely upon a person's conscience. 'Law' in modern usage is only that regulation which is enforced by political authority, whereas Muslim scholars use this word to cover every act of human behaviour, even acts of the human heart; for the *Sharīʿah* deals extensively with the intention, just as it does with the duties of prayer, fasting and alms-giving as well as with civil and criminal law.

MOTIVATION AND SANCTION

The entire sanction behind the *Sharīʿah* is a person's inner relationship with his Lord, his love and fear of Him, and his sense of responsibility and accountability to Him, here and after death. Much has been made of the punishments prescribed by the *Sharīʿah*, but it is far less widely appreciated that the Qur'ān and the Prophet have in fact laid down very few such punishments – and, where they have, they concern serious crimes against a fellow human being's life, property or honour. Because of this, perhaps, the *Sharīʿah* has been able to command a powerful and unparalleled following and obedience from Muslims down the ages, and, despite being often deprived of legal and political sanctions, has been accorded a remarkable adherence from one end of the world to the other.

Inner motivation is the main reason why the institutions created by the *Sharīʿah* – like family life, abstinence from alcohol, and chastity – have tenaciously survived for over fourteen centuries. The punishment for drinking is rarely enforced, yet the Muslim world has no alcohol problem. Punishment for adultery is also rare – except in one or two areas – yet the amount of extra-marital sex is very low. Divorce is easy to pronounce, but the divorce rate is extremely low.

LOVE AND LAW

The *Sharīʿah* experiences no tension between 'love' and 'law' or between 'faith' and 'deeds'. Both are integrated into a harmonious whole.

Guiding people to the *Dīn*, the Way, through the *Sharīʿah* is an act of God's greatest mercy, kindness and love. Wherever the 'sending down of the Book' is mentioned in the Qur'ān, the attributes of mercy, wisdom and omnipotence are also mentioned. *A sending down from the Most Merciful, the Mercy-giving* (41: 2). *We sent it down in the blessed night . . . a mercy from your Lord* (44: 3–4). *And following God's guidance is what a person's love for his Lord and Creator must lead to. Those who believe love God most* (2: 165). *But: Say: If you love God, follow me* [the Prophet] (3: 31). And only when one follows the Prophet out of love for God, is his love reciprocated by Him: *God will love you and will forgive your sins* (3: 31).

The very distinction between love and law is alien to the temper of Islam and incomprehensible in its vision. Love is all-embracing; how can it even conceive of displeasing the Beloved and ignoring the guidance given by Him? How can One who loves His creatures leave them wandering and groping in darkness to find answers to the complex problems of life?

MORAL IDEALS AND RULES OF CONDUCT

In Islam, faith is not an abstract theological dogma, nor an intellectual creed, nor a philosophical proposition. It must spring forth into action in day-today life, extending from the inner to the outer, from individual to social, from moral to legal. It is the *Sharīʿah* which translates faith and moral ideals into clear, definable, viable and concrete goals, forms and codes and brings them within the grasp of every ordinary man and woman; this is why it is one of the greatest blessings of God and one of the greatest vehicles for human progress.

If a person has to live a morally good life, if he has been created with a purpose, if he has to meet his Maker, then the moment he opens his eyes and becomes aware and conscious, he must know what to do and what not to do. And he must act in the certain knowledge that what he is following is universally and absolutely true and will please his Creator. Who else, then, other than his Creator should he look to for those answers? Herein lies the beauty of the *Sharīʿah*. Every person knows what his outward conduct ought to be to conform with his faith, his moral ideals. He has an answer to the eternal question: what is 'good'? It matters not whether he is illiterate or a scholar, he can confidently act.

Not that all ethical and moral problems have been solved and buried for ever. So long as a person is alive, he will continue to face difficult choices and dilemmas, old and new. This is a natural corollary of a worldview where a person has to battle incessantly for 'good' against evil. But, in the *Sharīʿah*, he has the means to find the best way to ease and facilitate his task.

INNER DIMENSIONS

To think that Islam emphasises submission to God merely in the outward conduct of life would be a gross misunderstanding. Islam grips the human being's inner self in equal, or even more emphatic, terms. Significantly, the Qur'ān prefers to address Muslims more as 'those who believe', and treats *īmān*, faith, and *ʿamal ṣāliḥ*, good conduct, as 'an integrated whole'.

Indeed, the Qur'ān and the Prophet, at almost every step, stress the importance of the inner relationship to God as compared to mere outward conformity. The true heart of the *Sharīʿah* is not at all formalistic. For example, although Prayers cannot be performed without turning to Makkah, the Qur'ān says, *it is no virtue merely to turn your face to the east or the west* (2: 187); charity is ardently desired, but an act of charity done for the benefit of the doer will bring no reward (2: 264); *it is not the flesh and blood of a sacrificial animal that God desires, but the Taqwā (God-consciousness) inside you* (22: 37). Furthermore, the Prophet declared, 'there are many who fast during the day and pray all night but gain nothing except hunger and a sleepless night' (*Dārimī*); and, finally, *only those who return to God with a pure and wholesome heart, Qalb Salīm, will deserve to be saved* (25: 89).

SHARĪʿAH AND *ṬARĪQAH*

Some in Islam, naturally enough, have concentrated more on developing the ways and means of purifying the inner self and of strengthening the relationship between themselves and God. The leading exponents of this approach, those known to be following a *ṭarīqah*, have been the Sufis. Much has been said about the conflict between the *Sharīʿah* and the *ṭarīqah*. But what we have said above gives the lie to the often propagated idea of any inherent or continuing dichotomy and tension between the two terms – both of which, interestingly enough, are of latter-day origin. (Early Islam used only Islam or *Dīn* which encompassed every aspect of a person's self.) Special circumstances may have led this or that person to lay more emphasis on a certain aspect; a few may even have been sufficiently misled to try to generate tension and conflict between the two or extol one at the expense of the other. But there were never two different Paths or two different expressions of a person's relationship to God. Interestingly, both *Sharīʿah* and *ṭarīqah* have exactly the same meaning – the Way. According to Ibn Taymiyyah, a person observing only the law, without its inner truth, cannot be truly called a believer; and, similarly, a person claiming to possess 'truth' which is at odds with the *Sharīʿah* cannot even be a Muslim.

Even, historically speaking, in early Islam, the two streams, of Sufis and the jurists never flowed separately. Ḥasan al-Baṣrī, the doyen of Sufis, is a major pillar of *fiqh* (jurisprudence) and *tafsīr* (exegesis); whereas Jaʿfar Ṣādiq, Abū Ḥanīfah, Mālik, Shāfiʿī and Aḥmad – the founders of the main schools of Muslim jurisprudence – find pride of place in Farīduddīn Aṭṭār's classical *Tadhkirah al-Awliyā'* (The Book of Saints).

In the Qur'ān and the *ḥadīth* both inward and outward are inseparably intertwined. For example, when the Qur'ān says, *who in their Prayers are humble* (23: 1), then Prayer is what one is likely to categorise as pertaining to the *Sharīʿah*, humility as to the *ṭarīqah*. Or, when it says, *those who believe, love God most* (2: 165), it may be said that the aspect of love fits closely with the spirit of the followers of a *ṭarīqah*, but, at the same time, the Qur'ān emphasises: *Say: If you love God, follow me* (3: 31). Thus Prayer and humility, love and obedience are inseparable, two sides of the same coin.

THE ETERNAL AND UNCHANGING

The *Sharīʿah* is for all times to come, equally valid under all circumstances. The Muslim insistence on the immutability of the *Sharīʿah* is highly puzzling to many people, but any other view would be inconsistent with its basic concept. If it is Divinely ordained, it can be changed by a person only if authorised by God or His Prophet. Those who advise bringing it into line with current thinking recognise this difficulty. Hence they recommend to Muslims that the 'legal' provisions in the Qur'ān and the concept of the Prophet as law-giver and ruler should be 'downgraded'.

But, as the manifestation of God's Infinite Mercy, Knowledge and Wisdom, the *Sharīʿah* cannot be amended to conform to changing human values and standards: rather, it is the absolute norm to which all human values and conduct must conform; it is the frame to which they must be referred; it is the scale on which they must be weighed.

Categorisation of Precepts

As we have already seen, the claim that the *Sharīʿah* is eternal and all-embracing does not in any way imply that every issue for all times to come has been decided. The mechanism through which the *Sharīʿah* solves a problem posed by an unspecified, new or changing situation can be best understood in the framework of the categorisation of its norms and rules and the role it gives to human reason in the form of *ijtihād*.

The code of behaviour and conduct laid down by the *Sharīʿah* divides human acts of heart and body into the following five categories:

- expressly prohibited (*ḥarām*);
- expressly enjoined (*wājib* or *farḍ*);
- disliked but not prohibited (*makrūh*), hence, permissible under certain circumstances;
- recommended but not enjoined (*mandūb*), hence there is no obligation to comply;
- simply without any injunction or opinion, and hence permitted through silence (*mubāḥ*).

It is not commonly realised what a great blessing has been imparted to the *Sharīʿah* by this categorisation: it enables the *Sharīʿah* to accord a vast expanse and degree of latitude to individual choice, freedom and initiative under varying human circumstances. Things which are prohibited or enjoined are few and a major part of day-to-day life falls in the *mubāḥ* category. Still more important and revolutionary is the principle that, in matters of worship, in a narrow sense, only what has been expressly enjoined or recommended, and nothing else, is obligatory or desirable; while, in matters of day-to-day life, whatever is not prohibited is permissible. This closes the door for any religious vested interests to impose upon God's servants additional burdens and duties in the Name of God as has so often been done in history; but at the same time it keeps wide open the options for resolving new problems.

Human Reason and Legislation

Total submission to God does not imply any lesser role for human reason. On the contrary, human reason has a very important and fundamental role to play in the *Sharīʿah* (except that it will be unreasonable for it to overrule its own God). No doubt the *Sharīʿah* is not rational in the sense that its authority does not rest in human reason; but it is rational in the sense that it cannot be meaningfully opposed to reason.

This role consists of understanding and interpreting the Divine guidance in new or changed situations; applying the Divine guidance to actual situations in human life; framing rules, regulations and bylaws for the implementation of the basic principles and injunctions; legislating in those vast areas where nothing has been laid down in the Original Sources. The conduct of the Companions of the Prophet and those who came after them, and the differences in opinions which emerged in the time of the Prophet himself, in the period immediately after him and among successive generations of Muslims, in all spheres of the *Sharīʿah*, bear ample testimony to the role of human reason in the *Sharīʿah*.

Permanence and Change

The role of human reason in the *Sharīʿah*, exercised through understanding and interpretation, *ijtihād* and consensus, *ijmāʿ*, provides it with a built-in mechanism to meet the demands of any changed human situation. The complexities of life and the novelty of the situations which the Muslims faced within fifty years of the Prophet's death bore no comparison to the simple life in Madinah. Yet the *Sharīʿah* successfully coped with all the situations, not only in that period, but for more than a thousand years afterwards, indeed, till the Muslims fell under the political subjugation of Western powers. This, in itself, is living testimony to its inner vitality and inherent capability to face any challenge.

What is important to understand is that none of what is stable and permanent in the *Sharīʿah* is of a nature as to need change. Where changes are necessary due to newly-emerging situations, the *Sharīʿah* has laid down broad principles only and left its adherents to work out the details. Where it has chosen to be specific there is in reality no need for change.

Again, it is only the changed human situations which the *Sharīʿah* caters for, and not for changes in primary and essential values and standards: the Divinely-given values and standards are final.

Historical Development

The issues involved in reviving the *Sharīʿah* in modern times can be better understood against the background of the history of its development.

The *Sharīʿah*, as the code of life derived from the Qur'ān and the *Sunnah*, in its present form, has developed over a long period of time. During the Prophet's life, he was available as the supreme source of guidance and all situations and issues could be referred to him. He either received a direct revelation or laid down the code by his own Prophetic knowledge, wisdom and authority. And, if a situation arose when he could not be approached, the Companions exercised their own judgements to find a solution in the light of the Qur'ān and whatever they had learnt from the Prophet. That he approved of this procedure is borne out by many instances.

For about 100 years after his death, as the Muslim society expanded and new situations arose, the Companions of the Prophet and the scholars trained by them used the same procedure of understanding, interpreting and applying the Qur'ān and the *Sunnah*, using their own reason and judgement. On the one hand, the *Khilāfah Rāshidah* (Rightly-Guided Caliphate) provided a central legislative and political machinery for this purpose. And, on the other, Muslims approached any Companion or trusted scholar of the Qur'ān and the *Sunnah* who was near at hand to find out answers to the problems they faced. They did not consider themselves bound to follow any one particular person and every Companion and scholar answered their questions to the best of his knowledge and wisdom without recourse to any organised body of jurisprudence.

After the period of the *Khilāfah Rāshidah*, Islamic political authority separated from the legal authority and could not play such an effective role; during the next 150 years, however, many Muslim scholars arose to answer the growing needs of Muslims. They gave definite shape to the principles and concepts which were already being used in determining the *Sharīʿah*, and also dealt with the ever more complex situations being faced by the Muslim society. It was during this period that great jurists like Jaʿfar Ṣādiq (d. 765 CE), Abū Ḥanīfah (d. 767 CE), Mālik (d. 795 CE), Shāfiʿī (d. 819 CE), and Aḥmad Ibn Ḥanbal (d. 886 CE) appeared. Each developed a circle of followers, although there were still no organised schools of law and jurisprudence – ordinary Muslims referring their problems to any scholar they could find. This is how a particular scholar came to be followed more in a particular region than another. By 965 CE, the principles laid down by these great scholars had developed into well-defined Schools of Thought and had begun to command the exclusive allegiance of scholars. Over the next 300 years ordinary Muslims also came to adhere to a particular School and owe exclusive allegiance to it. This happened, as explained, because they followed the School of Law to which the scholar or religious leader they found near and trusted belonged, or in some cases, to which the rulers and judges belonged. Inter-school debates and arguments also developed leading to, as often happens in such situations, a hardening of positions.

The fall of Baghdad, in the middle of the 14th century CE, was a watershed. The instinct for preservation became the foremost consideration in an age of intellectual disintegration and political instability. Although there was merit in this caution – the consensus that had been achieved after such tremendous effort by giants could not be allowed to be undone by pygmies – the unwillingness to think dynamically contributed to the decay and intellectual ossification of the *Ummah*.

The situation became worse after Muslims fell under the political subjugation of European powers; they, however, continued to live by the *Sharīʿah* as best they could. But they were no longer masters of their own affairs as an alien culture did its best to sever their links with their culture and traditions.

Ijtihād

Much ado has been made about the closure of the gate of *ijtihād*, the subsequent rigidity that set in and the need for making it wide open today. *Ijtihād* worked as a dynamic institution in the first five centuries of Islam. The giant intellectual upsurge generated by the study of the *Sharīʿah* has few parallels. Later, due to circumstances like the Mongol invasion and Western domination, the Muslims had to fall back upon formal law to preserve the identity of the *Ummah*. But even when the door was presumably closed, whenever new situations arose, efforts were made to find solutions. Of course, those solutions did not involve repudiation of the Qur'ān, the *Sunnah* and *ijmāʿ* – which is perhaps what irks some.

Ijtihād can only be done by those who have the ability and competence, knowledge and understanding, and, above all, the character and piety to undertake the crucial and sacred task of determining the *Sharīʿah*. Whatever may be said about the strictness and rigidity or otherwise of the qualifications imposed by the orthodox, the only criterion that will prevail in the final analysis is that any new *ijtihād* must find acceptance by the Muslim masses, for Islam has not left its revelations in the care of a 'Church'.

One thing is certain: Muslims will never accept, *en masse*, the *ijtihād* of a Hārūn al-Rashīd, a Kemal Ataturk, a Nasser or a Sukarno. An Abū Ḥanīfah, who died in prison and was lashed for his views, or an Aḥmad ibn Ḥanbal, who was persecuted and whipped for his opinions, are more likely to find acceptance by the sheer depth of their faith, steadfastness, fidelity, piety and knowledge. The ethics of the modernists are all too often based on expediency rather than on exemplary practice of the faith; no wonder they can make no headway.

What is required today is a generation of Muslim scholars who know the Qur'ān and the *Sunnah*, who fully understand the value of their heritage of fourteen hundred years, who are highly knowledgeable about Western thought and the strengths and weaknesses of modern times, who have the intellectual vigour and originality of thought to tackle problems afresh, and who, above all, possess the moral and spiritual qualities which bear testimony to their submission and fidelity to God and His Prophet. And such scholars must be supported by political rulers who will look to *ijtihād* not as an escape route but as the true way to live by the *Sharīʿah*.

Non-Muslims, both within Muslim countries and the Western countries, as well as international observers, will do well not to hinder the sometimes painful process of regaining self-identity, but rather seek to understand it.

SECTS AND SCHOOLS OF LAW

Will not various Schools of law and sects present formidable problems in the implementation of the *Sharīʿah*? Yes, to, some extent. As we know, countless scholars and hundreds of schools of thought blossomed during the first four centuries of Islam, its intellectual Golden Age, but only four have survived among the Sunnīs and most Shīʿas follow Jāʿfar as-Ṣādiq. The Ḥanafī School is predominant in Bangladesh, Pakistan, India, Afghanistan, West Asia and lower Egypt; the Maliki in North and West Africa; the Shāfiʿī in Indonesia and Malaysia; the Ḥanbalī and Shāfiʿī in Arabia; and the Jaʿfarī in Iran and parts of Iraq.

Although there have been periods of dogmatism, sectarian violence and rigidity in attitude (none, however, comparable in intensity to the religious wars of Europe), the differences between the various Schools pale into insignificance when compared with their similarities. Indeed, in essentials they hardly have any differences. Divergence occurs in the way that two courts, attempting to interpret the same law, may arrive at different conclusions. The differences may present problems, but they are not insurmountable. Although it may be difficult to return to the traditions of the earliest times of Islam, a solution is possible by allowing Muslims in each region to implement the *Sharīʿah* through a consensus of persons commanding the trust of the majority; while in personal law each sect should be free to follow its own legal system.

MUSLIM MINORITIES

Large Muslim communities now live in non-Muslim countries. Many have made the West their home, perhaps many more have known nothing but the West as their home. How can they live by the *Sharīʿah*? Obviously they have every intention of continuing to live where they are now and of making their own distinctive contribution to the societies around them. This contribution will be based on the rich culture of Islam, at the heart of which is the *Sharīʿah*. That a vast majority of them, under very difficult circumstances, still try to observe the *Sharīʿah* as best they can is a further testimony to its powerful roots.

Unfortunately, Muslims living in some non-Muslim countries face difficulties and hardships in their attempts to observe the *Sharīʿah*. The difficulties extend to very small and simple day-to-day matters such as their worship rites and what they may eat, drink and wear. In some places few real opportunities are available, for example, to offer Friday Prayers or to have appropriate diets in such institutions as schools, hospitals and prisons. Indeed, in some cases the majority of communities and their governments simply fail to acknowledge the existence of Muslims in their midst.

Efforts to assimilate Muslims into the majority culture at the expense of their observance of Islam will be of no benefit to the culture itself. Muslims who contravene the *Sharīʿah* would live with a sense of inner guilt deriving from the awareness that they have betrayed their own consciences.

CONCLUSION

Whatever reservations an outsider may have about specific provisions of the *Sharīʿah*, it should nevertheless be possible for him to appreciate the deep foundations, the solid framework and the breathtaking beauty of an institution which gave rise to one of the finest of human civilisations and which, to this day, continues to sustain and inspire every fifth person who walks on this globe. For the *Sharīʿah* literally means the Path to Water, the Source of Life.

24

Introdution to *Fiqh*

Sayyid Sabiq

Allah sent Muḥammad (pbuh) with the true way of worship of Allah and the complete code of law which provides people with the most honourable life and takes them to the highest degree a human being can attain. In a period of about twenty-three years, the Prophet completed his mission of inviting people to Allah and preaching His religion and gathering people into its fold.

THE UNIVERSALITY AND GOAL OF THE MESSAGE

Islam was not meant for a certain time or a certain generation or a certain people; in fact, it was a message for all of humanity, for all time. Allah says in the Qur'ān, *Blessed is He who has revealed to His slave the Criterion* [of right and wrong], *that he may be a warner to all of the peoples* (25: 1). He also said, *And We have not sent you* [O Muḥammad] *save as a bringer of good tidings and a warner to all people; but most people know not* (34: 28). And, *Say* [O Muḥammad]: *'O people, Lo! I am the messenger of Allah to you all* [the messenger of] *Him unto whom belongs the Sovereignty of the heavens and the earth. There is no God save Him, He gives life and He gives death. So believe in Allah and His Messenger, the Prophet who can neither read nor write, who believes in Allah and in His words and follow him that haply you may be led aright'* (7: 158). In an authentic *ḥadīth,* the Prophet said, 'Every Prophet was sent only to his people, but I have been sent to all people'.

That this message is universal can be illustrated by the following:

1. There is nothing difficult in this religion for any person to believe or act upon. The Qur'ān states, *Allah does not burden a soul beyond what it can bear* (2: 286). Also, *Allah desires ease for you, and He does not desire hardship for you* (2:185). And, *He has not laid upon you any hardship in religion* (22: 78). In *Ṣaḥīḥ al-Bukhārī,* it is recorded from Abū Saʿīḍ al-Muqbirim that the Messenger of Allah, upon whom be peace, said, 'This religion is easy. If anyone tries to make this religion difficult [upon himself], then it will overcome him.' In *Ṣaḥīḥ Muslim,* a *ḥadīth* says: 'The most beloved religion in the sight of Allah is the pure and tolerant worship of Allah.'

2. Those aspects that are eternal regardless of time or place, for example, matters of belief and worship, have been thoroughly explained in clear texts that encompass every aspect. No one can add or delete anything from them. Those aspects that are subject to change due to time or place, for example, affairs related to politics or war, and so on, have been explained with general guidelines useful for mankind in every age. These guidelines are to be used by leaders to establish truth and justice in their lands regardless of time or location.

3. The teachings of this religion aim at preserving faith, life, intellect, lineage, and legitimate earnings. These goals are definitely in harmony with the nature of mankind, easy for one to accept, and fit for every time, and place. Says Allah, *Say:* [O Muḥammad] *Who has forbidden the adornment of Allah which He has brought forth for His servants, and the good things of His providing? Say: Such, on the Day of Resurrection, will be only for those who believed during the life of the world. Thus, do We detail Our revelations for people who have knowledge. Say: My Lord forbids only indecencies which are apparent and fall under sin and wrongful oppression, and that you associate with Allah that for which no warrant has been revealed and that you tell concerning Allah that which you know not* (7: 156–157). He also says, *My Mercy embraces all things; therefore, I shall ordain it for those who ward off [evil] and pay the zakāh, and those who believe in our revelations, and those who follow the messenger, the Prophet who can neither read nor write, whom they will find described in the Torah and the Gospel* [which are] *with them. He will enjoin on them that which is right and forbid them from doing that which is wrong. He will make lawful for them all good things and prohibit for them only the foul; he will relieve them of their burdens and the fetters that they used to wear. Then those who believe in him, honour him help him, and follow the light which is sent down with him – they are the successful* (7: 156–157).

Islam seeks to purify the souls through the recognition of Allah and His worship and to reinforce the ties of people and to establish them on the basis of love, mercy, brotherhood, equality and justice This will bring happiness to people both in this life and the Hereafter. Says Allah in the Qur'ān, *He it is Who has sent among the unlettered ones a messenger of their own, to recite unto them His revelations and to make them grow, and to teach them the Scripture and Wisdom, though before they were indeed in manifest error* (62: 2). Allah also says, *We sent you not* [O Muḥammad] *but as a mercy for humanity* (21: 107). In a *ḥadīth* the Prophet says, 'I am a merciful guide.'

THE *SHARĪ'AH* OF ISLAM OR *FIQH*

The *Sharī'ah* is the most important aspects of Islam; it is the practical aspect of this message. But genuine laws, such as those related to worship, can only be a revelation from Allah to His Prophet, that is, from the Qur'ān or the *Sunnah*. Needless to say, the Prophet, upon whom be peace, did not go beyond conveying and explaining the message. Allah says concerning him, 'Your companion [i.e. Muḥammad] errs not, nor is he deceived, nor does he speak of [his own] desire. It is nothing but a revelation that is revealed to him' (*al-Najm*).

There are some general principles that Islam lays down which the Muslims are expected to follow. These are:

1. It is not allowed to speculate about events that have not happened until they actually occur. Allah states, *O you who believe! Ask not of things which, if they were made known to you, would trouble you; but if you ask of them when the Qur'ān is being revealed, they will be made known to you. Allah pardons this for Allah is Forgiving, Clement* (5: 101). There is also a *ḥadīth* in which the Prophet prohibited the discussion of events that have not yet occurred.

2. One should avoid asking too many questions which lead to speculation. A *ḥadīth* says, 'Verily Allah dislikes vain talk, asking too many questions, and wasting wealth.' The Prophet also stated, 'Allah has made certain things obligatory, so do not cause them to be lost. He has fixed certain limits, so do not transgress them. And He, without being forgetful, has been silent about certain things as a mercy, so do not search into them.' He also said, 'The person who has the greatest sin is one who asked about something that was not forbidden, and that thing was made forbidden due to his questions.'

3. One should avoid creating differences, splits or sects within Islam. Says Allah in the Qur'ān, *And lo! This nation of yours is one nation and I am your Lord, so keep your duty to Me* (23: 52). *And hold fast, all of you together, to the rope of Allah, and do not separate* (3: 103). *And do not dispute with each other lest you should falter* (8: 46). *Lo! As for those who sunder their religion and become*

schismatics (6: 159). *Of those who split up their religion and became schismatics, each sect exulting in its tenets* (30: 32), and *Be not as those who separated and disputed after the clear proofs had come unto them. For such there is an awful doom* (3: 105).

4. Any disputed issue is to be referred to the Qur'ān and the *Sunnah*. This is in accordance with Allah's words, *And if you have a dispute in any matter, refer it to Allah and the Messenger if you are* [in truth] *believers in Allah and the Last Day* (4: 54). *And in whatever you differ, the verdict therein belongs to Allah* (42: 100). This is because the religion has been explained in the Book. Allah says, *And We reveal the Scripture to you as an exposition of all things* (16: 89), and *We have neglected nothing in the Book* (6: 38).

The *Sunnah* explains how the Book is to be applied. Says Allah, *And We have revealed to you the Remembrance that you may explain to mankind that which has been revealed to them* (16: 44), and, *Lo! We reveal to you the Scripture with the truth, that you may judge between people by that which Allah shows you* (4: 105). The injunctions were completed and the teachings were made clear. Thus, says Allah, *This day have I perfected your religion for you and completed My favour to you and have chosen Islam for you as religion* (5: 3).

As such, there is no need for any differences for Allah says, *Lo! Those who find* [a cause of] *disagreement in the Scripture are in open schism* (2: 176). *But no, by your Lord, they will not believe* [in truth] *until they make you* [Muḥammad] *adjudicate between them and find themselves in agreement with what you have decided, and submit with full submission* (4: 66).

The Companions and those who followed them in the early pious generations followed the preceding principles. They did not differ among themselves save in a few questions, primarily because some of them had a better understanding of some verses or *ḥadīth* than the others.

When the founding *imāms* of the four legal schools appeared, they followed the same way as the people before them, except that some of them were closer to the *Sunnah,* such as those in the Ḥijāz, because of their familiarity with a large number *of ḥadīth* and reports from the earlier generations. Others were more familiar with juristic reasoning, such as those in Iraq, who did not have access to as many *ḥadīth* as the others.

These scholars did their best to teach the people their religion and offer them proper guidance, but they forbade people from following them blindly and told them, 'It is not allowed for anyone to say what we have said without knowing the evidence for our position.'

They made it clear that their school of thought was whatever the authentic *ḥadīth* stated. They did not have the intention of having the people follow them like they should follow the Prophet Muḥammad, upon whom be peace, who was protected from sin or mistake by Allah. All of them just intended to aid the people in understanding the commands of Allah.

But the people after them exaggerated their importance and began to follow them more and more blindly. Every group thought it sufficient just to follow what was found in their school of thought and to strictly adhere to it. They put the statements of their *imām* on the same level as that of the *Sharīʿah*. They went to such an extreme in their trust of their *imām* that al-Karkhī ventured as far as to say, 'Every verse or *ḥadīth* that differs from what the people of our school of thought follow either has a non-obvious explanation or it is abrogated.'

This blind observance of one *madhhab* caused the Muslim *Ummah* to lose the guidance of the Qur'ān and the *Sunnah*. The door to juristic reasoning was closed. The *Sharīʿah* became the statement of the jurists, and the statement of the jurists became the *Sharīʿah*. Anyone who differed from what they said was regarded as an innovator, whose words were neither to be trusted nor followed.

What deteriorated the situation further was the attitude of the rulers and wealthy who supported the institutes of learning. They limited themselves to one *madhhab* or to certain *madhāhib* only. This was one of the reasons why certain *madhāhib* were accepted at the expense of others, and why people turned away from independent juristic reasoning. In this way, they protected their wages and sustenance. Abū Zarʿah asked his teacher al-Balqīnī, 'Why doesn't Shaykh Taqiyyudīn as-Subkī exercise *ijtihād* or juristic reasoning when he is qualified to do so?' Al-Balqīnī had no response. Abū Zarʿah said, 'As far as I can see, there is nothing to keep him from doing so except jobs and positions, that are available to jurists of the four *madhāhib*, for such jobs are not available to those who depart [from these *madhāhib*]. They are not allowed to become judges, and people are discouraged from following their rulings by accusing them of innovations.' Al-Balqīnī agreed with his opinion.

By blindly following the *madhāhib* and losing the guidance of the Qur'ān and *Sunnah* and by closing the door to juristic reasoning or *ijtihād*, this *Ummah* lost its unity and entered into the den of the lizard, which the Messenger of Allah, upon whom be peace, had warned it about. As a result, the Muslim nation broke into different groups and sects to such an extent that they differed over whether or not it was permissible for a follower of the Ḥanafī *madhhab* to marry a woman of the Shāfiʿī *madhhab*. Some said that such a marriage would not be valid because the Shāfiʿī woman's faith was in doubt. Others said that such a marriage is valid by analogy to marriage with the 'people of the book'! Among other effects were: the spreading of innovations, the decline in teaching of the *Sunnah*, a decay in intellectual thought, and reasoning, and so on. This led to the weakening of the nation's integrity. They lost the purposeful life and hence progress and growth. With cracks inside, the outsiders were able to strike at the core of Islam.

Generations passed; and in every period, Allah would raise someone to renew His religion and guide His people. But whenever Muslims awoke, they would remain so only for a short while, for they would soon return to their previous state of existence or to something even worse!

Finally, the implementation of the *Sharīʿah,* by which Allah guides mankind, had reached a stage never reached before. Learning it became so degraded that it was seen by some as ruining one's intellect and thus a waste of time. This kind of attitude was of no benefit to Islam or to the life of the Muslims.

The scholars, oblivious of the changes around them, kept themselves occupied with the texts, commentaries, debates and discussions until Europe triumphed over the East. Muslims were shaken; they woke up to find themselves facing a new world. Astonished and amazed by what they saw, they began to reject their history, disrespect their forefathers and forget their religion. They followed Europe in its good as well as harmful aspects, in its beliefs and disbeliefs. Those who were ignorant took a negative attitude. They equated the *Sharīʿah* with decadence rather than progress.

Yet Islam called people back to their roots, back to the guidance of the Qur'ān and *Sunnah,* and challenged them to take their religion from these sources and spread this religion to others. By that, they would achieve the liberated life, and they would become truly happy.

Verily, in the Messenger of Allah you have a good example for him who looks unto Allah and the Last Day (33: 21).

25

Understanding Juristic Differences

Ahmad Zaki Hammad

'The problem with Muslims is that they cannot agree on anything.' I have heard this statement countless times in communities across the Muslim world. This is untrue. Our dilemma is that we do not know how to disagree.

There is a certain spirit of mercy and tolerance that must prevail when Muslims differ. That can only happen when a person begins to understand that the *Sharīʿah*, which touches all of human activity, is miraculously flexible.

Yet the message that Islam is a comprehensive way of life will be empty if we fail to agree on the mentality that one must come to the *Sharīʿah* with, and to recognise that understanding is a human quality which can naturally result in varied opinions and conclusions.

Amateur *faqīhs* (who seem to be everywhere) and, worse, those who have not had a chance to fathom the depths of the *Sharīʿah*, may be satisfied by their first or second or tenth encounter with a text or two, yet are shocked when they see others differing with their understanding.

Difference is not in itself evil. It is the Creator's signature across the universe, reflecting His splendour. But without a common knowledge for its causes, and Islam's ample room for it, differing can be dangerous.

KHILĀF AND *IKHTILĀF*

Among other things, the Arabs have applied the noun *khilāf* to a barren tree, a willow which bears no fruit. The place where it grows is called *wādī al-makhlafah*, the valley of fruitlessness.

Coming from the same root as *khilāf* (*kh-l-f*) *ikhtilāf* means dissimilarity or disagreement. Al-Rāghib al-Isfahānī, a lexicographer of Qur'ānic terminology, explains that if considering two things, '*Al-ikhtilāf* (or *al-mukhālafah*) denotes that each thing is on a path other than the path of its counterpart, in state or in statement. Another of its meanings is 'inequality'; things which are not equal being certainly different and distinguished from one another. As for *khilāf*, it means 'conflict,' connoting the meaning of *ikhtilāf* and exceeding it'.

The majority of scholars, however, do not distinguish in technical usage between *khilāf* and *ikhtilāf*. They use them interchangeably when describing conflict between persons based on differences of opinion, persuasion, belief, and matters of religion. In other words, the terms indicate discord in the points of view and positions of people.

Still, if the motive for disagreement is selfless, a matter of devotion to Allah, then, it is ultimately beneficial – in this world and the next. But the ends of self-serving dispute are punishment and suffering, here and in the hereafter.

ISLAMIC TEXTS AND *IKHTILĀF*

The Qur'ānic verses and the Prophet's utterances are unequivocal in urging Muslims to unity, solidarity, and a bonding commitment. Allah, the Exalted, states, *Hold firmly to the rope of Allah altogether, and do not become divided* (3: 103). Also, He says, *Truly Allah loves those who strive in His path in ranks as though they were a cemented structure* (61: 4).

Similarly, Allah has forbidden division and contentiousness in His statement: *Do not dispute or you will fail and lose your power; rather be patient. Indeed Allah is with the patient* (8: 46). And again, *Be not like those who divided and differed after Clear Signs had come to them. And it is those for whom there is a great punishment* (3: 105).

The Prophet also warned Muslims not to become divided; for 'indeed, those before you divided and they perished' (*Fatḥ al-Bārī*). The Prophet also has said, 'The Hand of Allah is with the Community, and whosoever secedes does so into the Fire.'

NATURAL DIVERSITY

Repeatedly, the Qur'ān urges us to observe and contemplate the overwhelming diversity in creation. Unique and variant forms and colours in our vast universe are clear signs and displays of the power of the Creator.

Surely in the creation of the heavens and the earth and the diversity of night and day there are signs for those of insight (3: 190). In another verse, *And of His Signs is the creation of the heavens and the earth and the diversity of your languages and colours* (30: 2).

Humanity's diversity is obvious. But it is not overwhelmed by things like colour and form. It includes natural gifts, talents, and temperaments. Dispositions differ to the extent that each one has his or her personal motivating forces. Even the anxieties that move people are different inside each individual. Indeed, natural diversity can affect each person's point of view.

Allah establishes in the Qur'ān that, *Had your Lord He so willed, He would have made them all a single nation, yet they will not cease differing* (11: 118).

Allah did not will to create a monolithic, uniform human species, equal and compatible in all ways. Rather, He cast human nature into various moulds and fixed firmly in it the capacity to bear diversity.

It is popularly attributed to the Prophet, peace be upon him, that he said, 'The Jews have split into seventy-one sects, the Christians into seventy-two; my Community will divide into seventy-three groups – all will be in Fire except one' (*Aḥmad bin Ḥanbal*). This *ḥadīth* is not acceptable as a justification for sectarianism among Muslims, nor does it deny the inherent evil of it. Rather, it is a warning to the intelligent to avoid the kind of diversity that leads to sectarianism.

BLAMEWORTHY DIFFERENCE

Disbelief in and rejection of the *Sharīʿah* is the most reprehensible type of *khilāf*, those holding that position being clearly astray. Indeed, it is a distinguishing characteristic of *kufr* or disbelief. The Qur'ān states: *So let those who deviate from His commandments beware, lest they be struck by an affliction or a severe punishment* (24: 63). Also, *Surely those who oppose Allah and His Messenger, they are the lowly* (58: 20).

A second form of blameworthy divergence of opinion lies in claiming things to be part of Islam that Allah has not prescribed. 'Various forms of error and misguidance', the Prophet said, 'would emerge from a people coming forth from the East. They recite the Qur'ān, yet it does not penetrate their beings any deeper than their throats. They fly out of Islam as arrows fly forth from their bows, and they return to Islam no more than a spent arrow returns to its archer' (*Fatḥ al-Bārī*).

A third type of difference takes place among the various legal Schools or *madhāhib*: the belief of some that their positions are correct and all others invalid. A statement from al-Karkhī, a Ḥanafī scholar, epitomises the aberrant perspective that comes with excessive commitment to one's legal School: 'The guiding principle with us [Ḥanafī's] is that every Qur'ānic verse which differs from our legal School must be interpreted as either being abrogated [by another verse] or improperly understood. In principle, every statement in dispute of a similar ruling of ours must be considered countered by our proof, so as to accommodate the School's final position.'

PRAISEWORTHY DIFFERENCE

Allah and His Prophet have commanded the Muslims to differentiate themselves from pagans or advocates of other beliefs and behaviour. In a number of *aḥādīth*, Muslims are bid to distinguish themselves from and not mimic 'the Magians'; 'the pagans' and 'the Christians and Jews'.

Likewise, the Qur'ān addresses the Prophet, *We have set you upon a sacred law in this affair. So consistently adhere to it and do not follow the vain desires of those who are devoid of knowledge* (45: 18). In the same light, the Prophet said, 'Whosoever imitates a people becomes one of them' (*Aḥmad bin Ḥanbal*).

Muslims should be distinct from non-Muslims including the celebration of pagan sacred festivals and customary social practices, dress, and other commonly distinguishing factors that conflict with Islam. Ibn Taymiyyah, however, held the following position: 'If a Muslim resides in a non-Muslim land that is either at war or peace [with Muslims], he is not compelled to oppose them in outward conduct because of the harm it may bring. In fact, it may be preferable or even mandatory for him to occasionally participate in their outward conduct provided that there is a religious benefit, such as inviting them to religion, repelling harm from Muslims, or other virtuous ends.'

The differences of opinion between schools of thought are also an acceptable form of difference if views are expressed with respect and are removed from bigotry.

WHY DIFFERENCES?

As we 'rethink' the original sources of Islam in our lives, we are bound to differ. Does that mean we can all be right in whatever well-intentioned decisions we make? Is it possible that all the various legal decisions are correct? Or is it the case that there are mistaken and correct ones?

Some jurists have opted for the idea that all conflicting judgements are accurate. Al-Qarāfī, for instance, is reported to have described the relationship between variant opinions qualitatively. He said the *Sharī'ah* encompasses all decisions due to its great breath. The majority of legal theorists, however, believed that the Truth in each case is only one, even though people may be unable to conclusively reach it. However, the *mujtahid* or legal practitioner who has fully and conscientiously exhausted his ability and missed the correct position does not commit a violation and is not blameworthy. On the contrary, he receives heavenly praise, as the Prophet stated; and people are free to follow these legitimate legal positions.

CAUSES OF LEGAL DIVERSIFICATION

Most legal diversity between scholars can be reduced to one, or a combination, of five causal factors.

1. The Nature of Arabic

First, Arabic, like other languages, has its native intricacies. Scholars classify this as linguistic ambiguity, by which they mean some phrases validly accept more than one meaning, where the alternate meaning is literal and not metaphorical.

In the Qur'ān there are some instances of this equivocal terminology. As such, scholars differed in their comprehension of what exactly Allah's intent was in certain instances.

The problem of a man engaging in non-conjugal sexual intimacy with his wife during her menstruation is a well-known example of this kind of differing. *They seek guidance in regard to menstruation. Say, it is a harm,* the Qur'ān reads. Also, *Refrain from your women during menstruation. Do not approach them until they have purified themselves* (2: 222).

What is the meaning of 'not approaching them' during menstruation? Prominent jurists like Mālik and Abū Ḥanīfah and a large number of other scholars, adopted the position that there should be total abstinence during menstruation. So they forbade that a man approach his wife for any type of sexual activity, except what had been clearly laid out in a *ḥadīth* of the Prophet's wife, ʿĀ'ishah, and others of his wives.

The Prophet approached his wives, even during their menstruation, enjoying intimate contact without intercourse. He would request them to wear a garment to cover the feminine organ.

Imām Shāfiʿī, in one opinion recorded of him, as well as the jurists Thawrī, Dāwūd (of the Ẓāhirī school) and Muḥammad bin al-Ḥasan (a Ḥanafī) interpret the command 'Refrain from your women during menstruation' to mean 'avoidance of the organ itself', that is, the place of menstruation.

Another significant cause of juristic divergence when it comes to language is the various Qur'ānic recitations, approved by the Prophet. A good example is the Qur'ānic verse referring to the washing of the feet in *wuḍū'* or ritual ablution. Does it state that we are obliged to 'wash' them or will a symbolic 'passing' of the hands over them suffice?

The underlying cause of the different opinions is the possible readings of the verse, *When you stand to pray, wash your faces, and your hands to the elbows, then wipe your heads, and feet to the ankles* (5: 6).

The discussion hinges on a point of Arabic grammar. Some scholars render the word 'feet' as *arjul<u>a</u>kum* (accusative). Others, like Ibn Kathīr, recited the same word as *arjul<u>i</u>kum* (genitive). This variation in recitation thus gives way to divergence in law.

The first group says the washing of the feet is mandatory. Of course, they look to the Prophet's *Sunnah* to verify their judgement. They cite a *ḥadīth* of the Prophet which establishes the obligation of foot washing in *wuḍū'*: ʿAbdullāh b. ʿAmr b. Al-Āṣ reports: 'The Prophet parted from us during travel. We eventually caught up with him, though we had [delayed] the late afternoon Prayer. When we made ablutions, we were merely wiping our feet, at which the Prophet cried out in his loudest voice, 'Woe from the fire to those who fail to include the feet up to the ankles.' He said it two or three times.' (*Bukhārī*).

The practice of the Prophet strengthens the statements recorded about him. He regularly washed his feet if he was barefooted, and wiped over his footwear if in shoes or leather socks. This is the opinion of most scholars, the stronger one according to Sunnī juristic literature, in terms of evidence and validity.

Now, the literalist looked at this word and, since it contained both meanings, said the obligation is both washing and wiping. Others, like Ibn Jarīr al-Ṭabarī (ninth century CE), saw it as a choice between the two, washing or wiping. Shawkānī has commented on these various legal opinions with great insight, and accuracy, I might add. 'As for those who have made wiping mandatory, they have not presented a clear decisive proof. This, even though they [in effect] differ from the Qur'ān and [in fact] with the consensus of the *ḥadīth* literature.'

2. Differing Methods of Analysis and Legal Approaches

The second problem relates to how a jurist approaches an issue and to what extent he can interpret texts. An important factor here is simply what sources a jurist deems valid, aside from the Qur'ān and *Sunnah*. This is a matter of method. The Ḥanafī, for instance, are known to give much weight to reason in their method. They use proof by analogy, called *qiyās*, extensively, holding it to be an important 'source' for the *Sharīʿah*. In other words, when they come to an unprecedented case, they derive an Islamic rule for it by making an analogy between the new case and a similar one that has a specific ruling in the Qur'ān or *Sunnah*. But some jurists reject *qiyās* as a valid source of the *Sharīʿah*. Indeed, some discredit its use completely. It is easy to see how this difference in method can lead to a difference in law.

Some Schools hold a particular source of law to be valid, but differ on how it may be constituted. *Ijmāʿ*, for example, is the consensus of the community, or *Ummah*. The Mālikīs readily acknowledge consensus as a valid *Sharīʿah* source. But they consider the community of Madinah – the city of the Prophet – to be the community of consensus.

The Shāfiʿīs, on the other hand, reject limiting consensus to Madinah, saying it is all Muslims at any given time, as represented by the community of scholars. Some think consensus can only be established by all Muslims from day one to the end of time, which means you couldn't have *ijmāʿ* until the Day of Judgement. Not a very useful source.

These differences in methodology affect the legal conclusions of various Schools. Let me try to clarify this by taking a case involving *qiyās*, analogy.

The Ẓāhirīs, who are literalists refuse analogy as a *Sharīʿah* source. So they would conclude that deliberate eating or drinking during Ramaḍān would not necessitate atonement, called *kaffārah*. The reason being that *kaffārah*, according to them, is established based on a *ḥadīth* that the Prophet uttered in regard to a particular incident, namely, intercourse between husband and wife during the fast of Ramaḍān. Since the *ḥadīth* did not specify eating or drinking during the fast, they do not necessitate atonement. But the majority of jurists made the analogy for deliberate eating and drinking during Ramaḍān based on this *ḥadīth*. They concluded atonement is obligatory for those who violate fasting by either eating or drinking, or intercourse during the actual fasting in Ramaḍān.

Now, we go to *ijmāʿ*. A number of reports related to the Prophet indicate that it is permissible to call the *iqāmah*, which tells us Prayer is imminent, repeating every phrase twice, exactly like the *adhān*, which is the call telling us Prayer is in. Yet *Imām* Mālik disagreed with this understanding, based on the fact that the practice of the Madinah community was contrary to it. Remember, he considered consensus, *ijmāʿ*, a *Sharīʿah* source, but limited it to the consensus of the scholars of Madinah.

As for the *iqāmah*, the second calling for Prayer, its words cannot be repeated (like the *adhān*). He says in his book *Al-Muwaṭṭā'*, 'This in fact is the practice of the scholars in our city [Madinah].'

Many other cases show the effect of juristic method on *Sharīʿah* rulings. So it is of the utmost importance to be aware of the characteristics of scholars' juristic thinking. This will go a long way to understanding the difference between their views.

3. Unfamiliarity or Uncertainty Regarding Specific *Ḥadīth*

This brings us to our third cause for legal divergence which relates to a jurist's lack of familiarity with a *ḥadīth*, or his doubt as to its authenticity. Incomplete knowledge or doubt of the Qur'ān cannot, of course, be used as a reason to justify dispute. This is because the Qur'ān has been reported by what is called *tawātur*, a continuous, overwhelming and reliable chain of reporters. Ignorance here is no justification, unlike with *ḥadīth*.

First, Muslims recognise that not all *aḥādīth* have been reported through *tawātur* from the Messenger of Allah. No one should find it strange that a number of jurists – even among the Companions – were unaware of some *aḥādīth*, either forgetting them or simply not hearing them from the Prophet.

Abū Bakr, for instance, the first Caliph, did not know the share of the grandmother in inheritance. But he asked various Companions until he found the answer with al-Mughīrah b. Shuʿbah and Muḥammad b. Maslamah. Both told him what they had heard the Prophet say.

Also, Abū Hurayrah, the Companion, used to say, 'Whosoever wakes up after dawn during Ramaḍān in a state of *janābah* (ritual impurity after sexual relations), his fasting is invalid.' He was not aware of the authentic report by the Prophet's wife, ʿĀ'ishah, that the Prophet sometimes heard the *adhān* for Dawn Prayer while in the state of *janābah*. Yet he continued his fast (*Muslim*).

Again, ʿAbdullāh b. ʿAmr b. Al-Āṣ used to instruct women who performed ritual bathing, *ghusl*, for either completing menstruation or giving birth, that they should untie or comb out their hair. ʿĀ'isha objected to this saying, 'What a strange position from the son of ʿAmr. Shouldn't he require them also to shave their heads? When I used to perform *ghusl* with the Prophet from a single vessel, I simply poured water on my head three times' (Muslim).

Understanding this cause of juristic difference and reflecting on it explains why legal divergence occurred even in the community of the Companions and their Successors. Knowledge of the Prophet's *Sunnah* and *aḥādīth*, which he taught, was learned by those who saw and heard him. Each one of them obtained as much as he or she could without any one of them enjoying mastery over it all. The Companions who travelled to various regions taught their Successors whatever they knew, who taught people after them, and so on, through the incredible – and unparalleled – system of *riwāyah*, transmission of *aḥādīth* from one generation to the next, until this day. It may not be an extreme position to say ignorance of *ḥadīth* in our time – after the monumental and exhaustive efforts of our predecessors to report the *Sunnah* and write it in the various collections – is not justifiable by any jurist. 'I do not know the *ḥadīth*' is not good enough. For virtually all of these *aḥādīth* texts are available to us, and the would-be jurist must begin by educating himself about them.

4. Apparent Conflict between Texts

Fourthly, there is the conflict between evidences. This is important, and requires, really, an excellent knowledge of a number of Islamic sciences. Sometimes it appears as if tension or conflict exists between separate *Sharīʿah* texts, that is, the Qur'ān and the *Sunnah*. In giving preference to one evidence over another, jurists varied in their approach to resolving apparent conflicts.

For example, the Prophet's *ḥadīth*, 'Whosoever touches his genitals should not pray without performing ablution' is in apparent conflict with another. The Prophet was asked about a person who touches his genitals during Prayer. 'Isn't it part of your body,' he answered, meaning, continue Prayer if it should occur.

The first *ḥadīth* is acknowledged by Shāfiʿī and Isḥāq b. Rahawī as being the latest statement of the Prophet. So it would abrogate the other reports on this topic. But Ḥanafī jurists have adopted the second *ḥadīth* as valid, expressing uncertainty about the authenticity of the first. It should be clear that the cause of difference is the apparent conflict between two *Sharīʿah* texts for one case, without it being decisive that one abrogates the other.

5. Unprecedented Occurrences not Specifically Addressed by the Texts of the *Sharīʿah*

The absence of a *Sharīʿah* text for an unprecedented case increases the likelihood of legal differing. The best examples here are the many issues and challenges that we now face. In the areas of economics, politics, and so on, we have in our hands few explicit texts stating the Islamic position or the *Sharīʿah* ruling. So jurists exert their efforts – in light of recognised sources of law, experience, and the general principles of *Sharīʿah*, both the spirit and the letter – to find solutions. It is self-evident that their Islamic rulings and conclusions will differ based on the extent of their knowledge and mastery of the issues.

This phenomenon occurs naturally as issues and cases seem to change, while the *Sharīʿah* texts are limited. Yet since Islam is the decreed way of life for humanity until the Day of Judgement, it is incumbent upon every generation to find solutions for new issues. Today's jurists should not freeze in their tracks, arguing that there are no texts to follow. We have an example of a case which the Companions had to deal with after the death of the Prophet for which they had no precedent. Yet they faced them.

The governor of Yemen during the caliphate of ʿUmar requested his Islamic judgement for a gruesome crime. A man, his wife, their servant, and a friend together killed a young boy, dismembered and stuffed the body in a leather container, and threw it in an abandoned well. When ʿUmar consulted with the Companions noted as jurists, a group said all must be executed for killing the young boy. Others argued that the killing of one human soul does not justify the execution of more than one person.

Ultimately, ʿUmar enforced the execution of all who participated in the boy's murder, ruling that were it the entire community of Sanā', the capital of Yemen, who participated in the slaying, all should be executed. ʿAlī b. Abī Ṭālib, among others, supported ʿUmar in this position.

THE WAY AHEAD

This Chapter on juristic dispute is a window to this important aspect of the world of Islamic law. It does not teach *fiqh, per se*, or its sources, but rather, the main causes and principles of juristic variance. It aims at helping to introduce a new attitude and a fresh way of thinking about the world of differing. In this direction, it is hoped that we can agree on the following 'heart-set':

1. Whosoever accepts true *tawḥīd*, Allah's Oneness, expressed in the Qur'ān and the *Sunnah*, is a brother or a sister to every Muslim and must be loved and accorded loyalty and support based on the integrity of that commitment.

2. The principal Muslim references are the Book of Allah and the *Sunnah* of His Messenger. Their interpretation must be based on the principles of the Arabic language, without contriving meanings.

3. If qualified, legitimately chosen leaders in a given Muslim community or association see fit to adopt certain juristic positions for the general welfare of the community, or give valid preference to some opinions over others, it is essential for the members to honour these positions. But blind or absolute loyalty to one person or a particular juristic School is not befitting of any Muslim. The *Sharīʿah* recognises the wisdom of following juristic authorities; learn the basis of their judgements and approach them with an open mind for guidance or correction – even if they differ with one's own bias or juristic affiliation.

4. All that has been reported to us from preceding generations (in harmony with the Book and the *Sunnah* of the Prophet) is accepted with awareness of the context involved. Insult, accusation, and innuendo regarding people of the past are beneath the dignity of a Muslim. The Qur'ān states: *That is a community that has passed on. For them is what they have earned. For you is what you have earned. And you will not be questioned about what they have done* (2: 134).

Remember this in your heart: juristic (*fiqhī*) dispute is forbidden if it leads to fighting, hatred, and fragmentation in the community, involving it in endless and senseless argumentation and disagreement. Co-operation in areas of agreement, tolerance of others, and understanding their point of view must be our attitude. Ḥasan al-Bannā frequently said, 'We co-operate in whatever we agree upon. And let us excuse one another in the areas where we disagree.'

Let our position towards *fiqhī* differences regarding the details of the *Sharīʿah* go only this far: 'Our opinion is correct, but liable to misjudgements; differing opinions are misjudgements, but plausibly correct.'

26

The Ethics of *Daʿwah* and Dialogue

Yusuf al-Qaradawi

The following represent several relevant and important points on the ethics of *daʿwah* and dialogue. I offer this *naṣīḥah* or advice, to all believers, especially the enthusiastic and sincere young Muslims whom I hold very dear. My reason for doing so is, as the Prophet Shuʿayb said, *'I only desire your betterment to the best of my power; and my success* [in my task] *can only come from Allah. In Him I trust, and unto Him I look'* (11: 88).

RESPECT FOR ALL PEOPLE

Islam teaches that all people are equal. This, however, should not be misunderstood or confused. There are certain differences, such as age, which must be observed and which require us to show politeness and respect. We must, indeed, observe the rights of relatives, spouses, neighbours, and rulers. Islamic ethics teach us that the young must respect the old, that the old must show compassion toward the young. There are many *aḥādīth* which command such attitudes: 'Respect for an old Muslim is a glorification of Allah' (*Abū Dāwūd*) and: 'A person who does not show compassion to the young, respect to the old, and gratitude to the learned is not one of us' (*Aḥmad*).

RESPECT THE RIGHTS OF THE FAMILY

Parental and kinship rights must be observed. Neither parents nor siblings should be treated with coarseness or disrespect on the grounds that they are transgressors, innovators, or deviants. These failings do no cancel their rights for kind and lenient treatment. Parental rights in particular are categorically expressed in the Qur'ān: *But if they strive to make you join in worship with Me things of which you have no knowledge, obey them not; yet bear them company in this life with justice* [and consideration], *and follow the way of those who turn to Me* [in love] (31: 15).

Similarly, one can learn a great deal from the Prophet Abraham's gentle and persuasive approach – as illustrated in the Qur'ān – in trying to lead his polytheist father to the Truth. Abraham persevered in his tender solicitude despite his father's brusque and repellent tone. What then if the parents are Muslim and kind? Even if they violate some injunctions of the *Sharīʿah*, they are still entitled to parental as well as Islamic rights.

RESPECT FOR EXPERIENCED ISLAMIC WORKERS

Consideration must be given to those people who have rich experience and who were very active in the field of *daʿwah*. If, for one reason or another, they become slack and lose their enthusiasm, we must not forget their contribution and neither defame nor discredit them.

This is the *Sunnah* of the Prophet, as evident in the story of Ḥāṭib ibn Abī Baltaʿah, who sent a message to the pagans among the Quraysh requesting protection for his children and relatives left behind in Makkah in return for information about the Muslims' preparations for the conquest of Makkah. When the message was intercepted and Ḥāṭib confessed, ʿUmar ibn al Khaṭṭāb was so outraged with this treachery that he requested the Prophet to let him punish Ḥāṭib by death. But the Prophet refused, saying: 'How do you know; perhaps Allah has looked at [the deeds of] the people [who fought in the Battle] of Badr and said to them: 'Do whatever you please for I have forgiven you [your past and future sins].' Ḥāṭib's early embrace of Islam and his courage and struggle during the Battle of Badr made the Prophet accept his excuse, thus reminding his Companions, and indeed all Muslims, of the special status of those who fought at the first Battle between the Muslims and the *kuffār* or disbelievers.

ABANDON UNREALISTIC IDEALISM

I advise the young to abandon your daydreams and your unrealistic idealism. You must come down to earth and identify with the masses, especially those who live from hand to mouth in the downtrodden parts of the world. In such places you can find the uncorrupted sources of virtue, simplicity, and purity in spite of 'necessity's sharp pinch'. There you can find the potential for social change, the opportunities for effort, struggle, movement, help, and reconstruction. There you can mix with the masses and show kindness and compassion towards the needy, the orphaned, the broken-hearted, the weary, and the oppressed. The realisation of such objectives, which is, in itself, a form of *ʿibādah*, requires collective effort, the formation of committees dedicated to eradicating illiteracy, disease, unemployment, lack of initiative, and harmful habits, such as, addiction to smoking, alcohol, and drugs; and on the other hand, to exposing and fighting corruption, deviation, oppression, bribery, and other practices. The struggle to relieve the suffering of the poor and to provide them with proper guidance is, indeed, a suitable form of *ʿibādah*, the significance of which many Muslims are unaware, even though Islamic teachings not only encourage the propagation of charitable deeds but commend them as individual and collective duties. Charitable deeds done for the welfare of the community are the best forms of *ʿibādah* and are considered branches of *īmān*, as long as those who do them do not seek praise and cheap popularity but only the pleasure of Allah.

Let us remind ourselves of those *aḥādīth* in which we learn that several acts, ranging from enjoining the common good and forbidding the evil and the desirability of removing harmful things are all charitable deeds. Abū Hurayrah relates the following *ḥadīth*: '*Ṣadaqah* is due on each joint of a person, every day the sun rises. The administration of justice between two persons is a *ṣadaqah*; assisting a person to mount his beast [i.e., mode of transport], or helping him load his luggage upon it is a *ṣadaqah*; and a good word is a *ṣadaqah*; and every step taken towards *ṣalāh* is a *ṣadaqah*, removing harmful things from a pathway is *ṣadaqah*' (*Bukhārī*).

Ibn ʿAbbās also related another *ḥadīth* to the same effect: 'A *ṣalāh* is due on each joint of a person every day'. A person in the audience said: 'This is the most difficult thing you have required of us.' The Prophet then said: 'Your enjoining the common good and forbidding that which is evil and undesirable is a *ṣalāh*, your help for the weak is a *ṣalāh*, your removing of dirt from a pathway is *ṣalāh*, and every step you take to the [prescribed daily] prayer is a *ṣalāh*.'

Buraydah related that the Prophet said: 'Each person has three hundred and sixty joints. He must give *ṣadaqah* for each one of them.' They [the Prophet's Companions] said: 'Who can afford to do so, O Apostle?' thinking that it was a financial *ṣadaqah*. The Prophet then said: 'Heaping earth upon some phlegm to cover it is *ṣadaqah*, removing an obstruction from a pathway is *ṣadaqah*' (*Aḥmad*).

There are many *aḥādīth* which rank cheerfulness towards other Muslims, helping the blind, the deaf and the weak, advising those who are lost and confused, relieving the distress of the needy, etc., as forms of *ʿibādah* and *ṣadaqah*. In this way, a Muslim lives his life as a vital source of virtuous deeds, either performing good or commanding it upon others, thereby guarding against the infiltration of evil. The Prophet said: 'Blessed is he whom Allah has made a key for righteousness and a lock against evil' (*Ibn Mājah*).

However, some enthusiastic idealists may argue that such social activities could hinder the propagation of Islam and the efforts to make people understand it. They believe that Islamic education is more obligatory than these social engagements. My reply is that social involvement is itself a practical *daʿwah* which reaches the people in their own environment. Calling people to Islam is not mere talk; *daʿwah* is participation in the affairs of others and the seeking of a remedy to their problems. Imām Ḥasan al-Bannā was quite aware of this and, therefore, established a charitable institution for social services and financial assistance in every branch of the Muslim Brotherhood he founded in Egypt. He was conscious that the Muslim is commanded to do charitable work just as he is commanded to bow down and to prostrate himself in *ʿibādah* for Allah. The Qur'ān says: *O you who believe! Bow down, prostrate yourselves and adore your Lord and do good that you may prosper. And strive in His Cause as you ought to strive. He has chosen you, and has imposed no difficulties on you in religion* (22: 77–78).

These Qur'ānic verses help us to define the Muslim's three-part role in life: His relationship with Allah whom he should serve through *ʿibādah*; his role in society which he should serve through charitable deeds; and his relationship with the powers of darkness and evil against which he should strive.

Enthusiastic idealists, however, might further argue that efforts should be concentrated on the establishment of an Islamic state which applies the *Sharīʿah* in all aspects of life within the state and works to call for Islam outside its borders. The realisation of this goal, they argue, will automatically solve all the foregoing problems.

The re-orientation of the Muslim lands to facilitate the establishment of an Islamic state which strives to unite Muslims under the banner of Islam is, of course, the duty of the whole *Ummah*. All *duʿāt* or Islamic workers must do their utmost to achieve this objective, employing in the process the best means and methods. But the realisation of this is conditional upon a number of imperatives, some of the most important of which are: to unite efforts, to remove obstacles, to convince suspecting minds of the nobility of the cause, to bring up Islamically orientated youngsters, and to prepare local as well as international public opinion to understand the Islamic faith and state. All this requires time and, indeed, perseverance. Until this is realised, Muslims must unite their efforts to serving their communities and to improving their societies. Such engagements will mould, prepare, and test the abilities of future generations for the leadership of the *Ummah*.

It is unacceptable for a Muslim who could, if he so wished, provide a cure for a patient at a public clinic or a charitable hospital to refuse to do so because he is waiting for an Islamic state to be established so as to provide such services. Nor would it be proper for a Muslim who could organise *zakāh* services to be indifferent to the miseries and distresses of the poor, the orphaned, and the old and widowed, by simply hoping that the future Islamic state would help through a comprehensive system of social welfare. It is equally improper for a Muslim to show indifference to the tragic and costly disputes between other Muslims claiming that these matters will be dealt with by the future Islamic state, which will reconcile people and fight the aggressor.

The duty of the Muslim is to strive against evil and to work for righteousness to the best of his abilities, no matter how little this might be. Allah says in the Qur'ān: *So heed Allah as much as you can* (64: 16).

The following may help to illustrate my concept regarding the desired Islamic state: An orchard takes a relatively long time to produce fruit. Is it then practical for the owner to do no other work, to reap no other fruit, but to only wait for his crop of desired fruits? Of course not. He must plant other fast-producing trees as well as vegetables to fertilise his land and to earn a living, nurturing at the same time his orchard which will eventually provide his anticipated and desired crop.

LIBERATION FROM PESSIMISM AND DESPAIR

Young Muslims must liberate themselves from the fetters of pessimism and despair and assume innocence and goodness in fellow Muslims. This optimism requires a conscious recognition of several important conditions:

1. Human Beings are Fallible

Human beings are not angels. They have not been created from light, but moulded from clay. They, like their father, Adam, before them, are all fallible. We learn from the Qur'ān: *We had already, beforehand, taken the covenant of Adam, but he forgot, and We found on his part no firm resolve* (20:115).

Recognition of our human fallibility and proclivity to temptation will enable us not only to tolerate and to cherish a sympathetic understanding of the faults and blemishes of others, but will encourage us to remind them to have faith and hope in Allah's Mercy and to warn them of Allah's anger and punishment. Allah addressed His Messenger, the Prophet Muḥammad: *Say:*

O My servants who have transgressed against their souls! Despair not of the Mercy of Allah: for Allah forgives all sins: for He is Oft-forgiving, Most Merciful (39: 53).

The possessive pronoun in 'My servants' signifies Allah's Love and concern for and indeed His Benevolence towards all people, which finds room for abundant mercy and forgiveness for all sins however great they may be.

2. Only Allah Truly Knows a Person

Remember that that no one but Allah knows what goes on in the innermost depths of a person. Therefore, we are obliged to judge people in accordance with what they profess and with what appears to us. If a person, for instance, confesses that 'there is no god but Allah, and that Muḥammad is His Messenger,' we should treat him as a Muslim. This is in keeping with the Prophet's *Sunnah*. This is why the Prophet would not punish the *munāfiqīn* or hypocrites, although he was sure they were plotting against him. When his Companions suggested that he should kill them to pre-empt their threat, he replied: 'I fear that the people would say that Muḥammad kills his Companions!'

3. Seek the Good in Everyone

We must recognise that every person who believes in Allah and in His Messenger cannot be devoid of some inborn good, however evil his practice may be. Involvement in major transgressions does not uproot a person's *īmān* unless the transgressor deliberately defies Allah and scorns His commands. Here, as elsewhere, we have to heed the *Sunnah* of the Prophet who used to treat wrongdoers as a physician would treat a patient, not as a policeman would treat a criminal. He was very kind to them and always listened to their problems.

The following example illustrates this point: a Qurayshi adolescent once came upon the Prophet and asked permission to fornicate. The Prophet's Companions were so outraged by the young man's request that they rushed to punish him, but the Prophet's attitude was totally different. Calm and composed, he asked the young man to come closer to him and asked: 'Would you approve of it [fornication] for your mother?' The young man replied: 'No'. The Prophet said: '[Other] people also would not approve of it for their mothers'. Then the Prophet repeatedly asked the young man whether he would approve of it for his daughter, sister, or aunt? Each time the young man answered 'No,' and each time the Prophet added that '[Other] people would not approve of it for theirs'. He then held the young man's hand and said: 'May Allah forgive his [the young man's] sins, purify his heart, and fortify him [against such desires]' (*Aḥmad* and *Ṭabarānī*).

The Prophet's sympathetic attitude clearly indicates a gesture of goodwill, a conviction in that inborn goodness of the human self which outweighs the elements of evil which could only be transient. So he compassionately and patiently discussed the issue with the young Qurayshi until he was able to convince him of its wrongfulness. Not only did he do this, but the Prophet prayed to Allah to forgive and guide him. Extremists could argue that leniency on this occasion was understandable, as the young man had not actually committed fornication.

Let us, therefore, consider the following example: during the lifetime of the Prophet there was an alcoholic who was repeatedly brought to the Prophet and was repeatedly punished, yet still persisted. One day when he was brought again on the same charge, someone from among the people said: 'May Allah curse him! How frequently has he been brought [to the Prophet to be punished]?' The Prophet said: 'Do not curse him. By Allah I know he loves Allah and His Messenger.' It is also reported that the Prophet said: 'Do not assist Satan against your brother.' The Prophet prevented them from cursing him because their action could create discord and ill-feeling between the man and his fellow Muslim brothers – his transgression should not sever the bond of brotherhood between him and other Muslims.

Deep contemplation of such examples and incidents amply demonstrate the Prophet's insight into the inherent element of goodness in people. We need, more than ever before, to study and follow the exemplary pattern that the Prophet has set for us. Those who indiscriminately accuse whoever makes a mistake of *kufr* or *shirk* must understand that they have to change their strategy and learn that a great deal of the corruption and perversion they abhor, results mainly from ignorance of Islam, bad company, or forgetfulness. The solution is to help people overcome and defeat all these problems. To be harsh, to accuse others of *kufr*, and to find fault with whatever they do only serves to alienate and estrange them. A wise person once said: 'Rather than cursing darkness, try to light a candle for the road.'

E. SELF–DEVELOPMENT

The Islamic Personality
Mahmud Rashdan

Revival of the Individual
Khurram Murad

Instruments of Character Building
Khurshid Ahmad

Spiritual Training in Islam
Asad Gilani

Watering the Seeds of Love
Said Ramadan

Guidelines for Better Living
Hasan al-Banna

Personal Evaluation
Riza Mohammed

27

The Islamic Personality

Mahmud Rashdan

What is the human being? What is his duty and place in the universe? What are the abilities and qualities that enable him to fulfil his duty? And finally, who if anyone, defines a person's responsibilities, and who gives him his abilities and characteristics?

To answer these questions, let us refer to the Qur'ān. When Allah was about to create the human being, He said to the angels, *I am placing a khalīfah or vicegerent on earth', the angels enquired, 'Will you place on it one who will cause corruption and one who will shed blood while we proclaim Your praise and glorify You?' But Allah, the all-Knowing, responded, 'Surely, I know that which you do not know'. And He taught Adam the names, all of them, then showed them to the angels and said: 'Tell Me the names of these, if you are truthful.' They said: 'Glory to You! No knowledge is ours except what You have taught us. Indeed, You are the all-Knowing, the all-Wise* (2: 30–32).

From this verse together with other related verses from *Sūrah al-Baqarah* we can draw the following conclusions: firstly, the human being is a creation of God. Secondly, he has the highest place in this universe among God's creations and thirdly, he is the vicegerent of God on earth, that is, his mission in life is to promote the development of this world with the very unique and distinctive qualities endowed upon him by God.

The human being also possesses a mind and the distinct ability to reason and to make decisions and choices. This distinctive nature means that, though he has instincts similar to those of animals, unlike animals, however, he has the ability to choose the time and manner in which to satisfy these instincts. Similarly, though he shares some qualities with the angels, he is distinctively different from them in that they do not have the ability to disobey God, but he has; and they do not have animal instincts but he does.

THE ISLAMIC PERSONALITY

The Islamic personality, therefore, is a balanced one. It can develop only by the balanced development of all the faculties and by satisfying all the dimensions of the human self. In short, the Islamic personality is the manifestation of the words of the Qur'ān, as exemplified by the Prophet Muḥammad, about whom God declares: *You have indeed, in the Messenger of God an excellent exemplar for whoever places his hopes in God and the final day, and who remembers Allah much* (33: 21).

Indeed Allah educated Muḥammad and elevated him to the highest level of character: *And you stand on an exalted standard of character* (68: 4). Moreover, when ʿĀ'ishah, the Prophet's wife, was asked about his character she replied: 'His character was the Qur'ān' (*Muslim*).

The fact that Muḥammad, like all other Prophets, was only a human is very illuminating because only then would it be possible for people to emulate him. The story of the few Companions who went to ʿĀ'ishah to enquire about the Prophet's devotions to Allah is very significant. The *ḥadīth* tells that when she described to them his long and fervent prayers, they resolved that they needed to do more because God had forgiven the Prophet and promised him Paradise. Thus, one of them resolved that he would never marry; another pledged to devote all his life to Prayer; and yet another vowed that he would fast the rest of his life. When the Prophet heard about their decisions, he became alarmed and announced in public that what the three men had decided to do was not the Islamic way and that whoever abandoned his example of moderation was not of his *Ummah* or community.

Islam, therefore, understands the nature of the human being and aims at fulfilling and developing all the dimensions of his personality in a balanced manner. Worship in Islam is not limited to the strictly ritual and spiritual forms. *ʿIbādah* or worship also includes eating, learning and marrying; because by engaging in these activities we are also fulfilling the will of God, to develop the truly human personality.

Nowadays, the problem with Muslims is not that they are indulging excessively in spiritual practices but rather that they have become very materialistic, failing to heed the call of Allah. Their exemplar is not that of the Prophet, but rather others who are mostly self-centred, materialistic and non-God fearing. Muḥammad, the example, was the tyrants' destroyer and many have become the tyrants' followers. Muḥammad, the man and the Prophet was generous but some have become niggardly; he was courageous, however, some tend to be cowardly; he was humble but some are arrogant; he was sincere, but there are many whose hearts are filled with hypocrisy.

Muḥammad's character was the Qur'ān; what is ours? How often do we study the Qur'ān to seek guidance? Indeed, how often do we read the Qur'ān?

REQUIREMENTS FOR PERSONALITY DEVELOPMENT

1. Study the Qur'ān on God's Terms

How then do we develop a truly Islamic personality? Firstly, we should aim to subject our whims and opinions to the instructions of the Qur'ān. We should not adopt our own opinions or pursue our own way of life and then seek to support the same by extracting bits and pieces from the Qur'ān. Instead, we should study the Qur'ān to see how close we are to the teachings of God and then try hard to close the gap.

When a cook uses a recipe book to prepare a meal, he is likely to follow the directions very closely. So is the case with the honest and diligent pharmacist when he fills a prescription. The Islamic personality is a Qur'ānic personality, and for the Qur'ānic personality to develop, the Qur'ān needs to be studied, synthesised and lived.

2. Connecting with Allah and Seeking His Pleasure

It is often true that whenever we are faced with a vexing problem we are likely to choose a solution that aims to please others. This approach, however, may make us do things not for the sake of God but rather for our own sake and that of others.

To illustrate the difference, let us consider two cases from Islamic history. The first concerns Khālid ibn al-Walīd. When ʿUmar became *Khalīfah*, the Battle of Yarmūk between the Muslims and the Romans was still in progress. The commander of the Muslim army at that time was Khālid bin al-Walīd. ʿUmar, however, sent orders to Khālid to pass the leadership of the Muslim army to Abū ʿUbaidah immediately. Khālid, however, waited until the Muslim army was victorious before he willingly passed his leadership to Abū ʿUbaidah. Upon doing this he said, 'I did not fight for the sake of ʿUmar. Rather, I fought for the sake of the Creator of ʿUmar.'

The second example concerns an outstanding Muslim warrior whose name remains unknown to this day. In another battle with the Romans during the Caliphate of Muʿāwiyah, the Romans had fortified themselves behind a strong wall. The Muslims sought to open a hole in the wall but failed. Finally, an unknown warrior risked his life and opened a hole in the wall, and the Muslim army was able to get through and win the battle. Yazīd, the leader, sought to identify this brave soldier and reward him. However, no one claimed the honour. Yazīd then commanded his soldiers, by God, that whoever knew the person should come forward and speak of him. Still, no one came forward. After a few days, one of the soldiers sought a private interview with the commander. He told Yazīd that he would tell him the name of the person who opened the hole, but that the person had three pre-conditions, before the information could be divulged. They were: that the soldier's name would not be mentioned to anyone; that the *Khalīfah* should not be written to in this regard; and finally, that no reward should be ordered to him. Yazīd agreed to meet these conditions. The man then said, 'I am the one you seek'. This humility, shown by the soldier, exemplifies how the Muslim should be more conscious of the reward from God, than of any worldly recognition.

BUILDING AN ISLAMIC SOCIETY

An Islamic society can be built only by Islamic personalities. However, one cannot build an Islamic society by merely knowing the stories and life histories of great Muslims of the past. The early Muslims had the vision and the courage to build a system within the framework of Divine revelations that would serve long after they had departed. Yet there are some today who, while working to revive the Islamic teachings, seek the fulfilment of their destiny and belief by living in and for the past, blindly following their leaders and ignoring their individual prerogative and responsibility of choice. Malik Bennabi, has said in this regard: 'The result has been to walk towards the future with backs turned to it and eyes fixed on the past in search of a faded glory, instead of seeking to build a new order, to which glory will come by right of accomplishment and not by right of inheritance.'

When we only dream of the past, we fail to build for the future and our precious present passes by. Accomplishment and success are a result of preparing for the future without breaking the faith and contact with the past, but also realising that constructive work can only be done in the present. Tomorrow never comes and yesterday never returns.

Muslims have abandoned their 'personality' and abdicated their leadership of mankind because they have broken their relationship with God, who exists in the past, the present, and the future. Because Muslims are constantly imitating, they become recessive and easily dominated by both indigenous tyrants and foreign imperialists and ideas.

Our predicament is reflected in the story of the crow that was not satisfied with the way God created him to walk. He was attracted to the way the pigeon walked and tried to imitate her. He could not, so he tried again and again but he failed; ultimately he decided to go back to his own way of walking which, to his amazement, he discovered he had forgotten. He ended up with something in between but uglier than either.

The Muslims of today, after generations of blind imitation, enjoy neither the Islamic personality nor the Western ways. They have failed on both counts. They are derelict in their duties as God's trustees on earth.

Our contemporary environment is complex, confusing and frustrating. The individual remains, however, the most significant entity of the universe and to ourselves as individuals, we must turn our utmost attention. The image and role which we seek to play will determine whether or not we will deserve the fulfilment of God's Promise.

Allah has promised such of you as believe and do good works that He will surely make them to succeed in the earth as He caused those who were before them to succeed others, and that He will surely establish for them their religion which He has approved for them, and will give them, in exchange, safety after their fear. They serve Me. They ascribe nothing as partner unto Me. Those who disbelieve henceforth, they are the miscreants (24: 55).

Therefore, we must demand, from ourselves first of all, an uncompromising awareness of ourselves, our being and our message. Thereafter we must work together, with others who share our faith and our destiny, to establish the Islamic way of life. There is a two-way relationship between the Islamic personality and the Islamic society. One cannot be truly fulfilled without the other.

Nations are not the outcome of irreversible destiny but they are the moulded product of people, usually of a few persons who have vision and courage. Every person, with no exception, can share that vision and help shape its outcome. No one is too small or too weak, too big or too strong, to become part of that process. The definition of our individual role cannot be imposed on us from outside; it has to develop from within and, no matter how others see us, our achievements will depend basically on our will and our actions.

The story of an observer passing by a construction site is quite illustrative. He asked each workman what he was doing – one said, 'I am carrying bricks.' The second said, 'I am earning a living.' But the third answered, 'We are building an institution of learning, and when it is finished, it will turn out scholars who will contribute to our civilisation. As for me, I am a part, a small part, of that project'.

28

Revival of the Individual

Khurram Murad

Individuals committed to the Islamic movement are like building bricks fused together to form a solid wall. Each individual, like a brick, must be strong and capable of withstanding the loads and stresses that it is called upon to bear. Just as each brick must be fully burnt and purified in a kiln and pass certain minimum standards, so too an individual has to go through a process of training and development in order to be effective within the edifice of the movement. But what is involved in this construction of the individual? What has the individual got to do in order to prepare himself for his role in the movement? These are fundamental questions – for a prerequisite to the revival of Muslim society, is a revival of the individual or the self.

THE KEY TO SUCCESS

The starting point in this process is what the Qur'ān calls the *qalb* or a person's heart. Look at yourself and you will find inside you a whole universe, emotions, desires, urges, instincts, which motivate you from within. The *qalb* does not mean the pump which pushes blood around the body, it means the centre or locus of the personality which is pumping motivations, desires and urges and which makes a person do what he wants to do.

The Qur'ān goes on to explain that this is the key to a person. His success depends not on what he is physically, nor on what he does, but on what lies at the centre of his personality. The Qur'ān declares that *except the one who comes to Allah with a sound heart on the Day of Judgement, none will be successful in His eyes* (26: 89). There is also a *ḥadīth* which states: 'Beware, there is a piece of flesh in the human body. If it is right, then the whole body is right and sound and if it is corrupted then the whole body is corrupted. Look, this is the heart' (*Bukhārī*).

According to the Qur'ān, the basis of corruption stems from within a person. The social institutions may be corrupt, there may be exploitation and abuse in the economic and political spheres, but the basis of all these diseases lies inside a person's heart. The Qur'ān says, *The disease* [is not somewhere in the body, it] *is inside their hearts* (2: 10).

What is it that stops a person from seeing right and doing right, that turns him blind? The Qur'ān explains, *It is not the eyes which go blind but it is the heart inside you which goes blind* (22: 46). This, then, is the basic starting point for the movement – to purify the heart and then summon it to the service of mankind, whether it be in government, in political institutions or in economic ventures. For those of us who are committed to Islam as a movement and who are involved in the path of *jihād*, attention should always remain riveted on keeping the heart, our centre, pure. Our whole attention must be focused on this continuous struggle. All the rites that have been prescribed by the Qur'ān reach out to purify the deepest regions of our selves. The Qur'ān states (regarding the animals sacrificed in charity), *It is not the flesh and blood that reach Allah, it is the taqwā within your heart that finds acceptance* (22: 37).

PURIFYING THE HEART

If the individual is the primary building block of society, then the heart is its foundation within each person. The question which arises now is how should we set about preparing this most basic of building bricks?

1. Submit the *Qalb* to Allah

First we must understand that the 'heart' must submit totally and exclusively to its Creator. It cannot be compartmentalised – we cannot dedicate one piece of it to Allah, and another to some other god, like wealth, status, career and so on. There is a beautiful verse in the Qur'ān which throws light on the absurdity of such a situation. It tells about some of the *mushrikīn* or idol worshippers who sacrifice animals and then say that one part of the animal is for Allah and another is for their other idols. The verse then states quite clearly that whatever is assigned to Allah is also, in reality, assigned to the idols, for Allah does not accept something divided. He is One, Indivisible, and wants us to be undivided in service to Him. So long as we remain divided within ourselves, so long as our heart lies in a hundred places, so long as our eyes are set in a hundred directions, so long as our destination is not one but many, we shall never be able to achieve that first condition for building a strong and pure personality.

Why do we allow divided loyalties to capture parts of our heart? Nothing of this world is going to be of use to us when we breathe our last, however hard we may have striven for it and however valuable it might seem to us. We must recognise that the prizes we should want are not the worldly possessions received from people like ourselves. It is only our Creator who can put a real value on our striving and bestow the real reward. *Shall I tell you of a 'business' which will deliver you of a tormenting punishment?* (61: 10). This 'business' amounts to a person committing his whole undivided being to Allah alone, and selling himself in order to seek His pleasure. This is the first step towards the building of the individual.

2. Love Allah

The second step is to love Allah. The Qur'ān says, *Those who believe love Allah more than anything* (2: 165). It does not say that one must love only Allah. Love is a blessing given to us by Allah which is manifested in so many aspects of life. In Islam, however, it must be foremost for Allah.

What is love? Perhaps it cannot be defined in terms which adequately reflect its nature and importance in a person's life. It is not possible to define it by a formula as we define a scientific fact, nor can we define it by a mathematical equation. But still each one of us knows what love is and can tell, from his own experience, the powerful force that it is, once it comes to reside in the heart. It becomes the overpowering force in life. It captivates you, it grips you, it moves you and you are prepared to do anything for the sake of it. Once love is there, what you do is not something which has to be imposed upon you, because you need imposition only for the things you do not love. *Īmān* or faith is something which must penetrate deep in our hearts and generate love for Allah and His Prophet, more than for anything else. Unless that happens inside you, you cannot even get the 'real taste' of *īmān*. According to one *ḥadīth* nobody can taste *īmān* unless Allah and His Prophet are more beloved to him than everything else.

But we must remember that this love for Allah and His Prophet is not of a kind to take us into the seclusion of a monastery. It is a love which makes us do our duty to Allah while we are in the street, at home or in the office

– everywhere we live as servants of Allah, willingly making every sacrifice required of us.

Whether or not we have that love is something for each one of us to closely examine. One of the criteria is that if you love something, one of your most intense desires is to get nearer to it. Now we have a way in which we can come nearer to Allah and 'talk' to Him, and that way is the *ṣalāh*. The Prophet said that when a person performs *ṣalāh*, he actually comes nearer to Allah and talks to Him. If you look at how you pray five times a day, you will have a barometer in your hand to find how much you love Allah. Once you are praying to Him, you are in front of Him, you are near to Him, you are talking to Him, you are responding to Him in gratitude and you are asking for His forgiveness. Prayer is not just a ritual in which you go through certain postures. The soul has to surrender itself exclusively to Allah and love Him. This love is like a seed which, as it grows, envelopes the entire personality. This will make you the sort of person the Islamic movement needs today.

3. Seek Nourishment from the Qur'ān

The next question is how to nurse and cultivate this seed of *īmān*. The most important nourishment for it is the Qur'ān. We know that the first workers of the Islamic movement got their training from the Qur'ān. It was their guide, their light, their leader. It is a treasure-house of soul-stirring inspiration and wisdom. We can and should spend hours in understanding the Qur'ān. There are thousands of pages of *tafsīr* to read. But we must know that the real test of benefiting from the Qur'ān lies somewhere else. The Qur'ān itself says that when people really listen to it their faith must increase. 'Where there is a fire there is smoke.' If the 'fire' of *īmān* has been lit inside the heart, there must be smoke, and you will see of those who truly listen to the Qur'ān, that their eyes begin to well up with tears which trickle down their cheeks. Nowadays, when we listen to the Qur'ān or read it, our hearts are not moved, nor do our lives change. It is as if water is falling on a rock and flowing away. Our task is to replace this hard rock with soft absorbent soil, so that the Qur'ān may nourish the seed that has been planted. We should always study the Qur'ān as if it is being revealed today. One of the greatest injustices we do to the Qur'ān is that we read it as if it was something of the past, and of no relevance to the present.

4. Build Brotherhood

The next method of sustaining the seed of *īmān* is to develop a strong bond of brotherhood. Brotherhood reinforces a person's life like nothing else. The Qur'ān says, *bind yourself with those who call upon Allah morning and evening*

(18: 27–28). As soon as you have planted the seed in your own heart, and you have recognised it in someone else and you find that he agrees with you, you feel ten times stronger. It has been proved experimentally that group life is one of the most powerful forces to stimulate and inspire a human being.

5. Invite to Allah's Way

The final method to nourish the seed of *īmān* is to strive and invite others to the path of Allah, the same path as you are following yourself. Again, if the faith is there inside you, this is a necessary outcome of it. As *īmān* increases you become aroused and you want to go out and tell everybody what you think is right or call upon them to join your mission and your brotherhood or group. Moreover, as your group grows, your *īmān* grows as well, each reinforcing the other, and that is how the whole of life becomes integrated and finds a path to the movement.

SUMMARY

To sum up: your person is the key to your movement and your 'heart' is the key to your person. Make your heart belong to Allah alone; let Him alone be the prize you seek. And let His Love be uppermost in your heart. Once it is so, every duty will turn into pleasure, to pray will be a delight, to indulge in politics for the sake of Allah will be a blessing. To nourish the seed of *īmān* and the love of Allah in your heart, you have three means at your disposal! First is the Qur'ān; second is brotherhood; third is *daʿwah*. We need people who will make every endeavour and offer every sacrifice to change the world around them through a social movement, in the light shown by the Qur'ān and the Prophet who brought the Qur'ān to us.

29

Instruments of Character Building

Khurshid Ahmad

This article focuses on some of the most important instruments of character-building that we are taught in the Qur'ān and *Sunnah*. They are: *dhikr, ʿibādah, tawbah* and *istighfār, ṣabr, iḥtisāb* and *duʿā'*. I shall give a very brief resume of them, leaving further elaboration to your own effort.

DHIKR

The first important instrument of character-building is *dhikr* or remembrance of Allah. We find that in the Qur'ān Allah says: *Surely in the creation of the heavens and the earth and in the alternation of night and day there are signs for people possessed of minds who remember God, standing, sitting, and lying on their sides, and reflect upon the creation of the heavens and the earth. 'Our Lord! You have not created this in futility. Glory be to You! Protect us from the torment of the Fire'* (3:190).

Who are these people? They are those who remember God in every position - standing, sitting and lying down, and who reflect upon God's creation of the heavens and the earth. They praise God and make *duʿā'* or supplication to Him. These are the three basic postures in which a person can be. So a Muslim is committed to *dhikr* in whatever position he may be.

Such *dhikr* can be in one's heart in a silent but conscious way. It can be by oral recitation – remembering God, whether in the form of reciting those *kalimāt* or 'words' and 'phrases' which we have been taught or simply by reciting from the Qur'ān. *Dhikr* does not relate to any particular situation or thing: it deals with all aspects of life – work and leisure. The importance of *dhikr* lies in the fact that it creates a psychological climate. In this climate one can protect oneself from the evil encroachments and inroads of the external environment wherever one may be. This is a kind of *ḥaṣānah* (immunity), or *ḥiṣār* (barrier). *Dhikr* is not difficult. While one is travelling, while one is on a train, wherever one can afford a few minutes, say *Allāhu Akbar* (Allah is the Greatest), *Subḥānallāh* (Glory be to Allah), *Lā ilāha illallāh* (There is no god but Allah). All this will give one a different psychological orientation, a different mental 'climate' from the anti-Islamic elements. In every situation one is able to preserve the Islamic ethos by *dhikr*.

The Prophet on one occasion explained the difference between one who makes *dhikr* and one who does not, as the difference between the living and the dead. Why? There is the cessation of life when one breathes no more; but even if physiologically one is alive and one is not 'breathing' the *Kalimātullāh* or the Words of God, breathing spiritually, then this is death.

Thus dhikr is one of the most important instruments of *tazkiyah* or purification. We have been taught how to make *dhikr* by God and His Prophet in a simple and clear manner. These methods are the most effective and they close the door of *bidʿah* or innovation.

One thing I should add is that *dhikr* not only provides a psychological climate for action, it also provides the inspiration needed for action. *Dhikr* enables a person to attain a position of honour which is unparalleled. Allah says in the Qur'ān, *As you remember Me so I shall remember you* (2: 152). Could you imagine any height for a human being that could be higher, where, when he remembers God, God also remembers him in return? One's Creator, Creator of the earth and the cosmos and all that exists, if you remember Him, He remembers you. If you remember Him here, then your *dhikr* is made in the entire universe. Thus, the importance of *dhikr* as an instrument of character-building is immense and of the highest priority.

ʿIBĀDAH

Each *ʿibādah* or act of servitude to God is also meant to be an instrument of character-building. As regards *ṣalāh* the Qur'ān states, *Surely, ṣalāh prevents indecency and evil* (29: 45). Further, the Qur'ān emphasises, that the purpose of *ṣawm* is to develop God-consciousness (2: 183). The very word *zakāh* comes from the same root-word as *tazkiyah*. *Zakāh* is that which purifies; it is a part of *tazkiyah*. And so is the case with each act of *ʿibādah*. *Ḥajj*, of course, is a culmination of all the formal aspects of *ʿibādah*. In *ḥajj*, the *ṣalāh*-element is present. The *zakāh*-element is there also in that one makes a monetary sacrifice to go for *ḥajj*. In *ḥajj* there is an element of abstinence. When one is in *iḥrām*, one has to abide by certain rules and avoid certain things. Thus, *ḥajj* is truly all the major acts of worship rolled into one.

TAWBAH AND *ISTIGHFĀR*

The third major instrument of character-building is *istighfār* and *tawbah*. *Istighfār* is repentance for one's sins, mistakes or aberrations. *Tawbah* is the act of returning to your Lord. Islam has not demanded of you that you must not commit mistakes, but that if you do commit mistakes you must recollect, repent, and return to your Lord. In the Qur'ān, God has said that the character of the Muslims is such that they do not persist in wrong doing. We might commit mistakes and sins, but we should try our best to avoid them. However, if a sin is committed, then, what we must do first is become conscious of it. We must not continue skidding into further commissions. Then there must be a conscious break with the act and we should return penitent to our Lord.

There are many words and phrases of *istighfār* which we have been taught and which we should say, but primarily, *istighfār* is a state of mind and *tawbah* is a state of resolve. The greatness of Islam is that is has raised human conduct from unconsciousness to the heights of consciousness. *Istighfār* and *tawbah* are acts of consciousness. If one makes a slip, one should stop, repent it and make a resolve not to commit it again. And as many times as this may happen, is as many times one has to make a resolve to return to God. This is part of God's *Raḥmah* or Mercy. He has not closed the doors of forgiveness once a mistake has been committed. If there is a repenting heart, a real repenting heart, you can come back to Him and find Him Forgiving.

ṢABR

Ṣabr basically means steadfastness. To cultivate *ṣabr* means to cultivate a spirit of perseverance and, in a way, this is part of the process of *istighfār* and *tawbah*, because *ṣabr* means that one must have perseverance to stick to the path of virtue and come to it whenever any mistake is committed or any aberration is made. It means that one has to carry on this task unceasingly, unswervingly. *Ṣabr* entails continuing with this in each individual act. It also means sacrifice, continuous sacrifice for one's brothers, for the cause of good, for the cause of Islam. It includes remaining steadfast in the face of the tempest of adversity. Muslims are those who have been charged with the duty of establishing and propagating the religion of Islam. In this lifelong struggle they have been asked not only to adopt the policy of *ṣabr*, but also of *muṣābarah* which is an intensive form of *ṣabr*. *Muṣābarah* or forbearance, if sufficiently understood and practised, is enough to meet all the challenges that confront *daʿwah* and is sufficient to overwhelm the forces that may otherwise frustrate us. Thus, one has to cultivate in oneself not only *ṣabr*, but also, *muṣābarah*.

IḤTISĀB

The next instrument of character-building, and perhaps, one of the most valuable is *iḥtisāb* or self-appraisal and self-criticism. In fact, the concept of *iḥtisāb* or *ḥisābah* is wider. It is social criticism as well as self-criticism because the twin commands of enjoining the good and forbidding that which is reprehensible (*amr bi'l-maʿrūf wa nahy ʿan'il-munkar*) are obligations on the Muslims that are of a social character. These twin commands also form part of *iḥtisāb*. From the viewpoint of *iḥtisāb*, we must try to criticise or appraise ourselves and we should be as honest, as frank, and, I could say, as 'cruel' to ourselves as we can. I would suggest that in appraising our behaviour we should be harsh on ourselves while being lenient with others. This should be the cornerstone of our policy, and if we stick with it, then only good will result, *inshā' Allāh*. The best method of self-criticism that I have found useful is to devote just two or three minutes, before going to bed each day for evaluation. Make it a habit; a conscious effort. Review your day so as to know how you spent it. Evaluate how you have spent your time, your money, the talents and resources that God gave you, the responsibility that has been entrusted to you. Assess each aspect of your life. Where you have succeeded offer *shukr* or thanks to Allah. Where you have failed make *istighfār*. This is the best form of self-criticism. And, indeed, the Prophet, upon whom be peace, has recommended doing your own self-appraisal before you are appraised on the Day of Reckoning. To do so would better prepare you for that fateful day. *Iḥtisāb*, is therefore, one of the most important instruments in *tazkiyah*.

DUʿĀ'

Another important instrument of character-building is that of *duʿā'*. *Duʿā'* means supplication, asking God's help, asking Him for everything that is needed. It is one of the most important instruments of *tazkiyah* because it is a snap-shot of all our ambitions. One's entire scale of priorities can be reflected in one's *du'ā'*. And we have been taught in the Qur'ān and the *Sunnah* what we should pray for and how. *Du'ā'* is something that must be offered regularly and with sincerity. The Prophet once said that some of our *du'ā's* are accepted just upon asking for them; some of them are fulfilled, not in the form in which one asked for them, but even better, and some of them remain unfulfilled. On the Day of Judgement one will find that the rewards for unfulfilled *du'ā's* are so great that one will wish that those *du'ā's* that had been fulfilled had not been, so that he could have the rewards of them in the hereafter. On that day ultimately, none of a believer's *du'ā's* go unrewarded.

SOCIAL NORMS FOR *TAZKIYAH*

There are also certain social norms for *tazkiyah* which concern behaviour patterns amongst Muslims and between Muslims and non-Muslims. In this connection, I shall only make a very broad suggestion, that if nothing else, one should read very carefully, again and again, *Sūrah Ḥujurāt* (Chapter 49). The verses of this *Sūrah* deal with the characteristics of believing men and women, their striving in the cause of Allah, the brotherly bond, their avoidance of ignorance and suspicion, derision and defamation of character and their conscious effort to achieve good-will in order to obtain Allah's Mercy. All the things that are necessary for social *tazkiyah*, at least in a rudimentary form, can be found in this one *Sūrah*.

30

Spiritual Training in Islam

Sayyid Asad Gilani

'The door of the heart opens inside and unless the one who lives in that house opens it from within, it cannot be opened.'

A *dā'ī* or Islamic worker who calls humanity towards the Truth, in reality calls towards obedience to Allah Almighty because the greatest reality and truth of this universe is that it has a Creator, the Master and the Ruler, Who is also its Nourisher, and who alone deserves worship and obedience.

The relationship between the creature and the Creator, if it is based on the Truth, is that the creature should worship the Creator and obey Him. This fact has been stated by the Creator of the universe Himself: *I have not created jinn and mankind except that they should worship Me* (51: 56). Hence, in all the activities of human life the most important purpose is that the Creator should be obeyed and worshipped. The greatest achievement for a person is to invite other human beings all over the world to bow down and worship Allah Who alone is their real Master.

The most distinct, honourable and holy group of people who came to this world to invite mankind towards worship of their Lord and Creator is the group of Prophets. The members of this group each in his own time and among his own nation, persevering and repeatedly gave the same message to all human beings, in the words of the Qur'ān: *O people worship Allah. You have no God other than Him* (11: 50).

Thus, the most reliable, trustworthy and holy group of human beings, that is the Prophets, concentrated on inviting mankind towards the worship of God because this reality is the greatest Truth of the universe. The Truth they taught is that the human being has been created by Allah and is His slave. The admission of this great Truth by people is the best acceptance of reality. The message of the Prophets was also conveyed by their followers and all other righteous people who followed them in their own age and time. That is why we can say that in the presence of Allah the invitation of mankind towards guidance and well-being and the Right Path, to be achieved through obedience to Allah, is the greatest work that can be done.

In the sight of Allah, the Most Exalted, the highest work for this world and the hereafter, and for the benefit and progress of mankind, is to call other creatures of Allah towards obedience and worship of their Creator. That is why it is necessary that people endowed with the best abilities should enter this work and, however busy they might be in their worldly pursuits, should put their share into this great work in order to fulfil and accept their trusts from Allah.

However, every job demands certain skills and expertise and the task of taking the message of Allah to His creatures also requires special capabilities and training. Allah Almighty, Himself, trained His messengers through particular methods. Sometimes He showed them His Signs in themselves and in the universe; sometimes this training was carried out by being brought up in the house of Pharaoh and then being made a shepherd; sometimes by way of the well and the prison and rising to the kingly throne. Sometimes by stages in the cave and the flight, or the *Hijrah*, to the final dominance of the Islamic system. After the messengers of Allah, whoever has to do the work of spreading the word of Truth will have to obtain special abilities through special training.

ACADEMIC TRAINING

When a person himself does not know what is the criterion of Truth, and how the Truth can be recognised and identified, and what are its features and boundaries, and from what it forbids us and what it commands us to do, how can he present the Truth to others and how can he know that he is in fact presenting the Truth? It is quite possible that he might present falsehood under the impression that he is presenting the Truth. Hence, for the message of Islam, its *dāʿī* should have a quest for the Truth and should be able to recognise it, should be aware of it and should follow it persistently. A person who wants to work for Islam will definitely have to undertake the following steps:

1. Development of Conscientiousness and Sensitivity

This is the very first step which is absolutely important for a *dāʿī* if he has come forth with the claim that he is going to spread the message of Islam. He must implement it in his own self. This is the very first demand which Islam makes on him. If he does not fulfil this demand, and leaves some aspects of his life blank, the responses of his audience will also be blank and the result will be that the audience will be distracted and dissatisfied. It is essential that he should weigh himself in the balance according to the criteria provided by the absolute Truth so that he might know his own weaknesses.

The *dāʿī* of Truth begins working when one catches hold of one's self and presents it in front of one's own conscience to be judged. This is the same thing as a soldier entering war who checks his weapons before he leaves. An alert and conscious mental attitude is required. The sign of an alert conscience is that it is pleased with doing good and sorrowful when something immoral occurs.

The event in which the Companion of the Prophet, ʿUmar, was involved in attacking his sister Fāṭimah, prior to his acceptance of Islam, was something which touched and awakened his awareness and sensitivity. ʿUmar saw his sister, who was weak compared with him and who would never even say a word, opposing him in a religious matter and saying: 'O ʿUmar, do what you will, but now Islam cannot be removed from our hearts.' His sister's courage, determination and refusal to be defeated or cowed down, woke up a new feeling and sensitivity within him. The future ʿUmar al-Fārūq was awakened and he felt that there was something special which had given his sister a new strength, so much so that she simply did not regard her brother's strength and power. It was his sister's courageous statement which sparked off the potential faith in ʿUmar.

The Blessed Prophet gave us a five-point self-analysis programme which can help us to check on our moral motivations, fear of Allah and determination to work for the true Faith. This consists of the following points:

- For what purpose is a person spending his precious life?
- For what purpose is he utilising his knowledge?
- From where does he obtain his livelihood and in what ways and methods does he spend it?
- In what activities does he spend his physical and mental energies?
- What portion or percentage of them is for the work of Allah?

This analysis, in itself, should be sufficient to help us identify whether or not we are ready to become the *dāʿī* for the religion of Truth.

2. Correct Motivation

After the awakening of sensitivity, comes the problem of motivation for working in the Way of Allah and the determination which is required here. As long as a person does not have the inner motivation to turn his face, his heart, his energies, his direction and his objectives towards the happiness which comes from acceptance of Allah's way, his own work will be erratic.

In Islam, the motivation to do good takes on greater importance than the good action itself. Fine motivation strengthens the good action and gives it sincerity and removes the desire for worldly rewards from it. The correct *niyyah* or motivation also gives courage, patience and determination.

Without *niyyah* no good deed can reach its conclusion. Hence, it is necessary for a believer to decide that he really wants to take the message of acceptance of Allah to all people and this is a right that Allah has on him, and unless he fulfils it he does not fulfil the purpose of creation. He has to realise that this is a social good without the fulfilment of which no good has any permanence or stability.

The *dāʿī* should feel strongly that he must take the message of the Lord of the universe to all His slaves who do not know it or who have lost the way or who are simply unaware, and in this task he will put his finest capacities and powers. He will not be shaken by the difficulties that might lie in the path, for these difficulties are only the provision for the journey. In this journey, opposition is to be expected. A true *dāʿī* is recognised by the fact that he takes the message of Truth and righteousness to the creatures of Allah, and in this effort if he faces opposition, obstacles, abuses, even physical harassment, beating and stones, he faces and accepts everything and leaves the results to his Lord and Master. In this work, no obstacle should stop him.

3. Acquisition of Knowledge and Righteousness

Islam, itself, is the knowledge of Truth and righteousness and there are only two sources from which it can be obtained: the Qur'ān and the *Sunnah*. The will of the Master of people can be found in the Qur'ān and the way to fulfil this will can only be understood from the way of life of the blessed Messenger of Allah to whom the Qur'ān was revealed. The *dāʿī* must have a permanent relationship with the Qur'ān. This is the Book from which he can obtain the Truth and guidance in its entirety. One who seeks the Truth cannot find it without utilising this Book. Hence, it is of great importance that the *dāʿī* reads the Qur'ān, understands its message and absorb its guidance with the help of those who have knowledge. He should allot some time to memorise as much of it as he can and also try to mould himself according to its precepts. Then he should try to walk in the footsteps of the pure being to whom the Qur'ān was revealed, because he alone is the standard and the model for the complete human being who wishes to see the Will of Allah reflected in human character. Thus, whoever wishes to hear the Truth speaking, can hear from the statements and teachings of the blessed Messenger.

4. Studying the Lives of the *Ṣaḥābah* and the *Ṣāliḥīn*

The best models in human form of Allah's teachings and the Prophet's example were the *Ṣaḥābah* or Companions of the Prophet Muḥammad and the *ṣāliḥīn* or righteous generations that followed them. These people are examples for us as they spent their entire lives in spreading the message of the *Dīn* (Islam). They were the embodiments of the Truth; they were the guided and the standard bearers of the forces of goodness, before whom the forces of evil were crushed and disappeared. In their habits and ways we can find the best examples of how to assert the good and how to avoid evil and wrong-doing. They did *jihād* for the Truth; they left their homes for the Truth; they gave their lives for the Truth. In fact, they sacrificed everything that they had. It is from them that the original message of Islam came down to us. They are examples for all times to come; in their fear of Allah, in the way they dealt with things and the way they performed their worship, in the exaltation of their character, in their faithfulness and truthfulness to Allah and His Messenger, and in their ability and desire to sacrifice and work for the Truth. It is very necessary for the *dāʿī* to study their lives and make them the torchbearers of their own lives.

5. Active Relationship with Allah

The strongest anchor for a *dāʿī* is a living, strong, stable and deep relationship with his Lord and Master. He should be aware that Allah, whose work he is doing, sees and watches over him. He should know that the forces of life and death, which are elements working for Allah Almighty, are also his helpers and they back him and support him when he works for Allah. The worker should feel that he is attached to that force which is Living, Eternal and Almighty, totally and absolutely higher than all human forces. That power supports him and helps him at every step. In every individual's heart it can open a way for the Islamic worker and in light and in darkness it safeguards, helps and supports him. Against the will of that Being, nobody can even shake a feather. He that is Allah listens to prayers that are not said aloud and knows the tumult which is in the heart. Thus true faith in Allah is of utmost importance, to the *dāʿī*. To fear Him is much more important than fearing anyone else. To seek His Pleasure comes before seeking anyone else's pleasure. One must strive to worship Him as one strives in no other field. The relationship with Him must be given priority over any other relationship. The call is towards Him and every sacrifice and effort is to be aimed at seeking His pleasure. That Allah be pleased with us is the real capital of our lives and it is for this pleasure that everything is to be sacrificed. In the words of the Qur'ān: *Surely my Prayers and my sacrifice, my life and my death are for Allah Alone, the Lord of the Universe* (6: 161). In short, the *dāʿī* should have the vitality to sacrifice all his loves for Allah's sake and to bear patiently all anguish for His sake and to accept all losses for His sake. In this way he should ponder and think of the Qualities of Allah and should love them and also fear them. He should find it more acceptable to fall into fire than to disobey or go against the teachings of the Creator. The remembrance of Allah should be dearer to him than anything else. He should pray for the sake of expressing his slavery to Allah. He should fast to obtain the pleasure of Allah and he should spend in the way of Allah to seek His Pleasure. Thus, when the *dāʿī's* relationship with Allah is correct, it gives him the strongest foundation for the building of a spiritual character in order to fulfil the demands of faith in Allah Almighty.

6. Love of the Prophet

After Allah, the being for whom the *dāʿī* must have limitless love, as part of his faith, is the person of the blessed Messenger, who brought human life out of a hellish condition on to the Path to Paradise. It was the Messenger who braved great suffering to open the way for us towards faith and Islam and acceptance of Allah Almighty. It was the Messenger, who through the *Hijrah*, opened the way for us to move from *kufr* towards *īmān*. It was he who confronted and clashed with the forces of *kufr* to make the difference between truth and falsehood very clear. He is the guide and leader of the caravan of humanity and a mercy for all the worlds, and till the Day of Judgement, he will be the leader of this caravan.

The blessed Messenger gave the lesson of civilisation to humanity. From savagery and brutality he brought a human being to nobility and urbanity. From darkness he showed the way towards the light of knowledge. He gave us the best law of justice and established human equality and obliterated the difference between master and slave. He exalted the position of women, made them the companions and friends of men and placed Paradise beneath the feet of mothers. He taught youngsters to respect their elders and taught the elders to deal with their youngsters with love and kindness. The world has not seen, and it will never see, the like of him in mercy, forgiveness and kindness. He was the embodiment of mercy and he was love and affection incarnate. He was the guardian and defender of the oppressed, the orphans, the needy, and the helpless of all humanity.

Our love for the Prophet of Allah is not only a recognition of what he has done for us but is a part of our faith. In fact, the heart in which there is no love for the Prophet, is devoid of true faith, even in Allah. For the Islamic worker, the Prophet's love lights the way, and following his example provides a standard of effort, determination and perseverance. It was in reference to this quality that the Messenger told ʿUmar: ''ʿUmar as long as I am not dearer to you than your own life itself, your faith is not complete.'

7. Thought for the Hereafter

Along with love for Allah and His Messenger, thought for the hereafter is also part of a *mu'min's* or believer's faith. Giving preference to the hereafter and preparing in this world for the hereafter is the first duty of the *dāʿī*. The Islamic worker, in fact, reminds people who are lost in the activities of this world of their return to their Creator.

The Qur'ān tells us that the complete final life is the life of the hereafter. The world as compared to it is as dew compared to the ocean. In this world, good and evil live side by side but in the hereafter there will be separate areas of living for the two antagonists. For the wrong-doers and criminals there will be Hell, and that is a horrible place indeed, and for the good, there will be Paradise, and that is a wonderful and joyful place. In the hereafter, the entire population of the world will be put into these two settlements and this division will be on the basis of belief and deeds done in this world. How did a person spend his life on earth? Was he faithful or was he a rebel doing what he willed? In this world, the life he lives is a test to find out whether he recognised his true Creator and obeyed Him or not. This work is only possible in a world where the real Creator and Master is hidden behind the curtain of His Signs and signification and the effort to move towards Him is ridden with difficulties and tribulations. The way towards the Creator is also blocked by the devil's most beautiful nets. Awareness of the hereafter is limited to one's inner being and conscience while the sweetness of the world is felt by every inch of a person's being. Thus, a person is put to the test and it is the *dāʿī's* work to recognise the reality and walk the Straight Path, show it to others and call them towards it.

There are various ways of developing a sensible and sensitive attitude towards the hereafter of which the most important is the study of the

Qur'ān's verses dealing with warnings and scenes of the Day of Judgement. Then there are various books of *aḥādīth* which should be studied. Then, off and on, one should visit graveyards to see the last signs of those who are on the journey to the hereafter. Once in a while the person should also visit a hospital to meet with those who are sick and so become aware of and know their condition.

CHARACTER DEVELOPMENT

Every true believer is basically a collection of three personalities. He is a Muslim, that is in all matters of life he is obedient to Allah and His Messenger. He is a *muballigh*, that is he does not try to keep knowledge of the Truth hidden within himself like a miser but shows it to all humanity in the best possible way. He is an activist and does all his work with vitality, and alertness, and with full attention, and in no work is he lazy. This is because spreading the message of *Dīn* (Islam) is a constant action and a perpetual *jihād al-Akbar* (supreme struggle for Islam). After the expedition of Tabūk, the Messenger of Allah while returning to Madinah said that: 'We are moving from the minor *jihād* to the major *jihād*.' Seeking self-subservience to Allah and seeking the pleasure of Allah is in itself a large *jihād* and this striving and *jihād* is characteristic of the Muslim's entire life.

We present from the Qur'ān an impression of the Muslim, *muballigh* and *mujāhid* who is the searcher for and propagator of the Truth. In *Sūrah al-Furqān* (see 25: 63–77), Allah says that his best creatures are those who:

- *Walk gently on the earth*
- *When the ignorant come up to them they say, peace be to you, and go away*
- *They spend their nights in the presence of their Lord, bowing and prostrating*
- *In spending they are not wasteful nor miserly but take a moderate course between the two*
- *Apart from Allah they do not worship anyone else*
- *Do not take any life unjustly*
- *Do not commit adultery*
- *Do not bear false witness*
- *When they pass something foolish they pass by with dignity*

And in *Sūrah al-Mu'minūn* (see 23: 1–11):

- *In prayer they are very conscious of their Creator*
- *They protect their private parts*
- *They stand by their trusts and their treaties and their words*

Then in *Sūrah Luqmān*: (see 31: 18–19):

- *Do not walk arrogantly on the earth*
- *Walk modestly and keep their voices low*

In *Sūrah al-Tawbah* (see 9: 112) other features of the believers are given:

- *Those who do not turn back*
- *Those who praise Allah*
- *Those who travel in Allah's way*
- *Those who bow and prostrate*
- *Those who forbid wrongdoing*
- *Those who safeguard the limits of Allah.*

PRACTICAL TRAINING

A worker for the Truth is not just a person of words. He strives to bring about a healthy but complete revolution in the lives of people. Hence, the real field is the field of action. He sows the seeds of change and regeneration in the lives of actual human beings and then prepares the harvest of a fine moral regeneration. He is never a hermit who goes quietly to his cave and finds his own way to salvation in isolation from everybody else. He never leaves the field of action where Allah has sent him to test and show his qualities. These would, indeed, be of no avail should he leave that field and go away. He is actually the audience of that great message of the Messenger of Allah: 'When any one of you sees wrong being done it is essential for him that he should change it with his hand, and if he does not have the ability to do so, then with his words, if he does not even have that ability, then he should hate it in his heart and should have the desire to eradicate it; this is the lowest level of faith. Those who do not hate wrong, even in their hearts, have not even a particle of faith'. That is why the Qur'ān commands in very clear words: *There should be a group from among you who should call towards goodness and should forbid wrongdoing and such are they who would earn salvation* (3: 104). This guidance evidently directs the *dāʿī's* practical work.

1. Practical Striving

The first practical thing to be done by the worker of Islam in his training is that he should do that which he thinks is the Truth. In fact, he does not even realise the natural results of his message, until he comes into the field and actually presents it to other people. As soon as he takes this step, there will be those hands of friendship which will be extended to help and support him, as well as those hands of animosity and hostility, which will try to stop him. Thus, immediately at the beginning of the struggle he will enjoy the pleasures of companionship in the struggle, and the pain of opposition. These two happenings, in themselves, are enough for his training. While meeting with friends, he will be able to map out a plan of work and while facing and removing opposition and difficulties placed in his way, he will have to think of the Prophet's methodology. He will have to learn the patience of the persecuted. Determination and perseverance will become a feature of his character and after having passed through the fire of test and tribulation, the real gold in him will emerge.

In this struggle, his near and dear relatives, friends and sympathisers may block his way fearing that he might spoil his worldly future. His opponents will also attempt to block his way so that he might not achieve that for which he is determined. This situation provides the kind of environment that is needed for fine tuning his character and it is in this atmosphere that the *dāʿī* develops towards becoming a successful worker for Islam.

2. The Companionship of the Good

The second practical method of training for the *dāʿī* is the companionship of the *ṣāliḥīn* or the righteous. The *dāʿī* has to remove himself from the friendship, love and companionship of those who are wrong-doers, and instead find the companionship and nearness of those who fear Allah and who love to do that which Allah has told them to do. This prevents him from being influenced by the forces of evil and also prevents him from becoming tolerant of the foolish and meaningless deeds and actions of wrongdoers.

3. Taking the Example of Better Workers

Another method of training and character-development is to observe those whose character, piety and fear of Allah are better than his. The *dāʿī* has been taught that in worldly matters he should look at those who are not as well off as he is, so that he might stay away from temptation and vain hope, and in religious matters, he should look at those whose character and morals are better than his, because to compare himself with them would help him overcome his own weaknesses.

If a person is observant he will find that in the companions around him there are all kinds of characters just like a bouquet of beautiful flowers of various shades and colours. One of them is always conscious of spiritual growth and another is full of good and happy spirits. One has a desire to spend in the way of Allah out of what Allah has given him. Another is strict in his prayers and worship. Another remembers Allah often and frequently repeats his various supplications. One is ahead of others in his sympathy and care for other people. Yet another is unique in his softness, his love and affection and good cheer for his fellow Muslims. One prays the *Tahajjud* at night while another, during the day, struggles hard in Allah's way and is alert and untiring in spreading the message of Islam. For the *dāʿī*, it is necessary to absorb all these qualities so that he might become like that bouquet of beautiful flowers.

4. Enjoining the Good and Forbidding the Wrong

Another method of the Islamic worker's training is enjoining the good and forbidding the wrong, and in so doing the *dāʿī* should not become upset about what others may say about him, nor should he fear anyone other than Allah. The Prophet said: 'By Him in whose Hand is my life, you must enjoin the good and that is obligatory upon you. Stop wrongdoing and catch hold of the hand of the wrongdoer and turn him towards the good. Otherwise Allah will mingle the evil of their hearts with yours and He will curse you in the same way that the Banī Isrā'īl (the tribe of Israel) was cursed' (*Tirmidhī*).

This shows, that in order to keep the light of goodness flaming, and to ward off the forces of evil, it is essential to fulfil this duty of enjoining right and forbidding wrong otherwise there will be no way out for a humanity that is trapped in its own system.

5. Society as the Mould of Training and Change

When a person comes forth with a message of truth it is not he alone who impinges on society; society itself notices his smallest mistake and forces him to maintain certain levels of moral quality. The *dāʿī* cannot call society towards something which he himself does not fulfil and it cannot remove a fault from the society which is to be found within himself. Thus, as soon as he comes forth with his *daʿwah*, from all sides he is viewed, as it were, with microscopes. His smallest weaknesses and faults are found out and placed squarely before him. It is not enough to just go forth and try to reform society. Society, itself, sees to it that there is no contradiction between what he says and what he does. Either he has to mould himself according to his words or he has to simply give up what he says. Sometimes, through society's criticism, and sometimes through the obstacles and tests that he faces, the worker for the Truth corrects, improves and develops his character and finally endeavours to make himself pure and fully sincere in his task. Thus, the society itself provides a training ground for the *dāʿī*.

6. The Struggle for the Establishment of Justice

The best method of training for the worker of truth is his struggle to implement and establish justice. The fact is that there are different stages and levels in the moral training of the standard bearer of truth just as, according to the *ḥadīth*, there are different levels of *īmān* or faith. The highest stage of *īmān* is to stop the wrong with one's hands. But the acquisition of the necessary power to stop wrong-doing is an obligation of the *dāʿī's*, which he can only ignore if he wants to devalue his other deeds as well. A worker for Islam must be motivated by the fact that justice be promoted in society. Unless he has this motivation, his character does not reach full development, nor does his spirit reach its full strength.

Undoubtedly, it is necessary that the worker for truth pass through all the stages of *īmān* and that he should possess firm faith in Allah and the Messenger and the hereafter; but it should be realised that verbal affirmation of the faith is, in itself, not enough. It must be accompanied by unhesitating resolve to carry out the commands of Allah and His Messenger in actual practice. If this is not so, mere words may even be the product of hypocrisy. Actions that are the natural consequences of faith are the true Islam that is needed. In our practical life, the actions of Islam should be evident, and these actions should demonstrate obedience to Allah based upon clear understanding, full realisation, sincere acceptance and a real desire to fulfil Allah's commands. These actions should reflect the fear of Allah and the love of his Messenger. It should become quite evident in the life of the Islamic worker that he must obey Allah. He does what he is told to do (by Allah) and stops what he is told not to do, and in all this, his desires and wishes do not come between him and his Lord.

However, it is not enough that he fulfils the rules and regulations as set down by Allah. These should be accompanied and carried out with deep enthusiasm and true spirit. Only in this way do those qualities emerge in the worker that are necessary for his task. He becomes self-propelled and moves ever-forward. He then becomes one of the Signs of Allah. How well a sage put it when he said: 'When I deviate even a little from obedience to my Master I see its influence in the rudeness of my son, in the negligence of my wife and in the wildness of my steed'.

Surely, the call to Islam is meant to 'make' different kinds of people and it must be full of wisdom and without superficiality. Those people who ignore human psychology and try to straighten crooked hearts merely through violent teachings, criticisms, taunts or mockery, usually break those hearts instead of straightening them. The door of the heart opens inside and unless the one who lives in that house opens it from within, it cannot be opened. The work of *daʿwah* is one of much wisdom. We have been commanded to do it in the best possible way. The Qur'ān says: *Call to the way of Allah with wisdom and with goodly teachings and discuss matters in the best possible way* (16: 125). It is necessary for the *dāʿī* to know the things that come in the way of training people and the things that spoil the effect of *daʿwah*. There are many such things but impatience is the worst of them all. Other such things which can be extremely harmful are: haste, harsh language, bad temper, violent statements. Similarly, it is necessary to know the kind of people that are careless and unheeding of the message of faith and those that are not ready to move towards the truth and do not feel its need at all. Among them are those who are in love with the world, who are intoxicated with power, who are involved in opportunism, who are habituated to comforts and those who are forgetful of the judgement in the hereafter. It is also important to know the kind of people that are best for the Islamic message and who may perhaps become its standard bearers and supporters of the mission. Among them are those whose natures have not been corrupted and merely by meeting and talking with them you can observe this. Among them are those who are thoughtful and who are used to pondering over things, trying to gain the best understanding. Among them are those who gain lessons from tragedies and disasters. There are also those searching for the true God, who ponder over Allah's Signs, who speak the truth, who are in the habit of being honest and who are courageous and brave. Such are particularly right for this mission. If the *dāʿī* takes his message to such people he can easily spread his message far and wide.

If the principles of academic training for the purpose of inner improvement and the principles of practical training for external discipline given above are adopted and the ways to moral decline are abstained from, the work of the Faith can be easily done. This, however, does not mean that one should not perform *daʿwah* until all these qualities are possessed within oneself. Only the ideal standard has been mentioned. It is the duty of every believer to go forth with the message. In this duty, each individual is responsible only for the qualities that he has; and so long as he tries his best, his Lord is the Most Forgiving, the Most Merciful. Allah is Gracious. He runs towards him who walks towards Him, and as for one who runs to his Creator, Allah exalts him even above the angels. None can comprehend the Graciousness and Blessings of this Master and Creator.

31

Watering the Seeds of Love

Said Ramadan

Someone with a long and outstanding involvement in Islamic work stretching over many years once remarked to me that Muslims have ignored the task which should be their specific concern, namely love of God and the strengthening of the ties of love among people for His sake. If a person should succeed in this task, he said, he would have set the firmest foundation in the depths of souls, sown the seed for every flourishing virtue and established an impregnable fortress against most external threats and tests.

This is so true. The word 'love' which people have so misused and abused, is that mighty word which distinguishes the followers of the Prophets and on which their societies were built. It is the 'elixir' which binds these followers to goodness, creating a true bond which even makes suffering seem sweet in its pursuit. By the same token it has fashioned the ties that bind them together – ties of the soul over and above the intellect, ties which are not subverted by differences of opinion. These ties are above materialistic interests and are not swayed by any particular passing whim.

LOVE IN THE QUR'ĀN

Indeed as you read the Qur'ān, you will find confirmation of the place from which this pure, noble love originates. You will find it discussed in:

1. The context of *daʿwah,* the purpose of which is to rekindle and arouse human hearts: *Say, if you want to love God, then follow me and God will love you* (3: 31).
2. The description of believers: *Those who have attained to faith in God, are most strong in their love of God* (2: 165).
3. The description of the relationship between the believers and their Lord and Sustainer: *He Loves them and they love Him* (5: 54).
4. The discussion of good and evil: *Indeed God loves those who do good* (2: 195), and *He does not love the aggressors* (2: 190).
5. The relationship between one believer and another in the form of God's grace, mentioned twice in one verse, which He has firmly bestowed on His servants: *And remember the grace of God on you. Behold you were enemies and He reconciled your hearts and so you became brethren through His grace* (3: 103).

LOVE IN THE *SUNNAH*

The life of the Prophet, may God bless him and grant him peace, was lived in the fullness of the Qur'ān. His life throughout was also filled with love. This, for example, is what he said as he sought to spread gentleness and love: 'Love God for all the grace and bounty He has bestowed on you all, and love me on account of the Love of God for me.'

Indeed, you will constantly witness this love in the Prophet's life; like a farmer in his nurseries nurturing the seeds of this emotion with irrigation and tender care, tirelessly doing this as part of his condition and calling. His is the situation of a person filled with love which overflows in those around him, bringing their hearts together through every means. You can readily see this in the narrations about the Prophet's noble character and behaviour:

1. Abū Saʿīd al-Khudrī relates that the Prophet was more shy and modest than a maiden in seclusion, and if anything was displeasing to him we would see it on his face. His was a kind and gentle face, so tender in appearance that he would not say of anyone what that person did not want to hear out of the shyness and generosity of his heart.

2. ʿAlī ibn Abī Ṭālib said: 'The Prophet was the most open-hearted of all people, the most truthful of speech, the tenderest in disposition and the most generous in relations.'

3. Al-Qādī Abū'l-Faḍl related: 'The Prophet united the hearts of his Companions and did not alienate them one from another. He would treat

honourably and generously any noble person of a tribe and confer the responsibilities of leadership on such a person. He was on his alert with some people but without denying them his cheerfulness and good disposition. He took care of his Companions giving each his due so that no one felt that he favoured another more. Whoever sat with him or approached him with a request, he treated him patiently until he left. Whoever asked of him any need was never sent away without some reassuring word. He was expansive in his cheerfulness to people. He was like a father to them and with him they enjoyed the same rights. He was always smiling, comforting and sociable.'

4. Jarīr Ibn ʿAbdullāh said: 'Since I became a Muslim, the Prophet was never out of my sight and whenever he saw me he was smiling. He would make jokes with his Companions, mix and chat with them, play with their children and sit them on his lap. He would respond to the invitation of the free and the enslaved, the captive and the needy. He would visit the sick in the farthest part of the city and accept an apology from him who apologised.'

5. According to Anas: 'He would never be the first to release a proffered hand and he would never stretch out his legs in the presence of a seated guest. He would be the first to extend the greeting of peace to whoever he met. While sitting, he would be the first to make room for his Companions. He was generous to whoever visited him, sometimes spreading out his garment for him and out of deference, offering his own cushion to his guest and prevailing upon him to sit on it if he refused. He would call his Companions by the names they liked best as a mark of honour and dignity to them and he would not interrupt the speech of anyone.'

As for the pronouncements of the noble Prophet himself, there is an abundance of his sayings on the subject. Abū Hurayrah for example reported that the Prophet said: 'The believer reconciles hearts in love and friendship and there is no good in anyone who is not disposed to be friendly to others nor entertains the love and friendship of others.'

The noble Prophet is also reported to have said: 'Around the Divine Throne, there are podiums of light. On them are people whose clothing is light and their countenances are light. They are not Prophets nor martyrs. The Prophets and the martyrs are delighted with them.' 'Describe them to us, O Messenger of God,' requested his Companions. The Prophet replied: 'They are those who loved one another for the sake of God. They kept each other's company for the sake of God and they visited one another for the sake of God.'

Indeed, the noble Prophet made affection springing from the heart a basic requirement in discharging the duties of brotherhood, without which faith is incomplete. This affection is not a favour which one grants to another. All this is implicit in his saying: 'No one of you has attained faith unless he loves for his brother what he loves for himself.'

Among those pleasant, evocative scenes that awaken deep-seated sentiments and strengthen the bonds of love is the story which the Prophet is reported to have related: 'A man once visited his brother in faith for the sake of God. So God designated an angel for him. The angel then asked him: 'Where do you wish to go?' 'I want to visit my friend.' 'Is there anything you need at his place?' asked the angel. 'No.' 'Is he a relation of yours?' 'No.' 'Why then (are you visiting him)?' 'I love him for the sake of God.' Thereupon the angel said: 'God has sent me to inform you that He loves you on account of your love, and He has undertaken to grant you Paradise.'

Even more weighty than this is the fact that the noble Prophet urged his Companions to compete with one another in mutual love when he said: 'Never do two friends love each other for the sake of God but the one more beloved of God is the one who has the stronger love for his friend.'

You have, thus, seen how the subject of love was nurtured in the first school of Islam and at the hands of its great teacher, may God's blessings and peace be on him. The great truths which the noble Messenger conveyed and on which he trained the first generation of Muslims are the only bases on which our new societies can be erected. Without them, our path will never be straight. For, the Truth will remain the Truth and human souls will always be the same.

32

Guidelines for Better Living

Hasan al-Banna

Your acceptance of Islam obliges you to seek continuous improvement in your condition. As you strive to please your Lord and earn the eternal reward and pleasure of Paradise, keep the following advice close to your heart.

1. Devote a daily period for the recitation of the Qur'ān. Aim to finish the whole of it within a month, but not before the end of three days.

2. Carefully recite the Qur'ān, listen to it, and ponder over its meaning. Set aside a period to study the *sīrah* or life history of the Prophet, and the history of the early Muslims. You should read many books. You should also read many books of *ḥadīth* and memorise at least forty *ḥadīth*. Last but not least, you should study the basics of the *ʿaqīdah* or Islamic faith, *fiqh* or Islamic jurisprudence and Islamic law.

3. Have a thorough medical check-up regularly, and get treated for any ailments diagnosed. Attach importance to physical fitness and self-defence, and stand aloof from all bodily weaknesses.

4. Avoid excessive use of coffee, tea and other stimulating drinks, and strive to abstain completely from smoking.

5. Show interest in the cleanliness and tidiness of your home and place of work. Be concerned with personal hygiene, for Islam was founded on cleanliness.

6. Always be truthful and never tell a lie.

7. Fulfil your promises and agreements. Do not resort to making lame excuses.

8. Be courageous and enduring. The highest degrees of courage are telling the truth in your own disfavour, keeping secrets, admitting mistakes and maintaining self control when angry.

9. Be serious and dignified. However, this should not stop you from enjoying jokes and laughing.

10. Be modest, careful, and sensitive to both good and bad things by expressing your happiness when experiencing good and gratitude when encountering bad. If you demand less than what you deserve, you will receive what you deserve.

11. Be fair in judging according to sound evidence. Your anger should not make you ignore the good in others and your blessings should not make you forget the bad in others. Always speak the truth, no matter how painful it is, even if it is against yourself and against the people dearest to you.

12. Be active, energetic and skilled in community services. You should feel happy when you offer a service to another person. You should feel compelled to visit the sick, assist the needy, support the weak, and give relief to the ill-fated, even if it is only a kind word of sympathy. Always rush to do good deeds.

13. Be compassionate, graciously excusing and forgiving towards others. You should be kind to all human beings and animals, and have good relations with everyone. Observe Islamic social injunctions. Be merciful to the young and respectful to the old. Make room for others in meetings and gatherings. Do not spy and backbite. Do not be noisy. Respect others' privacy, and neither condemn nor insult them.

14. Improve your reading and writing skills; increase your knowledge of the Islamic movement by reading about it. Read newspapers and magazines. Establish a personal library even if it is a small one. Delve deeply into your field if you are a specialist in science or the arts. Acquaint yourself with the general Islamic subjects to the degree which makes you capable of forming general judgements concerning day-to-day problems.

15. Undertake some economic enterprise, even if you are wealthy. Try to establish a private business, regardless of how small it may be or how busy or academically oriented you are.

16. Work, even though the pay is small, and do not quit unless the work is against Islam.

17. Perform your job in the best manner you can, and stand aloof from dishonesty and cheating. Observe your appointments, and never be late for work.

18. Be amicable in claiming your due, and hasten to give others their due in full, without procrastination.

19. Keep away from all forms of gambling, no matter what the incentive may be. Avoid unlawful means of livelihood, regardless of what quick profit lies therein.

20. Avoid the practice of charging interest (*ribā*) in all your transactions. Purify yourself from its putrid touch.

21. Contribute to the material gains encouraged by Islam by promoting private industry, especially Islamic enterprises.

22. Support *daʿwah* work by contributing some of your wealth to the Islamic movement. You must pay the minimally established amount of *zakāh* on your assets because this is the inalienable right of the poor and deprived.

23. Set aside a portion of your income to defray unforeseen expenses, no matter how small your income is, and never indulge in extravagance.

24. Strive as far as you can to keep alive the beneficial practices of true Islamic culture and for the elimination of practices alien to Islam in all areas of Muslim life. This includes greetings, language, dress, household furnishings, hours of work and rest, eating and drinking, and expressing joy and sorrow. Always refer to the purified practice of the Prophet for guidance in all affairs.

25. Avoid all newspapers, magazines, clubs, gatherings, and schools that oppose the principles of Islam, unless your reading and activities in such institutions are designed only to promote the good and oppose the bad.

26. Always be conscious of Allah; seek His pleasure with determination and resoluteness. Bring yourself closer to Allah through the performance of extra night prayers (*tahajjud*), fasting at least three days every month, contemplating on Allah and His Divine attributes and reciting the respected supplications of the Prophet.

27. Perfect your personal purity and cleanliness, and try to keep in a state of ablution (*wuḍū'*) as often as possible.

28. When you perform the daily prayers, do so on time, and always fulfil the rules. Try to pray in congregation and at the *masājid* as frequently as possible.

29. Observe the fast of Ramaḍān and go on the *ḥajj* as soon as you have the means. If you cannot afford to make *ḥajj*, make it one of the goals of your life and strive hard to undertake it.

30. Always cherish the intention of *jihād* and the desire to witness and sacrifice in the way of Allah, and prepare yourself for that.

31. Regularly renew your repentance, seeking Allah's forgiveness. Try to avoid pardonable offences as well as major sins. Devote a period of time every night before going to bed for self-criticism, reflecting upon the good or bad things you may have done throughout the day.

32. Avoid lustful thoughts, emotions, and occasions of sin, for example, by restraining your gaze from *ḥarām* things, urging your emotions to focus on good deeds, and keeping your heart and desires away from all that is forbidden.

33. Completely avoid intoxicating drinks and everything that causes impairment of the body or delays of the mind.

34. Do not take immoral people as friends. Keep away from places of immorality and sin.

35. Avoid all evil forms and places of entertainment, and in general, avoid the environment of arrogant and extravagant luxury.

36. Share the message of Islam everywhere you go.

33

Personal Evaluation

Riza Mohammed

As Muslims and workers of the cause of Allah, we must realise first and foremost, that all of us are going to be accountable for our deeds on the Day of Judgement. It is, thus, wise that we continuously assess ourselves in this world and make amends before that final judgement by Allah when we will not be given another opportunity to make up for our misdeeds. The Prophet said: 'Everyone starts his day and is a vendor of his soul, either freeing it or bringing about its ruin' (Muslim). 'Umar ibn al-Khaṭṭāb, in one of his famous sayings said, 'Judge yourselves before you are judged, evaluate yourselves before you are evaluated and be ready for the greatest investigation [the Day of Judgement].'

I therefore suggest to all of us, whether beginners, experienced workers, or responsible leaders, that they should have a daily period put aside for self-evaluation and scrutiny.

What follows is a questionnaire to prompt some guidance on how best to utilise these daily periods of reflection. Some points to note before starting the questionnaire are as follows:

- The best time to go through this questionnaire is at the end of each day.
- Do so on your own or with someone you trust fully.
- Answer each question as honestly and truthfully as you can.

- When you assess yourself, remember that Allah is your witness and that you are assessing yourself and your actions by His decree.
- Remember that a good judge is one who is neither unduly harsh nor unjustifiably lenient but truly and fully balanced.

QUESTIONNAIRE

1. Did I offer my five daily *ṣalāh* (prayers) on time?

Guard strictly your prayer, especially the middle prayer; and stand before Allah submissively (2: 238).

'The prayer most loved by Allah is prayer performed on time' (*Muslim*).

2. How many of my *ṣalāh* did I offer in congregation?

'A prayer in congregation is twenty-seven times more superior to one performed individually' (*Bukhārī*).

3. Am I satisfied with the quality of my *ṣalāh*?

'If a person performs two units of prayers without the distraction of any worldly thoughts, all his previous sins will be forgiven' (*Bukhārī*).

'When you stand for prayer, perform your prayer as if it were your last' (*Aḥmad*).

4. How much of the Qur'ān did I read with understanding?

Do they not then earnestly seek to understand the Qur'ān or are their hearts locked up? (47: 24).

5. How many verses of the Qur'ān did I memorise?

'Indeed the one who memorises nothing of the Qur'ān is similar to a deserted house' (*Tirmidhī*).

6. What steps did I take to help my family learn about Islam?

O you who have attained faith! Ward off from yourselves and those who are close to you that fire [of the hereafter] *whose fuel is human beings and stones* (66: 6).

7. What did I do to fulfil my duties as a *dā'ī*?

Encourage one another in truth and encourage one another in patience (41: 33).

8. Have I treated my parents with love and respect and have I given due consideration to all their needs?

Your Lord has decreed that you worship none but Him, and that you are to be kind to your parents, whether one or both of them attain old age during your lifetime; say not to them a word of contempt nor repel them but address them in terms of honour.

And out of kindness lower to them the wing of humility and say: 'My Lord, bestow on them Your Mercy as they cherished me in childhood' (17: 23–24).

9. Did I safeguard my tongue from useless speech?

'The faith of a person cannot be straight unless his heart becomes straight and his heart cannot be straight unless his tongue becomes straight' (*Aḥmad*).

10. Did I backbite or slander anyone?

'None of you should tell me anything about anyone, for I like to meet [anyone] of you with a clean heart' (*Abū Dāwūd*).

11. Did I commend others for the good things they may have done?

Kind words and the covering of faults are better than charity followed by injury. Allah is free of all wants and He is Most Forbearing (2: 263).

12. Did I fulfil my promises?

And fulfil your promise. Verily you will be answerable for [all] *your promises?* (17: 34).

13. Have I been just in all my dealings?

O you who believe! Stand out firmly for justice as witnesses to Allah even against yourself, or your kith and kin and whether they be rich or poor, for Allah can best protect both (4: 135).

14. What acts of *ṣadaqah* (charity) did I perform?

'There are 360 joints in the body and for each joint you must give a *ṣadaqah* (thanks or charity)' (*Bukhārī*).

15. Did I take an interest in my health (for example diet and exercise)?

'Health for one who fears Allah is better than wealth' (*Bukhārī*).

16. Did I safeguard my eyes from the influences of Shayṭān?

'A gaze is a poisoned arrow from Satan. Whoever abstains from it in fear of Allah shall receive from Him an increase in faith, the sweetness of which he will feel in his heart' (*Musnad* of *Ibn Ḥanbal*).

17. What and how much have I read to improve my understanding of Islam?

Of all His servants only those who know fear God (35: 28).

18. Did I practise what I read and said?

O you who believe! Why do you say that which you do not? It is most hated in the sight of Allah that you say that which you do not (61: 2–3).

19. Did I save a portion of my wealth?

Make not your hand be chained to your neck nor open it with a complete opening, lest you become blameworthy and destitute (17: 29).

20. Did I perform my work with proficiency?

Indeed Allah Loves that when you do a job you do it perfectly (*Baihaqī*).

21. Did I make *tawbah* (seek Allah's forgiveness)?

'Allah will continue to hold out His Hand at night so that he who sinned during the day might repent, and to hold out His Hand during the day so that he who sinned at night might repent till the sun should rise from the West' (*Muslim*).

22. Did I reflect on my accountability to Allah on the Day of Judgement?

And fear the Day when you shall be brought back to Allah. Then shall every soul be paid what it earned and none shall be dealt with unjustly (2: 281).

That day We shall seal up mouths and hands speak out and feet bear witness, to all that they did (36: 65).

23. Am I satisfied with the way I spent the day?

'Wise is the one who (continually) assesses himself and performs good deeds for the Life after Death. Foolish is the one who follows his desires and entertains very high hopes from Allah' (*Tirmidhī*).

REFLECTION

On answering each question, make a note of the following:

- What are my weaknesses and what steps am I going to take to remove them?
- What are my strong points and what steps am I going to take to improve them?

GLOSSARY OF ARABIC TERMS

adhān, call to Prayer
ʿadl, justice
ākhirah, Life after Death
Allāhu Akbar, God is the Greatest
ʿamal, work; action
anṣar, literally 'helpers,' meaning the Muslims of Madinah
ʿaqīdah, creed
ʿArsh, Throne of God
ʿawrah, private parts of the body
āyah, Sign or aspect of God's creation; a verse of the Qur'ān
bāṭil, falsehood
barakah, Blessing, Divine Grace
dāʿī (pl. *duʿāt*), one who invites to Islam
daʿwah, inviting to the Path of God
dhikr, the remembrance of God
dīn, religion, Way of Life
duʿā', supplication
dunyā, the world; this life as opposed to the life hereafter
faqīh (pl. *fuqahā'*), religious scholar
farḍ, an obligatory act
fiqh, Islamic jurisprudence
fitnah, corruption
fiṭrah, natural disposition to the good
ḥadīth (pl. *aḥādīth*), saying of the Prophet Muḥammad
ḥajj, pilgrimage to the House of God in Makkah
Alḥamdu lillāh, All praise is due to God
ḥalāl, that which is lawful or permissible in Islamic law
ḥaqq, truth
ḥarām, that which is unlawful or prohibited in Islamic law
hidāyah, guidance from God

ḥijāb, barrier or covering; often refers to a muslim woman's headscarf
hijrah, migration of the Muslims from Makkah to Madinah (622 CE)
ḥikmah, wisdom based on revelation of the will of God
ḥubb, love
ḥudūd, Divine sanctions
ʿibādah, act of obedience to and worship of God
iḥṣān, the perfect fulfilment of the Commands of God, beneficence
Injīl, the Scripture (Gospel) revealed to Prophet Īsā (Jesus)
ikhlāṣ, sincerity towards God
ijmāʿ, consensus
ijtihād, Islamic reasoning or judgement
ʿilm, knowledge, science
imām, leader
īmān, deep faith and trust in God
inshā' Allāh, if God wills
istighfār, seeking forgiveness from God
jahannam, Hellfire
jāhilīyah, ignorance; the pre-lslamic period
jamāʿah, group; congregation; organised community of believers
jannah, Paradise, the Garden
jihād, striving, struggling in the Path of God
kāfir, one who covers (the truth), disbeliever
khalīfah, trustee of God
khilāfah, trusteeship, caliphate
khuṭbah, sermon, speech
khimār, (female) headscarf
kibr, pride
kufr, ingratitude to God and disbelief in Him
malā'ikah, angel of God
maʿrūf, common decency
masjid, mosque; place of prostration
mujtahid, religious scholar qualified to exercise *ijtihād*
mu'min, believer
mushrik, polytheist
muttaqīn, the God-conscious ones
nafl, a supererogatory act
naṣīḥah, sincere commitment; good advice; sincerity
nifāq, hypocrisy

niyyah, intention
qiyāmah, resurrection; Judgement
qiyām al-layl, night-vigil; staying up for worship at night
qiyās, analogical reasoning
Rabb, Lord; Master
risālah, message (divine)
riyā', ostentation
raḥmah, mercy
rakā'ah, unit of Prayer
Ramaḍān, the ninth month of the Islamic calendar; the month of Fasting
ṣabr, patience, steadfastness, resoluteness
ṣadaqah, charity
ṣaḥābī, Companion of the Prophet Muḥammad
ṣalāh, five daily Prayers; one of the five pillars of Islam
ṣawm, fasting
shahādah, witnessing, acceptance of Islam
shāhid / shahīd, witness; martyr
Sharī'ah, the Way; Islamic law; the moral and legal code of Islam
shirk, polytheism; the gravest sin
shukr, gratitude
Ṣifāt, attributes of God
sīrah, biography of the Prophet
Subḥānallāh, Glory be to God
Sunnah, practice of the Prophet
sūrah, chapter of the Qur'ān
tafsīr, explanation of the Qur'ān
taqwā, God-consciousness
tasbīḥ, Praise of God
Tawrah, (Torah) Scripture revealed to the Prophet Moses
tawḥīd, the Oneness of God
tawwakul, trust in God
tawbah, repentance
tazkiyah, self purification
usrah, family; closely knit group
ustādh, teacher
ummah, the universal Muslim community
wuḍū', ablution in preparation for Prayer
zakāh, obligatory sharing of wealth with the needy

A SHORT BIBLIOGRAPHY ON ISLAM

THE ISLAMIC WORLDVIEW

Introductory Level

Islam, The Natural Way by Abdul Wahid Hamid. MELS, London, 1989.
Perhaps the best introductory book highlighting the main themes of Islam. It provides an interesting discussion on livelihood, family, neighbourhood, community, *Ummah*, interfaith interaction, global issues and the Hereafter.

Towards Understanding Islam by Sayyid Abul Ala Mawdudi. The Islamic Foundation, Leicester, 1981.
A lucid introduction and comprehensive view of Islam. It gives the rational basis of Muslim beliefs, the modes of worship and the wisdom behind them. Contains a section on faith and *Sharīʿah*.

Islam in Focus by Hammudah Abdalati. ATP, Indianapolis, USA, 1975.
Deals with the ideological foundations of Islam, giving an overview of all the basic concepts for example: righteousness, piety, life, sin and freedom. It has a section on the articles of faith and different aspects of individual and social life.

Islam at the Crossroads by Muhammad Asa. Dar al-Andalus, Gibraltar, 1980.
A thought-provoking treatise emphasising the original revolutionary spirit of Islam and challenging the intellectual dazzle of the contemporary West. The discussion on the place and role of the *Sunnah* is particularly useful.

What Islam is all About by Yahya Emerick. Islamic Book and Tape Supply, New York, 1997.
This is a basic textbook which covers the history of Prophet Muḥammad, the teachings of Islam, the history of the ancient Prophets, the study of the Qur'ān, the Islamic philosophy of the world and the life within it, Islamic law, *ḥadīth*, contemporary issues and much more.

Advanced Level

Tawḥīd: Its Relevance to Life and Thought by Ismail Faruqi, IIIT, Virginia, 1986.
This monumental work not only discusses *tawḥīd* as the axial doctrine of

Islam, but allows the reader to understand this doctrine from a number of different perspectives. In an endeavor to explain the simple truths of the doctrine, the author touches upon a broad spectrum of subjects including history, comparative religion and philosophy.

Islam and the Destiny of Man by Gai Eaton, ITS, Cambridge, 1992.
Explores what it means to be a Muslim and describes the forces that have shaped the hearts and minds of Islamic peoples. It also tells the story of Muḥammad and the early Caliphs, and delves into the Muslim view of man's destiny, the social structure of Islam and inner meaning of Islamic teachings.

Alim (CD-Rom). Islamic Softwear Limited, Houston, 2001.
Contains over 90, 000 pages of Islamic text and graphics, 80 hours of Qur'ān recitation in Arabic and English, 120 mins of video coverage, full Arabic searching capabilities, *Alim* provides a wonderful, easy and enjoyable way to learn about Islam.

THE QUR'ĀN

Introductory Level

The Message of the Qur'ān by Muhammad Asad. Dar al-Andalus, Gibraltar, 1980.
A highly recommended translation of the Qur'ān in a contemporary style with extensive explantory footnotes. The work is based on classical commentaries.

Way to the Qur'an by Khurram Murad. Islamic Foundation, Leicester, 1985.
This book aims to provide the reader with the necessary guidelines required to understand the Qur'ān. It contains chapters on what the Qur'ān means, how we should read it and why we should strive to understand it more fully.

'Ulūm ul-Qur'ān: Introduction to the Sciences of the Qur'ān by Ahmad Von Denffer. The Islamic Foundation, Leicester, 1983.
This book deals with the technical aspects of the study of the Qur'ān: history and transmission of the text of the Qur'ān as well as more recent issues such as Orientalists' views and recordings of the Qur'ān.

Concepts of the Quran: A Topical Reading by Fathi Osman. MVI Publications, Los Angeles, 1997.
An insightful and handy reference work which enables students to study specific Qur'ānic passages pertaining to larger themes. Topics covered include the faith of Islam itself, types of worship, moral values, Islamic law, among others.

Burnishing the Heart by AbdulWahid Hamid. MELS, London, 2003.
What is the human heart, why is there the need to burnish it, and how do we burnish it? These selections from the Qur'ān, with brief notes and a reflection on our state as human beings, are intended to provide some pointers.

Advanced Level

A Thematic Study of the Qur'ān by Muhammad al-Ghazali. IIIT, Herndon, Virginia, 2000.
The author uses a unique approach as he focuses on the organic unity of each *Sūrah* highlighting the logic or inherent reasoning that runs through the *Sūrah* and unifies its various components and images.

In the Shade of the Qur'ān (Vol. 1–7) by Sayyid Qutb. The Islamic Foundation, Leicester, 1999–2002.
A momumental *tafsīr.* Universally recognised as an outstanding contribution to Islamic thought and scholarship. The first seven volumes, to date, cover all the Chapters from *Sūrahs al-Fātiḥah* to *al-Aʿrāf.*

Towards Understanding the Qur'ān (Vol 1–7) by Sayyid Abul Ala Mawdudi. The Islamic Foundation, Leicester, 1988–2002.
An English rendition of *Tafhīm al-Qur'ān*. The first seven volumes, to date, covers all the Chapters from *Sūrahs al-Fātiḥah* to *al-Qaṣaṣ.*

Tafsir Ibn Kathir by Safiur-Rahman Al-Mubarakpuri (head of translation team). Darus Salam, Riyadh, 1998.
Major contribution to *tafsīr* literature in English. Translation of a classic commentary of the Qur'ān.

Understanding the Qur'ān: Themes and Styles by Muhammad Abdel Haleem. IB Tauris, London, 2001.
A linguistic approach to the study of the Qur'ān. The author shows how popular conceptions of Islamic attitudes toward women, marriage, divorce, war and society, differ radically from the true teachings of the Qur'ān.

Access to Qur'anic Arabic (3 books and 4 audio CDs) by Abdul Wahid Hamid Muslim Educational Literary Services, London, 1998.
This course offers a focussed, practical, step–by–step way to understand the Qur'ān. It uses only Qur'ānic vocabulary throughout. It covers basic grammarand structure of the language and provides help in using dictionaries and other essential reference material. This pack assumes that users can read and write the Arabic script. Learning aids include a textbook, workbook, and a book of Qur'ānic Selections for further study. For those

requiring training in reading and writing the Arabic script and reading the Qur'ān, *Graded Steps in Qur'an Reading*, also by the same author, is a well-paced and extensively tested course.

THE ḤADĪTH

Introductory Level

In the Prophet's Garden by Fatima D'Oyen and Abdelkader Chachi. The Islamic Foundation, Leicester, 2002.
A thematically arranged anthology of *aḥādīth* presenting essential Islamic teachings on faith and practices, morals, manners, character and conduct. Serves as suitable introduction to the message of Prophet Muḥammad for non-Muslims, and those new to Islam.

A Day with the Prophet by Ahmad Von Denffer. The Islamic Foundation, Leicester, 1982.
A short but comprehensive guide for anyone who would like to know about the Prophet's daily life. This book offers a selection of sayings and invocations of the Prophet for various parts of one's daily routine.

Hadith and Sunnah – Ideals and Realities edited by P.K. Koya. Islamic Book Trust, Malaysia, 1996.
Compilation of 14 selected essays on *ḥadīth* and *Sunnah* of the Prophet, written by various authors.

Hadith Literature – Its Origin, Development & Special Features by M.Z. Siddiqui. Islamic Text Society, Cambridge, 1993.
Elucidates the science of *ḥadīth*, the process by which each *ḥadīth* was recorded, transmitted, and collected by scholars in the early years following Prophet Muḥammad's death.

The Complete Forty Hadith, (Imam an-Nawawi) translated by A.S. Clarke. TaHa Publishers, London, 1999.
Translation of Imam an-Nawawi's classic collection of *aḥādīth* with a substantive commentary on each.

Advanced Level

Riyaadus Salihin, (Imam An Nawawi) commentary by Hafiz Salahuddin Yusuf. Dar as-Salaam, Saudi Arabia, 1996.
Covering every aspect of Islamic belief and moral conduct, it selects approximately 2,000 hadith from the six major collections: Bukhārī, Muslim, Abū Dāwūd, Tirmidhi, An-Nāsa'ī and Ibn Mājah. It serves as an excellent *ḥadīth* primer and daily reader covering a wide range of topics.

Commentary on the Forty Hadith of al-Nawawi by Jamaal al-Din Zarabozo. Basheer Publications, New Jersy, 1999.
This work offers a detailed analysis of one of the most important *ḥadīth* selections. Each *ḥadīth* features the Arabic text, English translation, selected vocabulary in Arabic with English translation, general comments, circumstances behind the *ḥadīth*, brief biography of the narrator and then a detailed commentary that explains the *ḥadīth's* major subjects and lessons.

Lasting Prayers of the Quran and the Prophet Muḥammad by Ahmad Z. Hammad. Quranic Literacy Institute, Illinois, USA, 1996.
Discloses the height and depth, the length and breadth of spiritual energy from the sources of Islam. It teaches Muslims to be sensitive to their purpose on earth, to social interaction and to the creation's incessant need for and welcome access to God. It meets the needs of all those who turn to prayer.

Studies in Hadith Methodology and Literature by M.M. Azami. ATP, USA, 1992.
An introduction to the systematic process of classifying the sayings and described actions of the Prophet Muḥammad. Topics include: the recording of *ḥadīth*, chain of narration, criticism of *ḥadīth* and their grading on the scale of authenticity and backgrounds of the scholars who collected the *ḥadīth*. The book helps explain the role *ḥadīth* play in the development of Islamic rulings.

THE SĪRAH

Introductory Level

The Makkan Crucible; Hijrah: Story and Significance; Sunshine at Madinah by Zakaria Basheer. The Islamic Foundation, Leicester, 1981 1990.
Based on original Arabic sources and modern writings on the *Sīrah*, this set of books presents an analytical account of the major events in life of the Prophet.

Muḥammad: his life based on the earliest sources by Martin Lings. The Islamic Texts Society, Cambridge, 1995.
Remains close to the Arabic sources and is one of the best written works on *Sīrah* in English. The book reflects both the simplicity and grandeur of the story of Muḥammad's life.

The Eternal Message of Muḥammad by Abdur Rahman Azzam. Islamic Texts Society, Cambridge, 1993.
This translation of a great Islamic classic offers a simple yet profound interpretation of Islam. Azzam examines the social and economic ramifications of the Muslim state, one based on humane ideals of law and

justice expressed in the Qur'ān and one which can provide the foundation for a just society in the modern day.

Companions of the Prophet (Vol. 1–2) by Abdul Wahid Hamid. Muslim Educational Literary Services, London, 1995.
A classic work that provides a lively introduction to early Muslim history and inspiring models for Muslim values, attitudes and behavior. Here are the trials and triumphs of the early period of Islam as embodied in the lives of individual men and women.

Advanced Level

Life of the Prophet (Vol. 1–4) by Ibn Kathir. Garnet Publishing, London, 2001.
Compiled in the fourteenth century AD by a prominent scholar, it is drawn from the earliest and most reliable Arabic sources and offers one the fullest available account of the historical circumstances and personalities most important in the founding of Islam.

Life of Muhammad by Muhammad al-Ghazali. IIFSO, Kuwait, 1990 .
A comprehensive and useful analysis of the life of Prophet Muḥammad. In his usual style, Muhammad al-Ghazali gives his incite with great perception and authority. The translation is somewhat cumbersome but doesn't detract from the message of the text.

The Life of Muhammad by Muhammd H. Haykal, (translated by Ismail al-Faruqi). American Trust Publications, USA, 1976.
This book aims to reveal the character of the Prophet in the light of historic reality, and to bring out the essence of Islam as exemplified in the life of the greatest Muslim.

Muḥammad: Man and Prophet by Adil Salahi. The Islamic Foundation, Leicester, 2002.
A comprehensive source on many aspects of Prophet Muhammad's life. In this account of Muhammad's life from his childhood in the desert to his divine revelations and early preaching, the author places the story in an historical context, making an analysis of events which led to Muhammad's triumphant march into Makkah in 630 AD.

Hayat-as-Sahabah by M. Yusuf Khandahlawi. Idara Isha'at-e-Diniyat, New Delhi, 1985–1993.
This book provides comprehensive accounts of the lives of scores of the Companions of Prophet Muḥammad. Circulated initially in the Indian Sub-continent, this book has become very widespread and can be found in many mosques, madrassahs and libraries across the world.

WORSHIP, ETHICS AND LAW

Introductory Level

Fiqh us-Sunnah (Vol 1–5) by Sayyid Sabiq, American Trust Publications, Indianapolis, 1989–93 (First published in 1947).
These five volumes cover prayer and ablution, supererogatory prayers, fasting and almsgiving, funerals and *dhikr*, and *ḥajj* and *umrah*. An excellent guide to personal fiqh adopting a comparative approach, looking across the *madhhabs*.

The Lawful and the Prohibited in Islam by Yusuf al-Qaradawi. American Trust Publications, Indianapolis, 1984 (1st edition 1960).
This book clarifies what is lawful and what is prohibited and why it is so by referring to the Qur'ān and the *Sunnah*. It answers many questions faced by Muslims in their lives and attempts to refute the ambiguites and misconceptions about Islam.

Islamic Law: Its Scope and Equity by Said Ramadan. McMillan, London, 1970.
This book explains the methodology of Islamic Law and its application to practical problems of jurisdiction; it also elucidates the complex structure of Islamic legal thought.

Advanced Level

Fiqh az-Zakat by Yusuf al-Qaradawi. Dar al-Taqwa, London, 2000.
One of the most outstanding scholars of our time deals in depth with the legal rulings and philosophy of *zakāh* in the light of the Qur'ān and *Sunnah*. This book covers every aspect of *zakāh* in great detail; from those who are obligated to pay *zakāh*, the amounts they have to pay, as well as the types of wealth on which *zakāh* must be paid. It also deals with how *zakāh* is collected, its connection to Muslim governance, and its relation to society as a whole.

Islamic Awakening Between Rejection and Extremism by Yusuf al-Qaradawi. IIIT, Herndon, Virginia, 1991.
In times of worldwide revival of interest in Islam, this book attempts to explain why this interest has led some among the younger generation to tread the path of fanaticism and intolerance. Covering the subject very clearly, the book calls for a return to moderation as the true spirit of Islam.

Source Methodology in Islamic Jurisprudence by Taha Jabir al-Awani. IIIT, Herndon, Virginia, 1994.
This book attempts to simplify the most important method of research ever devised by Islamic thought during its most creative period, and bring

it to the understanding and appreciation of the modern learner, while relating its importance and relevance to the world of Islam today.

Principles of Islamic Jurisprudence by Mohammad Hashim Kamali. Islamic Texts Society, Cambridge, 1991.
Offers the most comprehensive, detailed presentation of the theory of Muslim Law in English. Used as a text book in many universities, this is an essential reference book for anyone with an interest in issues of *usūl al-fiqh* and comparative jurisprudence.

The Four Imams by Muhammad Abu Zahra. Dar al-Taqwa, London, 2000.
Provides a comprehensive, in-depth analysis of the four Sunnī *madhāhib* and their founders, giving details of their biographies and the method they used in reaching their legal conclusions.

SELF DEVELOPMENT

Introductory Level

Let Us Be Muslims by Sayyid Abul Ala Mawdudi, (ed. Khurram Murad).The Islamic Foundation, Leicester, 1985.
Based on Friday congregational addresses, this revised version covers such themes as *īmān*, Islam, the prayer, fasting, almsgiving, pilgrimage and *jihād*.

Dying and Living for Allah by Khurram Murad. Islamic Foundation, Leicester, 2001; *In the Early Hours* edited by Riza Mohammed. Revival Publications, Leicester, 2000.
Two essential books for each Muslim home. They provide advice on the subjects of spiritual and self-development.

The Muslim Character by Muhammad al-Ghazali. International Islamic Federation of Student Organisations, Kuwait, 1983.
Comprehensive analysis drawing extensively from the Qur'ān and *ḥadīth* on character traits essential for development of an Islamic personality.

Al-Ma'thurat (book and audio tape/CD) by Imam Hasan al-Banna. Awakening Publications, 2001.
This is a compilation of du'ās and dhikr from the Qur'ān and authentic *aḥādīth*. It is presented as a form of litany to be recited every morning and evening.

Training For Action (CDRom) by The Tarbiyah Department, Islamic Society of Britain, Birmingham, 2002.
A comprehensive CD containing syllabuses for self and group development. It includes copius reference articles and books available elctronically for study.

Advanced Level

Remembrance and Prayer: The Way of Prophet Muḥammad by Muhammad Al-Ghazali. The Islamic Foundation, Leicester, 1981.
Describes in detail how the Prophet used to remember Allah and pray to Him.

Iḥyā' ʿUlūm al-Dīn by Abu Hamid Al-Ghazali. Islamic Texts Society, Cambridge & The Islamic Foundation, Leicester.
Widely regarded as the greatest work of Muslim spirituality. The two Publishers have separately translated several chapters under the following titles *Remembrance of Death; Invocations and Supplications; Discipling the Soul and on Breaking the Two Desires; Poverty and Abstinence; Patience and Thankfulness; Intention, Sincerity and Truthfulness; Inner Dimensions of Islamic Worship; The Duties of Brotherhood in Islam.*

Morals and Manners In Islam by Marwan Ibrahim Al-Kaysi. The Islamic Foundation, Leicester, 1986.
A compendium of rules regulating Islamic conduct on the personal, familial, social and institutional levels. It covers a wide range of issues faced in daily life.

Training Guide for Islamic Workers by Hisham al-Talib. International Institute of Islamic Thought, Herndon, Virginia, 1991.
An invaluable reference manual for Muslim activists and leaders to learn the Islamic approach to practical management issues. Based on forty years of experience, it is used by individual Muslims and in training programs throughout the world. It touches on key issues in *daʿwah*, group dynamics, problem solving, team building, self-development, communication, leadership, youth camps and more.